THE AN
THE FRE

ALEXIS DE TOCQUEVILLE was born in 1805 into an aristocratic French family loyal to the exiled House of Bourbon and to the Catholic Church. He acquired liberal sympathies by studying French and English history and observing the folly of the restored Bourbon monarchy; liberty became his central political ideal. Impressive academic achievements and family influence led to a legal career in government service in 1827. It was as a junior magistrate at Versailles that he met Gustave de Beaumont, the man with whom he would travel to America to prepare a study of its penal system for the French government.

After a lengthy journey round the United States, Tocqueville and Beaumont published their report on prisons; then Tocqueville turned his attention to other work. The result of this was his hugely influential two-volume *Democracy in America*, the first volume of which was published in 1835 (at which point he also married Mary Mottley, an Englishwoman) and the second in 1840. The book secured both his reputation as a writer and thinker, and his election to the celebrated Académie Française in 1841.

In 1839 Tocqueville was elected to the Chambre des Députés, and remained a member of the French assemblies until 1851. He was Foreign Minister for five months in 1849 under Louis Napoleon Bonaparte. In 1850–51 he wrote his *Recollections* of the 1848 French Revolution.

His last work, *The Ancien Régime and the French Revolution*, was published in 1856. He meant it to be the first volume of a grand study of the Revolution of 1789, but he did not live to complete it. He died in 1859.

GERALD BEVAN was educated at King Edward's School, Five Ways, in Birmingham, St John's College, Cambridge, where he studied Modern and Medieval Languages, and Balliol College, Oxford. His career in the teaching of French, Latin and Religious Studies ended in 1993 at St Albans School as Director of Studies and Head of Modern Languages. He specializes in French literature from the seventeenth, eighteenth and nineteenth centuries. Alongside his translation work, he teaches for the Workers Education Association offering courses in Philosophy, Psychology, Politics and Religion as well as Literature in English.

HUGH BROGAN is the author of the *Penguin History of the United States of America* and *Alexis de Tocqueville*, a biography published in 2006. A graduate of St John's College, Cambridge, he has worked at the University of Essex since 1974, and is now a Research Professor of history there.

ALEXIS DE TOCQUEVILLE

The Ancien Régime and the French Revolution

Translated and edited by GERALD BEVAN
With an Introduction by HUGH BROGAN

PENGUIN BOOKS

PENGUIN CLASSICS

Published by the Penguin Group
Penguin Books Ltd, 80 Strand, London WC2R ORL, England
Penguin Group (USA) Inc., 375 Hudson Street, New York, New York 10014, USA
Penguin Group (Canada), 90 Eglinton Avenue East, Suite 700, Toronto, Ontario, Canada M4P 2Y3
(a division of Pearson Penguin Canada Inc.)
Penguin Ireland, 25 St Stephen's Green, Dublin 2, Ireland (a division of Penguin Books Ltd)
Penguin Group (Australia), 250 Camberwell Road, Camberwell, Victoria 3124, Australia
(a division of Pearson Australia Group Pty Ltd)
Penguin Books India Pvt Ltd, 11 Community Centre, Panchsheel Park, New Delhi – 110 017, India
Penguin Group (NZ), 67 Apollo Drive, Rosedale, North Shore 0632, New Zealand
(a division of Pearson New Zealand Ltd)
Penguin Books (South Africa) (Pty) Ltd, 24 Sturdee Avenue, Rosebank, Johannesburg 2196, South Africa

Penguin Books Ltd, Registered Offices: 80 Strand, London WC2R ORL, England

www.penguin.com

First published 1856
This translation first published in Penguin Classics 2008

025

Translation and editorial matter copyright © Gerald Bevan, 2008
Introduction copyright © Hugh Brogan, 2008
All rights reserved

The moral right of the translator and editors has been asserted.

Set in 10.25/12.25 pt PostScript Adobe Sabon
Typeset by Rowland Phototypesetting Ltd, Bury St Edmunds, Suffolk
Printed and bound in Great Britain by Clays Ltd, Elcograf S.p.A.

ISBN: 978-0-141-44164-1

www.greenpenguin.co.uk

Contents

Contents

Chronology

1805 Born in Paris, on 29 July to Hervé, Comte de Tocqueville, and Louise-Madeleine, Comtesse de Tocqueville, French Catholic aristocrats

1814 Napoleon falls and the Bourbon monarchy is restored under Louis XVIII

1820–23 Tocqueville studies at the Collège Royal in Metz, where his father is Prefect

1823–7 Tocqueville studies law in Paris

1824 Charles X succeeds to the French throne

1827 Tocqueville granted an appointment as a minor judicial officer in the Versailles court of law

1830 Charles X's edicts restricting suffrage and censoring the press spark a revolution on 27 July which brings his reign to an end

1830 The 'July' Monarchy of Louis-Philippe begins on 7 August

1831 Tocqueville and his companion Gustave de Beaumont arrive in Newport, Rhode Island, on 9 May, for their nine-month visit to America

1833 Tocqueville publishes Du Système pénitentiare aux États-Unis with co-author Beaumont; first visit to England

1835 January. Publication of Democracy in America Part I Second Visit to England

1835 Marriage to Mary Mottley, an Englishwoman

1836 Journey to Switzerland

1839 Tocqueville elected to the French Chamber of Deputies; writes 'Report on the Abolition of Slavery'

1840 Tocqueville publishes the two volumes of Part II of Democracy in America

1841 Journey to Algeria

1841 Tocqueville elected to the Académie Française

1846 Second journey to Algeria

1848 Revolution in Paris: Louis-Philippe abdicates the French throne on 24 February amidst growing popular demands by republican and socialist reformers for change

1848 Tocqueville elected in April to the Constituent Assembly for the Second Republic; later appointed French Foreign Minister by Louis Napoleon

1848 Louis Napoleon Bonaparte, nephew of Napoleon, elected President of the French Second Republic in December

1850–51 Stay in Italy: writes *Souvenirs*, his unfinished book on the 1848 Revolution

1851 Louis Napoleon forcibly dissolves the Assembly

1851 Tocqueville resists the *coup d'état* of Louis Napoleon, is arrested and briefly imprisoned

1852 Louis Napoleon declares himself Emperor, as Napoleon III

1852 Tocqueville begins *L'Ancien Régime et la Révolution*

1853 Studies at the Tours Archives

1854 Journey to Germany

1856 Death of his father

1856 Publication of *L'Ancien Régime et la Révolution*

1859 Having moved to Cannes for health reasons, he dies there of tuberculosis. He is buried three weeks later in his chateau in Normandy

Introduction

'Classic' is a word of treacherous and evasive meaning, whether we apply it to a writer or to a text. It seems to imply that the work in question is undeniably of permanent, universal value; at the very least, that it can make a solid contribution to its readers' enlightenment. Yet it is not self-evident that any book can have such universal validity. Charlotte Brontë despised *Pride and Prejudice*; George III thought that much of Shakespeare was 'sad stuff', though he admitted that one must not say so. To claim that a book is a classic because vast numbers of people have enjoyed it over a vast number of years simply begs the question, *why* have they enjoyed it? To call a book a classic is to make a high claim for it without making a case. Hence the need for introductions.

If applied to a work of history the term is even more difficult, for most historical writing is and ought to be perishable. To write history without being content merely to repeat whatever has been said before is to engage in a perpetual argument; and, as times change, as new discoveries are made and new minds come forward, the soundest analyses grow vulnerable. A classic work of history is normally one that is left to gather dust on a high shelf; a classic historian is one who is remembered for having done good work in his day, but is now read only by specialists. In the truest sense of the word, a classic author is one who is perpetually present. With few exceptions, the great historians have left the room.

Alexis de Tocqueville is one of the exceptions.

Open any of his books at any page and you will hear a living, individual voice, that most precious of literary achievements. It does not hector, its language is plain, the topics which it discusses are frequently as dry as the most tedious pedant could require; but it is agreeable. Not everyone will want to listen, and nobody is in the mood for the same author every day; but the chances are high that anyone who enjoys reading and thinking about history will from time to time gain profit and pleasure from reading Tocqueville, even though he has been dead for nearly a hundred and fifty years. His books are still alive. He is a classic.

These assertions ought to be enough to induce the curious, or some of them, to dip into Tocqueville, and then he must look after himself. But it is, unhappily, possible for readers thinking of trying *Democracy in America*, or *The Ancien Régime and the French Revolution*, or even the *Recollections* (*Souvenirs*, Tocqueville's most accessible book) to approach the business with a complication of preconceptions that may make Tocqueville, voice and all, hard to read and hard to understand. The chief difficulty of *The Ancien Régime* is its subject. The book was written between 1852 and 1856 to throw light on the great French Revolution of 1789, a topic which had already been discussed in innumerable speeches, books, pamphlets, articles and official decrees. Europeans – Frenchmen in particular – had been struggling with the legacy of the Revolution for two generations; it was a subject on which everybody had opinions, because it affected everybody; a topic of myth, ferocious disagreement and passionate partisan debate. Tocqueville could not expect an unbiased hearing for his contribution, but it is a tribute to his powers that not only was the book an immediate bestseller: even his critics took pains to answer him respectfully: they would have made themselves ridiculous had they tried to dismiss him out of hand. He enriched the great argument, which continues to this day: for the questions which it raised – questions about liberty, equality, nationalism, violence, dictatorship, justice and the right ordering of the world – are as pressing as ever. If the library on the Revolution was already large in Tocqueville's day it is now enormous – too big to be catalogued. Readers of *The Ancien Régime* will inevitably try to fit it into the framework provided

by other readings; will try to see how it sits with the views of
Georges Lefebvre, François Furet or Simon Schama (to invoke
some recent names) or with those of Carlyle, Michelet or Acton
(more remote ones). Yet the process is risky. In the hubbub of
debate we may lose Tocqueville's voice, which is the chief
reason for reading him. Readers will have to be constantly on
their guard, or they may not notice that *The Ancien Régime* is
more than merely an item of historiography, and Tocqueville
himself much more than an out-of-date theorist of the causes
of the Revolution.

   True, he does not quite escape the fate of obsolescence. There
is a paradox here. He is an absolutely limpid writer who
occasionally rises to great eloquence; his thought is complex
but his style, over which he took enormous pains, is simple. As
a result he is enjoyable and instructive at first reading, and each
new reading will yield new discoveries. But there will also be
new errors to detect. Tocqueville must first be read uncritically,
for his own sake; but after that, for the sake of understanding
the French Revolution, he can hardly be read critically enough.

   This contradiction will not be resolved by forcing his work
into other men's schemes. As he said himself, he belonged to
no coterie, no party; as a writer and thinker he was something
of a solitary, though his views were not always so unusual as
he supposed. At any rate, he was not a socialist, a republican,
or even a professor. Nevertheless, he was by background very
much a man of his time. He was born in 1805 into a noble
family of ancient lineage. Through his parents he was related
to an extraordinary range of French heroes, from Joan of Arc
to Marshal Vauban. His mother's grandfather, Lamoignon de
Malesherbes, was one of Louis XVI's reforming ministers and
then the king's chief counsel at his trial: this service brought
Malesherbes and half his family to the guillotine during the
Reign of Terror (Tocqueville's father and mother were lucky to
escape). Another close relation was François-René de Chateaubriand, the greatest French writer of the early nineteenth
century, who was briefly Foreign Minister under Louis XVIII.
A cousin was Comte Molé, whose political career was launched
by Napoleon and who served as Prime Minister for two years

under Louis-Philippe. Tocqueville's father served as prefect (or chief royal administrator) in several departments under the Bourbon Restoration, and was appointed to the Chamber of Peers in 1827. Various cousins figured conspicuously at the restored Bourbon court, in the Chamber of Deputies, and in the legal profession.

Tocqueville was a brilliant young man, whose promise was evident from the first: at his birth his father joked that one day he would be an emperor. He seemed destined for a distinguished career in the ranks of the French ruling elite. But the troubled times made all such prospects illusory. Tocqueville's life-course was wrecked again and again by revolution. No more members of his family were guillotined, but they were exiled, dismissed, denounced; and he himself was, among other adventures, briefly imprisoned when Louis Napoleon Bonaparte overthrew the Second Republic in 1851.

In a phrase, Tocqueville was a disinherited aristocrat, a fact which he regretfully accepted, for he knew that the age of democracy was coming. On the whole he was prepared to make the best of it. The 1830 Revolution was no surprise to him: he had long realized that the efforts of the Bourbon kings to restore the Ancien Régime could not succeed. The great question of the age, he thought, was whether democracy was viable, and in 1831 he travelled to the United States, then the only modern democracy in the world, in order to find out. He discovered that not only was politics democratic in America: so was society. It was a post-aristocratic country in which there was complete equality of rank and status: even the public hangman was greeted in the street as a respected fellow citizen. This equality of status profoundly impressed Tocqueville. Not only did it become the main theme explored in his great book, *Democracy in America* (1835–40); it was, he thought, the key to modernity. To succeed, all political and social institutions would from now on have to adjust to it. For the rest of his life he was preoccupied with trying to understand it. In the drive towards equality he discerned the central characteristic and consequence of the French Revolution.

The success of *Democracy in America* opened his way into

INTRODUCTION

politics, as he had hoped and planned: from 1839 to 1851 he
sat in the parliaments of the July Monarchy and the Second
Republic. Aloof in manner and independent in his opinions, he
was slow to master parliamentary life, but eventually his talent
brought him a measure of success (he served as Foreign Minister
for five months in 1849). However, his chronic ill health hampered him, and the Revolution of 1848, of which he deeply
disapproved, dislocated his prospects once more: he was a leading liberal, and if the forces unleashed in 1848 – socialist,
nationalist, Bonapartist, Catholic conservative – agreed on
nothing else, they all repudiated the liberals. Tocqueville had
grown weary of politics even before Louis Napoleon, who had
won election to the presidency of the republic, shut down the
National Assembly in 1851, and a year later made himself
Emperor, as Napoleon III.

Tocqueville never forgave this *coup d'état* and never accepted
the Bonapartist regime as legitimate, although it was frequently
affirmed by popular majorities in plebiscites and elections. To
him Napoleon III was merely a dictator, a usurper, a demagogic
military adventurer of the type which he had long feared that
democratic politics might produce (as it had produced the first
Napoleon in 1799). He was sure that the Second Empire would
end in disaster: it was lawless and reckless. He turned back
to authorship with relief, and the result, eventually, was *The
Ancien Régime and the French Revolution*.

Tocqueville was a writer of first-rate but narrow tastes and
abilities. It is not surprising that in his new-found leisure he
aspired to write something as good as *Democracy in America*,
to make another experiment in what, following Montesquieu,
he called philosophical history (he is often labelled a sociologist,
but that is surely a mistake: even in his *Democracy* his preoccupation was less with society in itself, with how it worked,
than with how it changed). His first thought was to obey a
long-felt impulse and write a study of Napoleon I, a figure
who fascinated him as he fascinated everyone in the nineteenth
century. He sketched two brilliant chapters on the circumstances which brought Napoleon to power, but then halted,
partly because the subject was politically dangerous, but chiefly

because of his scholarly instincts. It was not enough for him to begin in the middle. To explain Napoleon it was necessary to explain the Revolution, and to explain the Revolution it was necessary to explain the failure of the old order. Besides, Tocqueville was a born researcher. He turned eagerly to investigate the archives of Normandy, where he lived; and when his quest for health led him to spend a year in Tours, in the Loire valley, he worked in the archives there, too. In this way a dead, forgotten, but curiously familiar society began to live again before his wondering eyes.

He had exceptional luck. The young archivist at Tours, Charles Grandmaison, had recently completed the ordering of the vast legacy of paper left by the eighteenth-century administrators of Touraine – above all, by the Intendants, the king's delegates. Grandmaison knew exactly what Tocqueville needed; the new book would be laid on a deep documentary foundation.

Tocqueville was well equipped to exploit his good fortune. His father, as prefect in Anjou, Lorraine and elsewhere, had been a successor of the Intendants (part of Tocqueville's boyhood had been spent in the former palace of the Intendants at Metz); his own youthful training as a magistrate had given him first-hand experience of local government in France and its relation to the central administration. His researches at Tours (and later in the national archives in Paris) convinced him of what he had long suspected: that in spite of appearances the Revolution had not totally disrupted the continuity of French history; rather, it had in crucial respects taken up the work of the Ancien Régime and completed it. This became a central theme of the new book. Another, closely related, was centralization. This was understood to be the system by which the rulers in Paris, whether revolutionaries, dictators or constitutional monarchs, made all important and most unimportant political and administrative decisions for France. Tocqueville's central scholarly achievement (thanks to Grandmaison's help) was to establish that centralization was also in full force under the Ancien Régime; indeed, in crucial respects it *was* that regime, and the tradition of centralization was the most important

example of the continuity which, in Tocqueville's view, over-
rode revolutionary disruption. At the same time it caused that
disruption: the injustice, inefficiency and heedlessness of the old
order gave the French a revolutionary education, thanks to
which they eventually swept away all vestiges of the traditional
government – except centralization.

Tocqueville deplored centralization without ever showing
very convincingly what could replace it; and in opposing it he
aligned himself firmly with the traditions of his family and the
nobility against the dominant historical school of his day as
represented, for example, by Jules Michelet, who crowned his
rhapsodic chapter on the French provinces, in his *History of
France*, with a eulogy of Paris and centralization. Yet although
Tocqueville's contemporaries were astonished by his new
interpretation they enthusiastically recognized its substantial
validity and Tocqueville's power of mind. A historian could
hardly ask for more.

Perhaps if he had encountered a different sort of archive –
that of the Ministry of Finance, for instance – he might have
drawn a different picture. As Olwen Hufton has shown in her
remarkable study of eighteenth-century Europe, *Privilege and
Protest* (1980), the ramshackle finances of the Ancien Régime
were so inextricably bound up with private vested interests of
all kinds that reform, however necessary, was impossible; the
old order was doomed to bankruptcy, and its crash brought
down the whole structure of French society and government,
which had then to be rebuilt, brick by brick. Or had Tocqueville
systematically explored the archives of the Foreign Ministry –
which he did to some extent investigate – he might have discovered that, as T. C. W. Blanning has shown in his *Origins of
the French Revolutionary Wars* (1986), the weakness of the
French state in the 1780s was putting France's standing as a
great power in jeopardy, which, for a nation so numerous, rich
and intellectually active – the leader of European civilization –
was absurd. France was on the brink of a great renewal which
proved, as she remade herself and half Europe, to be one of the
prodigies of history. This was a theme which Tocqueville, by
talent and training, was fully capable of handling; indeed, it

was one of the things which he really wanted to do, as the first five chapters of his book demonstrate. In a sense, *The Ancien Régime* was meant to be a mere prologue to the great philosophical history of the Revolution which he did not live to write.

But it was and is more than that. It is actually unlikely that different sources would have generated a significantly different book. Tocqueville sought out administrative archives because they would enable him to give historical expression to ideas he had long held. *The Ancien Régime* is in many respects both a monograph and a political pamphlet, but it is primarily a confession of faith, even a *cri de coeur*. 'The book I now offer to the public is in no way a history of the Revolution, which has been tackled too brilliantly for me to dream of redoing it in my turn; this is a study of that Revolution.' Tocqueville saw both the last century of the old order and the Revolution itself as episodes in the tragic struggle between competing impulses – which should have collaborated – towards equality and liberty. Equality he had long thought to be inevitable; though he was full of nostalgia for a (largely imaginary) age of aristocratic freedom, he despised those who clung to the unjust and inefficient structures of the past. Liberty was his lifelong passion. In his eyes the greatness of 1789 was that it claimed liberty for France and tried to realize it. He hoped that by recalling that moment of glory he could do something to disgust the French with the despotism of Napoleon III and induce them to forgive the crimes and follies of the liberals which since 1830 had unintentionally done so much to bring about the revival of Bonapartism. The old monarchy, by levelling its subjects under what Tocqueville liked to call its 'administrative tutelage', had given the French all too strong a taste for a grovelling, selfish, materialistic equality, and had rendered them all too acquiescent in centralized, authoritarian government; but neither the monarchy nor subsequent regimes had succeeded in rooting out a spontaneous taste for liberty which had blossomed in 1789 and might yet do so again.

Here we reach the essence of Tocqueville's life and thought. His ideas had been deeply influenced by visits to the United

States and the British Isles, and by his many British and American friends; but in the end his conception of liberty cannot be disentangled from his idea of France.

He detested the greed and selfishness which he saw, or thought he saw, all round him. Liberty, for him, was a school of virtue in which men learned to be citizens by exercising their rights and carrying out their duties. It was as citizens that men (and women, too, though he laid no stress on this point and never showed any interest in giving women the vote) attained their fullest, highest stature as human beings. This explains the cold anger with which he denounced the first Napoleon (and, by implication, the third) for setting up a parody of a free state:

> ... a government, stronger and much more autocratic than the one the Revolution had overturned, subsequently centralized the whole governmental machinery once again, suppressing all those dearly bought freedoms and putting empty shams in their place. So the voting rights of electors who were unable to access the truth or to join together or to have a choice, went by the name of sovereignty of the people; the slavish and silent assent of assemblies replaced a free vote on taxes. The principal guarantees of law, free thought, free speech and writing, along with the capacity to govern itself were removed from the nation – that is, all that had been most valued and noble in the victories of 1789. All this still did not stop the government's appropriating the great name of the Revolution.

He admitted, indeed he asserted, his political passion:

> A Frenchman would hardly be allowed not to have feelings when he speaks of his own country and muses about his times. I confess, therefore, that the study of our former social order, in all its aspects, has never entirely removed the present from my gaze.

Liberty, he felt, was the only corrective for the vices of Frenchmen, new and old. Only liberty could drag them away from the worship of money and their preoccupation with their small private affairs and could make them:

notice and sense at every moment their own country over and around them. There are times when liberty alone can replace the love of personal comfort with higher and more active enthusiasms, can provide ambition with loftier aims than the acquisition of wealth and can shed enough light to lead people both to see and to judge the vices and virtues of men.

He claimed that human nature was on his side:

Is there a man whose soul is so mean as to wish to depend on the whims of a single member of his community rather than to obey the laws he himself has helped to establish, that is, if he thinks his nation exhibits the virtues necessary to make a proper use of liberty?

Note the qualification: not only is it characteristic of Tocqueville's realism, so that he was always ready to modify a generalization for the sake of accuracy, it also encapsulates his entire political career, during which he could never wholly trust the voters, or give himself wholeheartedly to demagogic parties whether of the Left or the Right.

Tocqueville clung to the hope that the French were a virtuous nation, but in the last chapter of his book he sketched a devastating portrayal of its character which was hardly a vote of confidence:

When I contemplate this nation in itself, I find it to be more extraordinary than any of the events in its history. Has there ever appeared on this earth a single nation so full of contrasts and so excessive in all its actions ... unruly by temperament yet better suited to the arbitrary and even violent authority of a king than to the free and orderly government by leading citizens; today the declared enemy of all obedience, tomorrow devoting to servitude a kind of passion which nations best suited to slavery cannot manage; led by a thread as long as no resistance is offered; ungovernable as soon as an example of such resistance appears somewhere; thus always tricking its masters who fear it either too much or too little; never so free that one need despair of

enslaving it nor so enslaved that it cannot still break its yoke;
fitted for everything but excelling only in warfare ... the most
brilliant and the most dangerous of European nations ...

Only France, he concluded, could have made the Revolution.

Tocqueville had long ago given up any pretension to say
more of the future than that it was inevitably uncertain; it was
a fog into which he peered with quite as much misgiving as
hope; but choices would have to be made, and he was convinced
that scientific understanding of the past, of what had brought
France and the modern world into such difficulties, was necessary in order to choose rightly. This was the justification of his
book. 'Without a clear idea of the former society, its laws, its
failings, its prejudices, its sufferings and its greatness we will
never grasp what the French have done during the sixty years
which have followed its downfall.'

It was the faith of a historian and to understand it completely
perhaps it is necessary to make comparisons with other historians – with Michelet, for instance, who dominated the
interpretation of the Revolution in Tocqueville's day. Michelet
did not look to the past to explain the Revolution, but to the
Revolution to explain the past; to Michelet, only 1789 gave
meaning to French history. In most respects (not all) he was the
antithesis of Tocqueville; he was quite as great a scholar and
artist; his ambitions and achievement as a historian were vaster;
his is still the version of French history that everyone begins
by learning; but today Tocqueville (who nowhere mentions
Michelet) seems to be having the last word. In spite of many
mistakes of omission and commission he contributed hugely to
the understanding of the revolutionary epoch (his portrayal of
the peasantry on the eve of the crisis is especially striking);
indeed, he was the chief originator of modern methods of
investigating it, as his end notes, which take up a third or so of
his text, amply demonstrate. He and Michelet are both immor-
tals (and not just because both were elected to the Académie
Française, whose forty members were known as *immortels*);
both were among those who realized the ambition for historians first uttered by Thucydides, each giving their country 'a

possession for ever'; Tocqueville in his cool fashion was as eloquent as Michelet, and much more judicious. In an amazingly lucky shot Chateaubriand prophesied his achievement when in 1807 he publicly reminded Napoleon that, under Nero, Tacitus had already been born. This enraged the Emperor, who did not like being compared with Nero, nor the implication that future historians would condemn him; and Chateaubriand did not know how right he was, for at that time Alexis de Tocqueville was only two years old. But the bowman had hit his mark, for of all the great historians Tacitus is the one Tocqueville most resembles, and not merely because they both liked to make derogatory references to the Emperor Augustus, the nephew (actually, great-nephew) of an uncle, like Napoleon III. We still read Tacitus's relentless chronicle of the crimes of the Caesars because of the human conviction of his picture, because of the moral passion which informs it, because of his unique prose style, even though we probably do not share all the values and prejudices of the artist, and although modern scholarship has corrected his picture in many details. Similarly, Tocqueville's merciless examination of the Ancien Régime is informed on every page by a vision to which we cannot help responding, for it was that of a great man and a great writer. He made quite as many mistakes as Tacitus, but he had this advantage – that the questions which obsessed him, of liberty, equality and fraternity, still preoccupy us, or ought to; his pages are still challenges to thought and a call to arms.

There lies the justification for calling his book a classic.

Further Reading

Brogan, Hugh, *Tocqueville* (London: Fontana, 1973).
—*Alexis de Tocqueville: Prophet of Democracy in the Age of Revolution* (London: Profile Books, 2006).
Furet, François, *Interpreting the French Revolution*. Translated by Elborg Forster (New York: Cambridge University Press, 1981).
Herr, Richard, *Tocqueville and the Old Régime* (Princeton: Princeton University Press, 1962).
Jardin, André, *Tocqueville: A Biography*. Translated by L. Davis (New York: Farrar, Strauss & Giroux, 1988).
Kahan, Alan, *Aristocratic Liberalism* (New York: Oxford University Press, 1991).
Lively, Jack, *The Social and Political Thought of Alexis de Tocqueville* (Oxford: Clarendon Press, 1962).
Mayer, J. P., *Alexis de Tocqueville* (New York: Viking Press, 1966).
Pierson, George Wilson, *Tocqueville and Beaumont in America* (New York, Oxford University Press, 1938).
Siedentop, Larry, *Tocqueville* (New York, Oxford University Press, 1994).
Tocqueville, Alexis de, *Democracy in America*. Translated by Gerald Bevan (London: Penguin Books, 2003).
—*Recollections: The French Revolution of 1848*. Translated by G. Lawrence. Edited by J. P. Mayer and A. P. Kerr (Edison, New Jersey: Transaction Publishers, 1987).

Translator's Note

The text used for this translation is the fourth edition published in December 1858 – the last published in Tocqueville's lifetime.

I have retained the same layout of paragraphs as in the French text while rearranging the structure of sentences to ease the French into the idiom of English. It is evident that this remarkable man was always more concerned about the accuracy of his 'study' than about embellishing his language with colourful expression or, as he put it, he sought 'an ideal perfection of language'.

Alexis de Tocqueville wrote his recollections (*Souvenirs*) of the events of 1848 published in an incomplete form first in 1893. The year 1964 saw the definitive version of this most attractive of works.

The ordering of this translation of Tocqueville's last book is simple. Professor Brogan's Introduction is followed by the text itself, comprising a foreword by the author and three books. In addition, Tocqueville wrote an extensive series of Notes to be found after the main text. The author's notes are signposted in the text by the use of superscript numbers.

This edition has a glossary which follows the author's own notes. Most of the references in the text and Notes will be covered, especially the legal and financial terms. Tocqueville himself has explained many of the latter in his Note 73. Consequently only the fiscal categories used in the text find themselves in the Glossary.

Certain terms have been retained in the French as they are unique to French history. However, these are to be found in explanatory entries in the Glossary. The 'Ancien Régime' has been retained as the 'Old Regime' would be out of place.

It had been hoped to quote Edmund Burke and Arthur Young in the original English. However, it has become apparent that Tocqueville could be reckless in his treatment of both authors, quoting from memory or from inaccurate transcriptions, even attributing to Young views he did not hold (or at least publish). I have, therefore, decided to translate Tocqueville's renderings and to add something in the Glossary. This will quote at least the sources of the excerpts for the reader to follow up.

In many of the characters and references explained in the Glossary we can see Tocqueville's liberal leanings, his feeling for the dispossessed and his enthusiasm for liberty and equality.

I have resisted the temptation to expand phrases and sentences beyond the style used by Tocqueville in order to render the broad meaning of the French. Tocqueville has a lucid and economic approach to language and I have aimed to reflect this in the idiom of the English I have adopted.

Alexis de Tocqueville, although from an ancient aristocratic family, felt passionate about liberty and equality. It is no surprise that he had throughout his life been an acute observer of the political landscape which followed the French Revolution and a keen participant in the affairs of government. This book represents the opening study of the roots of that momentous event and there is a pervading wistfulness that he compiled only the notes for a second book.

While he does not entirely escape the preoccupations of an intellectual, he shows little pretentiousness. This modest devotion to his theme gives the reader the unfussy style which is more concerned with the struggle to pursue an historical study of integrity than to promote himself. He claims in the book to have been fearless in his desire to describe an era as it is represented in the original documents. His handling of original source material is exemplary. All these features add to the huge success Tocqueville still continues to enjoy in the English-speaking world. It is our hope that this translation matches up to the achievement of this remarkable and attractive commentator.

I would wish to acknowledge the help offered to me by a

number of colleagues and friends. Professor Hugh Brogan of the Department of History in the University of Essex has, in addition to writing the Introduction to the book, made a series of useful and authoritative suggestions from his intimate knowledge of Tocqueville and his works. As with the translation of *Democracy in America* for Penguin Classics in 2003, Monique Meager, Maîtrise de la Sorbonne, contributed to aspects of French life and history, aided by her friend Christian Darlot, whose enthusiasm for French history and political ideas has provided invaluable background information. Above all, Gay Scase, formerly Head of Languages at St Albans School, Hertfordshire, has prepared typescripts and computer discs of the various drafts of the book, interpreting and making critical judgements in the translation and without whose help this project, like the previous one, could not have been realized.

Richard Collins, my copy editor for this second Penguin volume, has been the perfect companion, exhibiting a wit, humour and stylistic elegance so necessary in the final stages of the book.

Gerald Bevan
St Albans
February 2008

THE ANCIEN RÉGIME
AND
THE FRENCH REVOLUTION

Contents

BOOK 3

AUTHOR'S FOREWORD

The book I now offer to the public is in no way a history of the Revolution, which has been tackled too brilliantly for me to dream of redoing it in my turn; this is a study of that Revolution.

No nation has devoted more effort than did the French in 1789 to distinguish, as it were, the two periods of their destiny, to create a gulf between what they had been up to that point, and what they sought to be from then on. With this in mind they adopted all kinds of precautions to avoid carrying anything of their past into their new state. They imposed every kind of restriction upon themselves, so as to form an identity quite different from that of their forefathers. To sum up, they neglected nothing, so as to make themselves unrecognizable.

I had always judged that they had been considerably less successful in this unusual endeavour than had been thought abroad or at first among themselves. I was convinced that, quite unwittingly, they had held on to most of the opinions, customs and ideas of the Ancien Régime with whose help they had engineered the Revolution which destroyed it and that, unintentionally, they had exploited the remnants of the old order to erect the structure of the new social order. Consequently, to reach a true understanding of the Revolution and its achievements, we should leave aside for the moment the France we have before our eyes in order to investigate the final resting place of the France which is no more. That is my aim in this book, though I have experienced more difficulty in achieving success with this than I would have believed possible.

The early years of monarchy, the Middle Ages and the

Renaissance have stimulated extensive studies and have been the subject of profound research work. These have acquainted us not only with the events of those times but also, at a governmental as well as a national level, with the laws, customs and spirit of those different periods. Until now no one has yet made the effort to view the eighteenth century in this way or from such a close vantage point. We reckon that we have a thorough knowledge of French society of that time because we see clearly its brilliant surface, because we grasp the most detailed history of the most distinguished characters who lived there and because critical and well-penned studies have succeeded in making us familiar with the great writers who made it famous. We have, however, only a confused and often mistaken conception of how it transacted its business, of how its institutions actually functioned, of the precise relations of class to class, of the social conditions and feelings of those who could be neither seen nor heard and of the underlying source of attitudes and customs.

I have attempted to delve into the heart of the Ancien Régime, so close to us in years yet concealed from us by the Revolution.

To fulfil this aim not only have I reread the well-known books produced by the eighteenth century but also I have set out to study many works which, while being less well known and deservedly so because they are composed with little skill, reveal even more accurately perhaps the true motivations of the age. I have worked hard to scrutinize all the public documents in which Frenchmen were able to publish their opinions and preferences as the Revolution loomed. The reports of the Estates and, later, of the provincial assemblies, have provided me with many insights on this matter. Above all, I have used the registers of grievances (*cahiers*) prepared by the three Orders of State in 1789. The originals of these notebooks represent a long series of manuscript volumes which will stand as witness to this former French society, as the ultimate expression of its needs and the authentic revelation of its final ambitions. This is a unique document from history. Even that has not satisfied me.

In countries where public administration is already strong, few ideas, needs, grievances, few interests or enthusiasms fail sooner or later to come to its notice. By examining its archives, not only does one gain a precise idea of its public procedures but the entire country is on display. Any foreigner granted access today to all the confidential correspondence which fills the dispatch boxes of the Ministry of the Interior or of the Prefectures would soon know more about us than we do ourselves. In the eighteenth century public administration, as readers of this book will realize, was already very centralized, very powerful and wonderfully energetic. It was evident that people might be helped, or hindered, or liberated by it. Promises or subsidies were lavishly available. Not only was the general conduct of affairs already influenced by it in a thousand guises, but also the destiny of families and the private life of every man. Furthermore, the lack of publicity meant that no one feared exposing even his most secret weaknesses to its view. I spent a very long time studying the remaining reports of such administrations both in Paris and in several of our provinces.[1]

As I anticipated, I found in them a living record of the Ancien Régime, its ideas, its passions, its prejudices and its habits. In them, every man spoke his own language freely and disclosed his inmost thoughts. Thus I managed to acquire considerable knowledge about this older social order not available to contemporaries, since I had before my eyes material not presented to theirs.

The more I progressed in this study, the more surprised I was to see, at every turn, in the France of that period many characteristics which strike us still today. I encountered a host of feelings which I believed had been born with the Revolution, a host of ideas which, until then, I had thought had sprung from it alone and a thousand customs which we felt had been given to us only by the Revolution. On all sides I came across the roots of present-day society deeply implanted in this ancient soil. The more closely I drew near to 1789 the more distinctly could I make out the spirit which had caused the shaping, the birth and the growth of the Revolution. I perceived the features of this Revolution gradually unfurling before my gaze. It was already signalling its make-up and its spirit. It was its real self. Not only did I find in its first struggles the reason for what it was to become but, still more perhaps, the forecast of what it was finally to create. For the Revolution had two distinct phases: the first occurred when the French appeared to aim for the entire abolition of the past; the second when they attempted to recover a vestige of what they had abandoned. As a result, a large number of constitutional laws and customs from the Ancien Régime disappeared suddenly in 1789 only to resurface a few years later, just as certain rivers plunge underground only to re-emerge a little further on, showing us the same water but between new banks.

The central objective of this work which I am placing before the public is to explain why this great revolution, which was stirring simultaneously throughout almost the whole continent of Europe, should explode in France rather than elsewhere, why it emerged, as it were spontaneously, from the very society it was to destroy and how the old monarchy could finally collapse in such a comprehensive and precipitous fashion.

My view is that the work I have undertaken should not stop there. If time and strength do not fail me, I intend to follow, through the twists and turns of this long revolution, those very Frenchmen with whom I have recently lived on such familiar terms under the Ancien Régime and who were shaped by that same régime; to watch them shifting and changing according to events, yet without altering their natures and emerging endlessly before our gaze with a slightly different, but always recognizable, appearance.

My first task will be to range with these men over the opening years after 1789 – a time when the love of equality and freedom had an equal share of their hearts; a time when they wished to found not only democratic but also free institutions; not only to destroy privileges but to acknowledge and sanctify rights. These were times of youth, enthusiasm, pride, generous and sincere passions, the memory of which, despite mistakes, men will preserve forever and which, for years to come, will disturb the sleep of all those wishing to corrupt or enslave them.

As I rapidly trace the course of this revolution, I shall attempt to show what events, mistakes, miscalculations led these same Frenchmen to abandon their initial aims and, turning away from freedom, to want nothing more than to serve the master of the world on an equal footing. I shall show how a government, stronger and much more autocratic than the one the Revolution had overturned, subsequently centralized the whole governmental machinery once again, suppressing all those dearly bought freedoms and putting empty shams in their place. So the voting rights of electors who were unable to access the truth or to join together or to have a choice, went by the name of the sovereignty of the people; the slavish and silent assent of assemblies replaced a free vote on taxes. The principal guarantees of law, free thought, free speech and writing, along with the capacity to govern itself were removed from the nation – that is, all that had been most valued and noble in the victories of 1789. All this still did not stop the government's appropriating the great name of the Revolution.

I shall stop at the point when the Revolution appears to me to have virtually accomplished its work and created the new social order and then I shall review this social order itself, attempting to discern in what manner it resembles that which preceded it and in what manner it differs, what we have lost in that mighty upheaval and what we have gained from it. Finally, I shall try to look into our future.

One section of this second work is already sketched out but is, as yet, undeserving of publication. Shall I be granted the time to finish it? Who can say? The destiny of individuals is much more difficult to perceive than that of nations.

I hope I have written the present book without bias but I do not claim to have written it without passion. A Frenchman would hardly be allowed not to have feelings when he speaks of his own country and muses about his times. I confess, therefore, that the study of our former social order, in all its aspects, has never entirely removed the present from my gaze. Not only have I set out to discover what disease defeated the patient but also how he might have avoided death. I have proceeded like those doctors who attempt to stimulate some form of life into every lifeless organ. My aim has been to compose a picture which was strictly accurate but which, at the same time, might be instructive. Thus, every time I encountered in our forefathers some of those male virtues which would be most necessary and which are now virtually non-existent – a true spirit of self-reliance, the leaning towards high ambitions, faith in ourselves and in a cause – I highlighted them. Similarly, when in the laws, ideologies and customs of those times I came across some of the deficiencies which had destroyed the old order and which still plague us, I have been careful to cast light upon them so that, in discerning the damage they have inflicted upon us, the more easily we might grasp what they could again do to us.

I confess that, to achieve this aim, I have not shrunk from offending anyone, either individuals or classes, opinions or memories, however respectable they may have been. Often it is with regret that I have done so but always it is without remorse. I hope that those whom I might have displeased will forgive me out of consideration for the impartial and honest intention I am pursuing.

Maybe several will accuse me of having betrayed in this book an excessive zeal for freedom, which, I am told, is scarcely of any great concern in present-day France.

I simply ask those who might level such a reproach at me to have the kindness to reflect that this enthusiasm of mine is of very long standing. For over twenty years ago I was writing almost word for word what you are about to read here about another social group.

In the dark depths of the future three obvious truths can already be seen. The first is that all our contemporaries are driven on by an unknown force which we can hope to govern and moderate but are unable to overcome. At times these forces push them gently forward, at others they propel them to the destruction of the aristocracy. The second is that, at the heart of all societies in the world, those societies which, over a long period of time, always have the greatest difficulty escaping from an absolute government are precisely those in which the aristocracy has disappeared, never to reappear. The third and final truth is that nowhere is despotism bound to produce more damaging effects than in such societies since, more than any other system of government, it fosters the growth of all those defects to which these societies are especially prone and it drives them accordingly in the very direction they were already favouring as a result of a natural inclination.

In such communities, where men are no longer tied to each other by race, class, craft guilds or family, they are all only too ready to think merely of their own interests, ever too predisposed to consider no one but themselves and to withdraw into a narrow individualism where all public good is snuffed out. Despotism, far from fighting against this tendency, makes it irresistible since it deprives all citizens of all shared enthusiasms, all mutual needs, all necessity for understanding, all opportunity to act in concert. It confines them, so to say, to private life. Men were already moving towards isolation; now despotism confirms it. They were cooling in their feelings for each other; despotism freezes them solid.

In such kinds of society where nothing is settled, every man feels endlessly goaded on by his fear of sinking or by his passion to rise in that society. Just as money has become the principal sign of social class and the means of distinguishing men's position, it has acquired an unusual mobility, passing as it does continuously from hand to hand, altering the social condition of individuals and raising or lowering the status of families. Almost no single individual is free from the desperate and sustained effort to keep what he has got or to acquire it. The desire to grow rich at all costs, the taste for business, the passion for gain, the pursuit of comfort and material enjoyment are thus the most common preoccupations in despotisms. Those preoccupations spread with ease throughout all classes of society; they even affect those very classes which had been most free of them up to that point; shortly they would weaken and debase the entire nation, if nothing emerged to check them. Now the fundamental feature of despotism is to encourage and spread these preoccupations. Such demoralizing passions come to its aid, filling men's imaginations and diverting them from public affairs, making them shudder at the very idea of revolution. Despotism alone can provide them with that state of secrecy and obscurity which makes greed an easy option and favours the making of dishonest profits by outfacing dishonour. These passions would have been strong enough without despotism; with it they are rampant.

On the other hand, only freedom is an effective defence

against the natural weaknesses of such societies and is able to support them on the slippery slope. In fact, freedom alone can deliver citizens from the isolation imposed upon them by the very independence of their social condition, forcing them to draw closer together. Only freedom encourages and reunites them in the daily need for the mutual understanding, inspiration and delight of sharing the conduct of public business. Only freedom is capable of tearing them away from the worship of money and the petty daily upsets in their personal affairs so as to make them notice and sense at every moment their own country over and around them. There are times when liberty alone can replace the love of personal comfort with higher and more active enthusiasms, can provide ambition with loftier aims than the acquisition of wealth and can shed enough light to lead people both to see and to judge the vices and virtues of men.

Democratic societies which lack freedom can still be wealthy, sophisticated, attractive, even impressive, deriving power from the influence of their like-minded citizens. In such societies we encounter private virtues, kindly fathers, honest businessmen, exemplary landowners and even good Christians whose home country is not of this world and the glory of whose faith fosters people like that in the midst of the deepest moral corruption and the most depraved governments. The Roman Empire, in the final days of its decline, had many such in its population. However, I daresay that what we will not meet in such societies are great citizens, still less a great nation. I do not shy away from maintaining that, as long as equality and despotism co-exist, the general quality of hearts and minds will inexorably decline.

I was thinking and speaking in this vein twenty years ago. I confess that, since then, nothing has happened in this world to cause me to think or speak otherwise. And, having openly championed liberty in an age when it was in favour, no one will accuse me of bad judgement if I continue to do so when it is being abandoned.

Besides, people should realize that, in this, I reflect the views of most of my opponents more closely than they may themselves suppose. Is there a man whose soul is so mean as to wish to depend on the whims of a single member of his community rather than to obey the laws he himself has helped to establish, that is, if he thinks his nation exhibits the qualities necessary to make a proper use of liberty? I do not think such a man exists. Even despots accept the excellence of liberty. The simple truth is that they wish to keep it for themselves and promote the idea that no one else is at all worthy of it. Thus, our opinion of liberty does not reveal our differences but the relative value which we place on our fellow man. We can state with conviction, therefore, that a man's support for absolute government is in direct proportion to the contempt he feels for his country. I am asking for a little more time before I convert to such an opinion.

I trust I can claim in all modesty that the book I now offer to the public is the result of a great deal of work. One quite short chapter has cost me more than a year of research. I could have overloaded the pages with footnotes; I have chosen rather to insert a small number of these at the end of the volume and to refer the reader to the relevant pages in the text. In these notes will be found material which illustrates and proves my point. I could supply many more examples, if anyone thought that this book merited their asking for them.

BOOK ONE

CHAPTER I

CONFLICTING OPINIONS OF THE REVOLUTION AT ITS OUTSET

There is nothing more capable of inspiring cautiousness in philosophers and statesmen than the history of our Revolution, for never were there events more profound, with more distant roots in the past, so long in preparation and yet less foreseen.

Despite his ability, Frederick the Great had no inkling of it. He was close to it, yet failed to see it. Furthermore, by his actions he anticipated its ethos. He was a precursor and already, one could say, a promoter. He could not see what it was from the advance signs and, when it finally came into sight, the new and extraordinary features which were to mark it out from the host of countless previous revolutions at first eluded everyone's notice.

Abroad, the Revolution was the object of universal curiosity, everywhere evoking in the mind of nations a sort of indistinct idea that a new age was in the making and a vague hope for change and reform. But no one yet suspected what form it was to take. Kings and their ministers even failed to see this mysterious warning which was troubling the nation when it appeared. In the first instance, they thought of it as one of those periodical diseases to which the constitution of all nations is subject and which simply opens up new fields to the political manoeuvres of their neighbours. If they happened to express the truth about it, it was unwittingly. It is true that Germany's principal rulers, meeting at Pillnitz in 1791, declared that the danger threatening the French royal family was shared by all the former European powers and that likewise all were in jeopardy. At root, however, they had no such belief. Secret documents from that time reveal to us that, in their view, these were clever stratagems with which to conceal their own plans or to falsify them for the public gaze.

As for them, they knew full well that the French Revolution was a local and passing event, which they needed only to exploit to their advantage. With that in mind, they hatched up plans, made preparations, contracted secret alliances and quarrelled among themselves at the sight of these imminent spoils, splitting and uniting into different camps. They got ready for almost every contingency except for what was actually to happen.

The memory of their own history and their long-standing practice of political liberty gave the English more enlightenment and experience. Thus they became quite aware, albeit through an impenetrable veil, of the image of a great revolution in progress. Yet they could not make out its shape and the effect it would soon have upon their fate and that of the world was concealed from them. Even Arthur Young, journeying through France at the very moment when the Revolution was about to break out and, aware of its imminence, was still sufficiently unaware of its reach that he wondered whether the outcome would be an increase of privilege. 'As for the nobility,' he said, 'if this revolution bestowed upon them even more power, I think that would do more harm than good.'

Burke, whose loathing for the Revolution radiated through his mind from its birth, even he for a few moments was uncertain when it happened. His first prophecy was that France would be weakened and virtually destroyed by it. 'We may assume,' he said, 'that France's military capacity has for a long time been removed, maybe forever, and that men of the following generation will be able to echo the words of this ancient writer: *Gallos quoque in bellis floruisse audivimus.* (We have heard that the Gauls, too, once excelled in war).'

Judgements of an historical event from close to are no better than those coming well after it. On the eve of the Revolution

in France, no clear idea of its aims yet existed. From the many
records, only one or two reveal a real fear of the populace.
What they dreaded was that the political power of the royal
house, or 'the Court' as it was still called, was bound to be
maintained. They were troubled by the weakness and the brief
hold on power of the Estates-General. They were alarmed that
the latter would be damaged. The nobility, in particular, was
exercised by this apprehension. Several of these documents
suggested that the Swiss Guards should swear an oath never to
assault French citizens even in the event of riot or revolt. If the
Estates-General were free, all abuses would easily be removed;
reform required much effort but was easy enough to achieve.

Meanwhile, the Revolution followed its own course. No
sooner did the head of this monster make its appearance, than
its peculiar and terrifying character emerged. It first destroyed
the political and then the civil institutions; it changed the laws
and then the customs, procedures and even the language. After
wrecking the fabric of government, it undermined the foundations of society and seemed, in essence, to aim at challenging
God himself. Soon, when the Revolution itself spilled abroad,
using methods unknown before then, new tactics, murderous
slogans, 'opinions supported by arms', as Pitt would say, a
totally unheard-of power came to beat down barriers, smash
royal crowns, trample nations underfoot and, stranger than
strange, managed to rally these last to its cause. As all these
things exploded into being, a new point of view emerged. What
had, in the first instance, seemed to the rulers of Europe and
the politicians an event not out of the ordinary in the life of
nations, now appeared to be such a new event, in such opposition to all that had happened before in the world, yet so
widespread, so grotesque, so indecipherable, that the human
mind looked upon it with open-mouthed disbelief. Some felt
that this unknown power would drive human societies to their
complete and terminal dissolution, since nothing appeared
either to feed or to flatten it. It could not be arrested by men
nor could it control its own momentum. Many judged it to be
the evident behaviour of the Devil himself. As M. de Maistre
voiced as early as 1797, 'The French Revolution has a demonic

character.' Others, in contrast, perceived in the Revolution the benevolent workings of God whose aim was to reinvigorate not only the face of France but of the whole world by creating some type of new humanity. In the works of several writers of that period, we encounter something of this religious fearfulness which Salvanius experienced at the sight of the barbarians. Burke, developing his own thoughts on the matter, exclaimed: 'France stripped of her former government or rather of any government, resembles an object of contempt and pity rather than the scourge and terror of the human race. But from the grave of this murdered monarchy springs a deformed, grotesque creature, more terrifying than any of the monsters which have overwhelmed and enslaved the human imagination. This strange and ugly being advances straight to its goal, neither afraid of danger nor halted by remorse, deriding all accepted truths and all normal routines. It knocks to the ground those that cannot even understand how it came into existence.'

To the men of the time was this event indeed as unusual as it seemed? Was it as unprecedented, as deeply disturbing and reinvigorating as was supposed? What was its real meaning, its actual character? What were the lasting effects of this bizarre and terrible revolution? What precisely did it destroy? What has it created?

The time for investigation and judgement seems to have arrived. Today we are positioned at that exact moment when we can best decipher and assess this important event. We are far enough from the Revolution to experience only a pale version of the enthusiasms which disturbed the sight of those who led it, yet near enough to be able to empathize with the spirit which guided it and to understand it. Soon it will be difficult to do such a thing, since those great revolutions which are a success conceal the causes which have inspired them and thus they run beyond our capacity to understand because they were so successful.

CHAPTER 2

HOW THE FUNDAMENTAL AND ULTIMATE INTENTION OF THE REVOLUTION WAS NOT, AS WAS THOUGHT, TO DESTROY RELIGIOUS POWER NOR TO WEAKEN POLITICAL POWER

One of the opening assaults of the French Revolution was against the Church and among the passions to which the Revolution gave life, the first to be kindled and the last to be extinguished, was the anti-religious. Even when the enthusiasm for liberty had faded away, when men had been reduced to buying peace of mind at the cost of slavery, the rebellion against religious authority still subsisted. Napoleon, who had succeeded in overcoming the libertarian spirit of the French Revolution, struggled in vain against its anti-Christian spirit. Even in our own time we have seen men who believed that, by exhibiting their contempt for God, they could cover up their cowardice before the least significant government officials. These men abandoned all the most liberal, noble and exalted revolutionary doctrines, while priding themselves on keeping faith with its essence by retaining their irreligious stance.

And yet today it is easy to be convinced that the war against religions was simply a minor event in this great revolution, a prominent but fleeting feature, an ephemeral result of the ideas, passions, individual details which preceded and prepared for it, rather than the spirit at its centre.

Eighteenth-century philosophy is correctly considered as one of the main causes of the Revolution and it is quite true that this philosophy is profoundly anti-religious. But it must be carefully noted that in it there were two quite distinct and separable trends.

In the first reside all those new or revitalized opinions which connect with social conditions, civil and political principles of the law, such as, for example, the natural equality of men, which leads as a consequence to the abolition of all racial, class and professional privileges, the sovereignty of the people, the predominance of social power, the uniformity of rules ... Not only are all these doctrines the causes of the French Revolution, they virtually create its foundation. They represent all that is fundamental, lasting and authentic in its characteristics as far as that time saw it.

In the second part of their doctrines the political and social commentators of the eighteenth century, known as the 'Philosophes', attacked the Church in a sort of frenzy. They attacked its clergy, its hierarchy, its institutions, its dogmas and, in order better to overturn them, they set out to uproot the very foundations of Christianity. However, this aspect of eighteenth-century philosophy, having taken root in the conditions that the Revolution itself was destroying, was gradually to disappear with those conditions and to end up buried, as it were, in its own triumph. I shall add but one word more in a final effort to make my meaning clear for I intend to return to this great theme elsewhere. It was far less as a religious faith than as a political institution that Christianity had stirred these uncontrolled loathings. It was not that priests claimed to regulate the affairs of the other world but that they were landowners, lords of the manor, exactors of tithes and administrators in this world; not that the Church was unable to find a place in the new order of society about to be created but because it occupied at that time the most privileged and most powerful place in the old society which people were concerned to reduce to dust.

Simply look how the passage of time has highlighted this truth and has daily kept it in the spotlight. Just as the political achievement of the Revolution was consolidated, its anti-religious campaign foundered; as all the former political institutions it attacked have been destroyed, as the agencies of government, the centres of power and the class system, which were particularly hated, have been overcome for all time; as – and this is the last sign of their defeat – those very hatreds they inspired have died down and, as finally the clergy has increasingly distanced itself from all that fell with them, we have seen the power of the Church gradually restored and strengthened in men's minds.

And do not think that this phenomenon is peculiar to France. There is scarcely any Christian Church in Europe which has not received a new lease of life since the French Revolution.

To believe that democratic societies are by their nature hostile to religion is to commit a great mistake. Nothing in Christianity, not even in Roman Catholicism, is totally contrary to the ethos of these societies and several aspects are very favourable to them. Furthermore, the experience of every century has revealed that the most vigorous roots of religious feeling have always been planted in the hearts of the people. Every religion which has perished found its last refuge in the people and it would be odd if those institutions which tend to uphold the ideas and passions of the people should involve the necessary and permanent outcome of thrusting the human spirit towards irreligion.

What I have just said about religious power I shall say all the more strongly of social power.

When men saw the Revolution overturn both every institution and every custom which had hitherto sustained social hierarchy and constrained them within the rules, they were able to feel that its result would be to destroy not only the social order of the individual but all order, not such and such a government but the power of society itself. Men were bound to conclude that its nature was fundamentally anarchic. Yet I am bold enough to maintain that this was still only a superficial view.

Less than a year after the outbreak of the Revolution, Mirabeau wrote secretly to the king: 'Compare this new state of affairs with the Ancien Régime; thereby you will see the grounds for reassurance and hope. One set of the edicts promulgated by the National Assembly – and the most weighty – is clearly favourable to monarchical government. Is it therefore of no consequence to be without *parlements*, the Independent Provinces, the priesthood, the privileged classes, the nobility? The idea of forming a single class of citizens would have been to Richelieu's liking; this level ground facilitates the exercise of power. Several years of absolute government would not have done as much for royal power as this single year of revolution.'

That was the kind of understanding of the Revolution that comes from a man capable of leading it.

Since the French Revolution did not simply have the aim of changing the former government but of abolishing the old structure of society, it had to attack simultaneously every established power, destroy every recognized influence, blot out tradition, create fresh social customs and habits, somehow drain the human mind of all those ideas upon which respect and obedience had been founded up to that time. That was the source of its strangely anarchic character.

But remove this debris and you will see an extensive unified power which has attracted and absorbed into its centre all the fragments of authority and influence which previously had been scattered between a group of secondary power bases, social orders, classes, professions, families and individuals, all of which were spread throughout the body of society. Never had such a power been seen in the world since the fall of the Roman Empire. The Revolution created this new power, or, rather, this power emerged autonomously from the ruins caused by it. The governments it founded are, it is true, more fragile but a hundred times more vigorous than any of those it overturned – fragile and vigorous for the same reasons, as will be explained elsewhere.

This is the simple, shapely and majestic structure that Mirabeau was already espying through the dust of the half-demolished institutions of this older age. Despite its great size this object was as yet invisible to the eyes of the crowd; but gradually time laid it before everyone's gaze. Today it fills the eyes of princely rulers who contemplate it with admiration and envy, not only those who owe their beginnings to the Revolution but even those who are most alien and hostile to it. All are straining to destroy immunities, abolish privileges within their territories. They muddle the distinctions of class, equalize social conditions, replace the aristocracy with civil servants, local charters with uniform regulations. They concentrate on this revolutionary work with unflagging effort. If they encounter any obstacle, they often borrow from the Revolution its methods and its slogans. When the need arose they were seen championing the poor against the rich, the commoner against the nobleman, the peasant farmer against his lord. The French Revolution was equally their scourge and their teacher.

CHAPTER 3

HOW THE FRENCH REVOLUTION WAS A POLITICAL REVOLUTION WHICH FOLLOWED THE LINES OF RELIGIOUS REVOLUTIONS AND WHY

All civil and political revolutions have been restricted within the boundaries of their own countries. The French Revolution did not have its own territory. Furthermore, its effect, to a degree, has been to remove from the map all former frontiers. We observed it uniting or dividing men despite their laws, traditions, personalities or language; it turned fellow citizens into enemies, strangers into brothers. It would be truer to say that it created, beyond the separate nationalities, a common intellectual homeland where men of all nations could become citizens.

Search through all the annals of history and you will not find a single political revolution which has had this same character; you will find something similar only in certain religious revolutions. Consequently, we must compare the French Revolution to religious revolutions, if we wish to use an analogy to make ourselves clear.

Schiller was right to note, in his history of the Thirty Years War, that the great Reformation of the sixteenth century had the effect of suddenly drawing together nations which hardly knew each other and of uniting them closely through this new fellow feeling. At that time, in fact, Frenchmen were seen fighting Frenchmen while Englishmen came to their aid. Men born in the far-off Baltic advanced deep into Germany to protect Germans of whom they had previously never heard. Every foreign war assumed something of the character of a civil war.

In every civil conflict foreigners would appear. The former interests of each nation were forgotten for new ones; issues of territory were superseded by those of principle. All the rules of diplomacy were thrown into muddle and confusion, much to the astonishment and grief of the politicians of that period. Precisely the same happened in Europe after 1789.

The French Revolution was, therefore, a political revolution which evolved in the manner of religious revolutions and assumed something of their character. Notice the individual and characteristic features in which it finally resembled them. Not only did it spread far and wide as they did but, like them, it advanced through preaching and propaganda. Here was a political revolution which inspired converts; one which was promoted as passionately among foreigners as it was fostered with enthusiasm at home. That was a new sight to behold! Amid all the unheard-of facets which the French Revolution revealed to the world, this was certainly the most novel. But let us not stop there. Let us attempt to look even more deeply to discover whether these similar effects did not stem from some hidden similarity in its causes.

The usual feature of religions is to consider man in isolation without pausing to wonder what the common foundation of laws, customs and traditions of a country might have contributed on the individual level. Their principal aim is to order the general relations of man to God and the general rights and duties of man to man, with no attention paid to the particular form society adopts. The rules of behaviour they display relate less to the man of a particular country or period of history than to a son, father, servant, master or neighbour. Thus resting upon the basic structure of human nature itself, these rules can be acknowledged equally by all men and can be relevant everywhere. Consequently, religious revolutions have often enjoyed such vast canvasses and have seldom been confined, like political upheavals, to the territory of one nation or even of one single race. If we are keen to examine this subject even more closely, we shall discover that the more religions have this abstract and universal character which I have just noted, the more widely have they spread, whatever the differences of law, climate or men.

The pagan religions of antiquity, which were more or less linked to the political constitution or the social state of each nation, while preserving even in their doctrines a certain national and often municipal character, were usually confined within the boundaries of one area which they scarcely ever left. Sometimes they bred intolerance or persecution but missionary zeal was almost entirely unknown. Thus no great religious revolutions occurred in the West before the advent of Christianity, which, passing with ease beyond all the barriers that had halted pagan cults, took no time at all to overcome a majority of the human race. I think I can say, without lacking respect towards this holy religion, that it owed its triumph in part to the fact that it had freed itself, more than had any other cult, from every special link with a single nation, government, social state, historical period or race.

The French Revolution evolved in reference to this world in exactly the same manner as religious revolutions acted in relation to the world beyond the grave. It viewed the citizen in an abstract fashion, unrelated to any particular society, just as religions viewed man independent of time or country. It did not simply seek to determine the individual rights of the French citizen but the general duties and rights of men in the political sphere.

So, it was because the French Revolution harked back to the universal and, so to speak, to the most natural as far as social structure and government were concerned, that it has been able to appear comprehensible to all and to be worth imitating in a hundred places at once.

Since it appeared to aim at the regeneration of the human race much more than at the reform of France, it kindled a passion which the most violent of political revolutions had failed to arouse before. It inspired the missionary spirit and fostered propaganda as a result of which it was able to assume that air of a religious revolution which so terrified people at the time. Or rather it became itself a species of new religion, barely formed, it is true. Godless, without ritual or an afterlife but which, nevertheless, like Islam, has flooded all the Earth with its soldiers, apostles and martyrs.

We must not, however, think that the methods it used were

entirely without precedent or that all the ideas it engendered were completely new. Over the centuries, there have always been, even at the heart of the Middle Ages, agitators who, in order to change particular customs, have appealed to the universal laws of human societies and who have undertaken to establish the natural rights of mankind against the constitution of their own country. But all these efforts have failed. The same firebrand which set eighteenth-century Europe alight had been easily snuffed out in the fifteenth. In order for such arguments to bring about revolutions, certain changes in social conditions, customs and manners must already have occurred so as to prepare the human mind to let itself be influenced by them.

There are times when men are so mutually incompatible that the notion of one single law being applicable to all is virtually unintelligible to them. At other times it is enough to show them, from a distance and in a blurred form, the image of such a law for them to recognize it immediately and to pursue it.

The most extraordinary aspect is not that the French Revolution employed the methods which we have seen it use or conceived the ideas that it did. The most novel aspect was that so many nations had reached this point of development that such methods could be effectively exploited or such ideology easily welcomed.

CHAPTER 4

HOW ALMOST THE WHOLE OF EUROPE HAD EXACTLY IDENTICAL INSTITUTIONS AND HOW THESE INSTITUTIONS WERE EVERYWHERE FALLING INTO RUIN

The nations, which overturned the Roman Empire and finally formed our modern nations, differed by race, country and language; they resembled each other only in their barbarism. Once established on the soil of the Empire, they entered upon a long clash of arms characterized by large-scale confusion and, when at last they became stable, they found themselves separated by the devastation they had caused. Since civilization had almost disappeared and public order was destroyed, communication between men became difficult and dangerous. The great European Society split into a thousand small societies which existed as distinct and hostile units each living independently. Yet within this incoherent mass there developed suddenly a uniform system of laws.

These institutions were not imitated from the Roman legal system; they were so unlike it that Roman law[2] was called upon to modify and abolish them. Their character is original and distinguishes them from all other laws that men have devised for themselves. These laws share a close similarity and, taken as a whole, form a body of law whose parts are so closely knit that the articles of our modern codes are not more compactly united. These were astute laws adapted for the use of a semi-barbarian society.

How such a legislative system could finally have taken shape, spread and become the norm in Europe it is not my aim to investigate. What is certain is that, in the Middle Ages, it was extant more or less everywhere in Europe and that, in many countries, it prevailed to the exclusion of all other systems.

I have had the opportunity to study the political institutions of the Middle Ages in France, England and Germany. As I progressed in this work, I was filled with astonishment at seeing the extraordinary similarity found between all these legal systems and I wondered how such different nations, whose contact with each other was so slight, had managed to adopt for themselves such similar laws. It was not that they revealed endless variations and an almost infinite degree of detail according to local circumstances but that their fundamentals were the same everywhere. Whenever I lighted upon a political institution, a rule of law, a power in the ancient German legislation, I knew in advance that, were I to investigate, I would discover something exactly similar in France and in England. And indeed I never failed to do so. Each of these three nations helped me to a better understanding of the other two.

In all three countries the government was conducted in accordance with the same rules, the political assemblies were formed from the same elements and were armed with the same powers. Their society divided in the same way; the same hierarchy was found among different classes; the nobles occupied identical positions with the same privileges, features and disposition. These were not different kinds of men but essentially the same men everywhere.

The town constitutions were alike; rural districts enjoyed the same style of government. The social conditions of peasants were little different; the land was owned, settled, cultivated similarly and the farmer was subject to the same taxes. From the Polish borders to the Irish Sea, the manor and its court, the fiefdoms, the holdings paying quitrent, the feudal services and rights, the guilds were identical. The names were sometimes the same and, what is still more noteworthy, one single ethos inspired all these similar institutions. I venture to maintain that the social, political, administrative, judicial, economic and literary institutions of fourteenth-century Europe shared more resemblances than perhaps they have at the present time when civilization seems to have taken care to clear every path and remove every obstacle.

It is no part of my theme to relate how this former European constitution[3] gradually lost its power and fell into decay. I simply state that in the eighteenth century it was in partial ruins everywhere. The disintegration was generally less pronounced in the east of the continent and more so in the west but every country manifested this process of ageing and disintegration.

This gradual collapse of the institutions peculiar to the Middle Ages can be followed in their archives. We know that each manor owned registers of land ownership called *terriers* in which, through the centuries, they recorded the boundaries of the fiefs, the holdings paying rent, the dues payable, the obligatory feudal services and the local customs. I have seen the *terriers* of the fourteenth century which are masterpieces of drafting, clarity, precision and intelligence. They become obscure, ill-formed, incomplete and muddled as they move into more recent times, despite the general progress of knowledge. It would appear that political society drifted down into barbarism at the very time when civil society was finally achieving enlightenment.

Even in Germany, where the old European Constitution had maintained its original features more effectively than in France, some of the institutions it had created were already everywhere being destroyed. But we can best judge the ravages of time less by observing its losses than by viewing the state of its remaining features.

Those urban institutions, which in the thirteenth and fourteenth centuries had transposed the chief German towns into small, prosperous and enlightened republics,[4] still existed in the eighteenth but offered nothing more than an empty show. Their legal conditions appeared to be as vigorous as ever – the magistrates they appointed had the same names and appeared to perform the same functions – but the activity, energy, shared patriotic feeling, virile and productive virtues which they inspired had vanished. These ancient institutions had inwardly collapsed without losing their original shape.

All the powers of the Middle Ages that still remained were attacked by the same disease and displayed the same disintegration and the same slow decline. Still more, everything which was associated with the old constitution and had retained an almost clear imprint of it, without exactly belonging to it, directly lost its vitality. From that contact the aristocracy became infected with senile decay. Political liberty itself, whose achievements had permeated the whole Middle Ages, appeared to be stricken by barrenness wherever it still bore the particular characteristics it had gained from the medieval period. Wherever provincial assemblies had preserved their ancient constitution in an unchanged state they halted the progress of civilization rather than fostered it. It might be said that they were alien and almost impervious to the new spirit of the time. Further, the heart of the people kept away from them and turned towards the royal households. The antiquity of these institutions had not made them respected. Quite the contrary, they lost any credit even as they grew old and, strange to relate, they inspired all the more hatred as they seemed less capable of causing harm through their increasing decay. 'The present state of things,' said a German writer, a contemporary and friend of this old regime, 'appears to have become generally painful for everyone and occasionally contemptible. It is strange to see how people now judge unfavourably everything that is old. New impressions come to light at the heart of our families and upset their orderliness. Even our housewives no longer wish to put up with their old furniture.' Yet in Germany, at the same time as in France, society was thriving and enjoyed a growing prosperity. But pay the following careful attention – for this feature completes the picture – everything which was alive, active and creative was recent in origin, not only new but in conflict with the past.

Royalty shared nothing in common with the royalty of the Middle Ages, possessed other powers, occupied another position, had another spirit and inspired other feelings; the administration of the state extended everywhere, settling upon the remnants of local powers; the hierarchy of public officials increasingly replaced the government of the nobility. All these new powers acted according to procedures and followed ideas which men of the Middle Ages had either not known or had condemned. These had their links in fact to a state of society beyond their experience.

In England also, where one's first impression would have been that the ancient constitution of Europe was still flourishing, the same was happening. If we were to ignore the old names and to dismiss the old patterns, we would find, from the seventeenth century onwards, a feudal system substantially abolished, classes melding into each other, the nobility removed, an aristocracy open to all, wealth turning into power, equality before the law, equal taxation, the freedom of the press and the public reports of debates. All these new principles were unknown to medieval society. Now the gradual and skilful introduction of these novelties into the old feudal order, precisely ensured its rejuvenation without risking its dissolution and filled it with fresh energy while leaving intact the ancient organizations.

Seventeenth-century England was already a fully modern nation which had merely preserved within its centre, as if embalmed, a few relics of the Middle Ages.

It has been necessary to cast a swift glance beyond the boundaries of France to help our understanding of what follows, for whoever has restricted their studies and observations only to France will, I venture to say, understand nothing of the French Revolution.

WHAT WAS THE REAL WORK OF THE FRENCH REVOLUTION?

The aim of all the previous chapters has been to illuminate the subject and to arrive more easily at the solution of the question which I posed at the beginning. What was the real objective of the Revolution? What, in short, was its essential character? Why exactly was it set in motion? What did it achieve?

The Revolution was not set in motion, as some have believed, to destroy the dominance of religious beliefs; essentially, despite appearances, it was a social and political revolution. Within the group of similar institutions, it did not aim to perpetuate disorder, making it somehow permanent, nor (as one of its main opponents asserted) to *bring method* to anarchy but rather to increase the power and rights of public authority. It was not to alter the character of the current civilization, as others have thought, nor to bring progress to a halt, nor even to modify the essence of those basic laws which supported human societies in the West. When we detach the Revolution from all those chance events which have briefly changed its appearance in various eras and in different countries, so as to view it in its own right, we see quite clearly that the only effect of this revolution has been to abolish those political institutions which have prevailed unopposed for several centuries in most European nations and which we normally describe as feudal, in order to replace them with a more uniform and simple social and political regime based upon social equality.

That was enough to create an immense revolution. For, aside

from the fact that the ancient institutions were still entwined and connected to almost all the religious and political legislation of Europe, they had, in addition, inspired a host of ideas, opinions, habits and customs which clung to them, as it were. A hideous upheaval was needed to destroy them and, at the same time, to extract from the body of society that part which was attached to all its members. This made the Revolution appear yet greater than it was. It seemed to destroy everything because, what it did destroy, affected everything and in some way was part of everything.

Radical though it may have been, nevertheless the Revolution was much less innovative than is generally supposed, as I shall demonstrate later. What can truly be stated is that it completely destroyed or is in the process of destroying (for it is still an enduring influence) everything of the ancient society which derived from the aristocratic and feudal institutions, which was linked to them in any way at all and which bore the *slightest* impression of them in any way whatever. It preserved from the old world order only that which had always been alien to these institutions or could exist without them. What the Revolution was not in any way was a chance event. Admittedly it took the world by surprise. It was nevertheless only the accompaniment to a long period of effort and the sudden, violent outcome of a task undertaken by ten generations of men. If it had not taken place the old social edifice would nonetheless have continued to collapse, here sooner, there later; it would simply have gone on collapsing bit by bit instead of crumbling at one fell swoop. The Revolution finished off suddenly by a convulsive and painful effort, without a period of transition, throwing caution aside and without any consideration, what would have automatically been finished gradually and by slow degrees. Such was its achievement.

It is surprising that what today appears so easy to see remained as tangled and hidden as it was even to the most far-sighted observers.

'You wished to correct the abuses of your government,' said Burke himself to the French, 'but why stir up novelty? Why did you not adhere to your old traditions? Why not limit yourselves

to recovering your old freedoms? Or, if you found it impossible
to recover the obliterated character of the constitutions of your
ancestors, why did you not cast a glance in our direction where
you would have found the ancient common law of Europe?'
Burke did not perceive what lay beneath his gaze, namely that
the Revolution itself must abolish this ancient common law of
Europe. He did not spot that this and nothing else was what it
was about.

But why did this Revolution break out in France rather than
elsewhere when it was everywhere in a state of readiness and
threatening every country? Why did it have certain features in
France which have not been found anywhere else or only partially so? The second question surely deserves to be asked and
the aim of the following books will be to examine it.

BOOK TWO

CHAPTER I

WHY FEUDAL RIGHTS HAD BECOME MORE HATED AMONG THE PEOPLE OF FRANCE THAN ANYWHERE ELSE

At the outset one fact is surprising: the Revolution, whose real aim was to abolish everywhere what was left of medieval institutions, did not break out in those countries where these more firmly entrenched institutions most inflicted their oppression and violence upon the people but in those where they least did so. Consequently, their yoke became most unbearable where it was, in fact, least burdensome.

At the end of the eighteenth century, almost no part of Germany[5] had seen the abolition of serfdom; in most parts the people remained all but tied to the land, as in the Middle Ages. Almost all the soldiers who formed the armies of Frederick the Great and Maria Teresa were serfs in the true sense.

In the majority of the German states in 1788, the peasant could not leave the lord's estate and, if he did so, he could be tracked down everywhere he went and brought back by force. He was subjected to the jurisdiction of his lord who kept an eye on his personal life and punished his excesses and laziness. He could neither rise in rank nor change his work, nor marry without the approval of his master. A great part of his time had to be devoted to the latter's service. Several of his adolescent years were to be spent in the domestic service of the manor house. Forced labour (la corvée) for his lord was in its heyday

BOOK TWO, CHAPTER I

and could take up to three days of a man's week in certain countries. The peasant it was who rebuilt and maintained the lord's buildings, who transported his produce to market, drove him around and was responsible for taking his messages. The serf could, however, become a landowner but always with uncertain tenure. He was obliged to cultivate his fields in a specified way under his master's eye. He could neither sell them nor mortgage them at will. In certain cases, he was forced to sell the produce; in others, he was prevented from doing so. As far as he was concerned, farming his land was always obligatory. Even his inheritance did not pass entirely to his children; a part of it was usually retained by the manor.

I did not seek out these regulations in obsolete laws; I came across them even in the code drawn up by Frederick the Great[6] and published by his successor at the very same moment that the French Revolution had just broken out.

Nothing of that kind had existed in France for a long time: the peasant came and went, bought and sold, negotiated and worked as he pleased. The last shreds of serfdom could be seen only in one or two recently conquered provinces of eastern France; everywhere else it had completely disappeared and even its abolition went back to such a distant time that its date was forgotten. Scholarly research of our time has proved that, from the thirteenth century, it had vanished from Normandy.

But, in France, a quite different revolution had come about in the social conditions of the people; the small farmer had not only ceased to be a serf, he had become a landowner. This fact is still so poorly understood and, as we shall see, has had so many consequences, that I may be allowed to pause a moment to examine it.

It has long been believed that the division of property dated from the Revolution and had been a product of it. The opposite is proved by all kinds of evidence.

At least twenty years before this Revolution we encounter agricultural societies complaining already that the land was being excessively sub-divided. 'The division of inheritance,' said Turgot about that same time, 'is such that the bequest which was enough for one single family is being split between five or six children. These children and their families can no longer live from the land alone.' Necker said, a few years later, that there was in France *a large number* of small rural properties.

I came across a secret report lodged with an Intendant not long before the Revolution: 'Inheritances are divided in a fair but disturbing way. Since each child everywhere wants his share of everything, the plots of land are split and split again ad infinitum.' Would you not think that this was being written today?

I have taken infinite pains to reconstruct to a degree the land register of the Ancien Régime and have sometimes managed to do so. According to the law of 1790 which established a land tax, every parish had to draw up a list of properties in existence within its boundaries. These lists have mostly vanished. Nevertheless, I have unearthed them in a certain number of villages. By comparing them to the administrative rolls of today I have observed that, in those villages, the number of owned properties reached half, often two-thirds, of the present number. This will appear quite remarkable if you think that the total population of France has grown by more than a quarter since that time.

Already, as in our own day, the love of the small farmer for property was excessive and all passions born in him for the ownership of land were aflame. 'Land is always sold above its value,' said an excellent contemporary observer. 'This results from the passion all inhabitants have to become landowners. All the savings of the lower classes, which elsewhere are invested in private funds and in public bonds, are devoted in France to the purchase of land.'

Amid all the novelties which Arthur Young noticed when he visited us for the first time, none struck him more forcibly than the wide division of the land among small farmers. He states that half the land of France belonged to them exclusively. 'I had no idea,' he often says, 'that such a state of affairs existed.' In fact, such a state of affairs existed nowhere at that time except in France or in its immediate neighbourhood.

There had been peasant landowners in England but there were already fewer of them. Everywhere in Germany a certain number of free peasants had always been observed who owned areas of land with full rights of possession.[7] The particular and often strange laws governing the property of the peasant farmer can be found in the oldest of German traditions. But that sort of land ownership had always been an exception to the rule and the number of these modest landowners was very small.

At the end of the eighteenth century, the districts of Germany, where the farmer was an owner and almost as free as in France, were situated for the most part along the Rhine;[8] this was also where the revolutionary zeal of France spread most rapidly and was most fervently felt. The parts of Germany, on the other hand, which have been the most impervious to this zeal are those where nothing similar has been found. A fact worth noting.

Believing, therefore, that the division of land ownership dates in France from the Revolution would be to make a common mistake; this phenomenon is much older than that. It is true that the Revolution sold all the Church lands and a large part of the land belonging to the aristocracy but, if one wishes to consult the actual minutes of these sales, as I have from time to time had the patience to do, one will see that most of these lands were bought by people who were already landowners. The result was that, even if the property changed hands, the number of owners increased much less than is imagined. There already was an *immensity* of the latter, to pick up the ambitious, though on this occasion accurate, expression of M. Necker.[9]

The effect of the Revolution has been not to divide the land but to free it up for a brief moment. All these smallholders were, in fact, considerably restricted in the use of their land and endured many privations which they were not allowed to shake off.

These burdens were doubtless heavy but what made them appear unbearable was precisely the circumstance which ought to have seemingly lightened the pain for them. These same farmers had been freed, more than anywhere else in Europe, from the government of their lords – another revolution no less important than that which had made them landowners.

Although the Ancien Régime is still quite close to us in time, since we daily come across men who were born under its laws, it already seems to be lost in the obscurity of the past. The radical revolution which separates us from it has the same effect as centuries would have – it has cast a veil over everything it did not destroy. Thus few people exist today who might give a precise reply to this simple question: how was the countryside administered before 1789? In fact, it cannot be answered with any accuracy or in any detail unless you have studied, not the books, but the administrative archives of that period.

I have often heard it said that the nobility had for some long time ceased to take part in the government of the state and had hung on to the administration of the countryside to the very end. The lord governed the peasants. This very much looks like a mistaken view.

In the eighteenth century all parish affairs were conducted by a certain number of state officials who were no longer agents of the manor and no longer chosen by the lord. Some were appointed by the Intendant of the district, others elected by the peasants themselves. It was the duty of these authorities to assess taxes, repair churches, build schools, summon and preside over the parish meeting. They supervised the municipal lands and controlled any use of them; they instituted and defended lawsuits in the name of the community. Not only did the lord not continue to control the administration of these minor local affairs, he did not even supervise them. Each parish official served under the government or the direction of the central administration as we shall demonstrate in the next chapter. Furthermore, one almost never saw the lord acting in the parish as the representative of the king nor as the intermediary between the king and the inhabitants. He was no longer charged with the implementation of the general state laws – summoning the militia, raising the taxes, publishing the commands of the king or distributing the king's charity. All these duties and rights belonged to others. The lord was, in real terms, merely an inhabitant separated and isolated from everyone else by immunities and privileges. His social position, not his power, was different. The Intendants took care to write letters to their sub-delegates that *the lord was only the first citizen*.

If you move away from the parish and consider the canton,

you will see exactly the same picture. Nowhere did the aristocrats govern, either together or as individuals; that was peculiar to France. Everywhere else the characteristic features of the old feudal society had been in part preserved; the ownership of the land and the government of the inhabitants were still linked.

England was administered as well as governed by the main landowners. In those very areas of Germany where the rulers had had the greatest success in escaping the control of the nobility in general state business – for instance, Prussia and Austria – they had left the aristocrats for the most part to administer the countryside. Even if, in some places, they had gone so far as to rein in the lord, they still had not anywhere usurped his position.

In truth, the French nobility had not had contact with public administration for a long time except for one aspect, namely justice. The leading members of the nobility had retained the right to appoint their own judges to decide certain lawsuits on their behalf and, from time to time, issued police regulations within the confines of the manor. But the royal authority had gradually curtailed, limited and reduced the lord's justice to such a degree that those lords who continued to exercise it, viewed it less as a power than as a source of revenue.

All those rights peculiar to the nobility found themselves in the same position. The political aspect had vanished; the monetary portion alone had remained and sometimes had considerably increased.

I now wish to speak just about that area of useful privileges which, par excellence, went by the name of feudal rights because these are the features which especially affected the people at large.

Today, it is not easy to state what these rights were still composed of in 1789, for their number had been very large and their range extraordinarily wide. Several had already disappeared from among them, or been transformed, so that the meaning of the words describing them was then already confusing people and has become extremely obscure for us today. Nevertheless, on consulting eighteenth-century experts in feudal law and researching closely local usage, we can see that all those rights still in existence can be reduced to a small number of main types. It is true that all the others still existed but only as isolated instances.

Traces of statutory forced labour demanded by the lord could be found almost everywhere but half obliterated. Most of the tolls on roads were reduced or removed, though there were few provinces where you did not encounter several still intact. In all provinces the lords levied dues on fairs and markets. We know that in the whole of France they enjoyed exclusive hunting rights. In general, they alone could own dovecotes and pigeons. Almost everywhere they forced the peasant farmer to grind his grain at their mill and process his grapes in their wine press. One universal and very burdensome right was that called *lods et ventes*, which was a tax paid to the lord whenever land was bought or sold within the boundaries of the manor. In short, everywhere the land was burdened with rents, property costs, dues in cash or in kind payable to the lord by the owner, which the latter could not redeem. One common feature ran through all these variations: all these rights were tied more or less to the land or its produce; they all hit the peasant farmer.

We know, too, that the Church lords enjoyed the same advantages, for the Church, which had different beginnings, a different destination and a character other than feudalism, had, nevertheless, in the end, linked itself closely with that system. Although it had never been entirely incorporated into this alien body, it had been so deeply impregnated by it that it became virtually embedded in it.[10,11]

Thus, by virtue of their ecclesiastical duties, bishops, canons and abbots owned fiefs or quitrents.[12] Normally the convent had the lordship of the village in which its land was situated. It had serfs in the only part of France where there were still some. It employed forced labour, levied dues on fairs and markets, had its own oven, mill, wine press and stud bull. Furthermore, clergy, in France as throughout the Christian world, enjoyed the right to collect tithes.

But what matters to me here is that throughout Europe we can see that the same feudal rights, *exactly the same*, still existed and that, in most continental districts, they were much more burdensome. I will cite the single example of the lord's right to forced labour. In France it was rarely encountered and was mild; in Germany, it was still found everywhere and was harsh.

Furthermore, several of the rights of feudal origin, which had so outraged our forefathers and which they viewed not merely as contrary to both justice and civilization – tithes, irredeemable land rents, permanent charges, land purchase and sale taxes, what they called in the rather exaggerated language of the eighteenth century the *enslavement of the land* – all these were still to be found, to some extent, among the English and several can still be seen there even today. They do not stop English agriculture from being the most advanced and the most productive in the world and the English nation hardly notices their existence.

Why, then, have these same feudal rights aroused in the hearts of French people such a powerful hatred that it has survived the object of that loathing and thus seems ineradicable? The reason for this phenomenon is that the French peasant had become a landowner on the one hand and, on the other, had completely freed himself from the dominance of his lord. There are yet other reasons of course but I think these to be the chief ones.

If the peasant had not owned the land, he would not have been aware of several of the burdens which the feudal system imposed on agricultural property. How does tithing matter to someone who is merely farming the land? It is only levied on the farmer's produce. How does land rent matter to the man not owning the land? How do the restrictions on land-use matter to the farmer who exploits the land for someone else?

On the other hand, if the French peasant had still been governed by his lord, the feudal rights would have seemed to him much less intolerable because he would have seen them only as a natural consequence of the constitution of the country.

When the nobility possesses not only privileges but also powers, when it both governs and administers, its individual rights can be greater while being less obvious. In feudal times the nobility was viewed with almost the same eye as we view the government today. The burdens it imposed were tolerated in the light of the guarantees it offered. The nobles possessed annoying privileges, enjoyed rights that people found irksome but they safeguarded public order, dispensed justice, had the law upheld, came to the help of the weak and directed public business. As the nobility ceased to conduct these affairs, the weight of its privileges seemed more burdensome and its very existence was, in the end, no longer understandable

I would ask you to picture for yourself the French peasant of the eighteenth century, or rather the one you know now, since he is still the same. His social status has changed but not his temperament. Look at him – as the documents I have quoted have drawn him – so passionately wedded to the land that he devotes all his savings to buying it and at any price. To acquire it he must first pay a fee, not to the government but to the other landowners in the vicinity who are as alien as he is to the administration of public affairs and almost as powerless. Finally, he takes ownership, puts his heart into the land with the seed he sows. This small corner of earth, which belongs solely to him in this vast universe, fills him with pride and independence. And yet, these neighbours arrive to drive him from his fields and force him to go and work elsewhere without payment. Were he to try and defend his crops against their game, these same men stop him. The same men wait at the river crossing in order to exact a toll from him. He comes across them in the market, where they sell him the right to sell his own produce. When, returning home, he wishes to use the remainder of his corn for himself – this very corn which has grown beneath his own eyes and by his own hand – he cannot do so until he has sent it to the mill for grinding and to the oven for baking, both of which these men own. A share of the income from his small domain goes to pay their fees and these are permanent and irredeemable.

Whatever he does, everywhere on the road he encounters these troublesome neighbours who disturb his pleasure, impede his work, eat his produce. When he has finished with these, other black-coated men make their appearance to take from him the best of his harvest. Imagine the position, needs, character, passions of this man and reckon up, if you can, the rich vein of hatred and envy which has accumulated in his heart.[13]

Feudalism had remained the greatest of our civil institutions when it ceased to be a political one. In its reduced state, it aroused even more hatred still and it can truly be stated that the destruction of one of the medieval institutions had made the ones remaining even more detestable.

CHAPTER 2

THE CENTRALIZATION OF THE ADMINISTRATION BELONGS TO THE ANCIEN RÉGIME AND IS NOT THE WORK OF THE REVOLUTION OR OF THE EMPIRE AS IS MAINTAINED

When we had political assemblies in France, I once heard a speaker say about the centralization of the administration: 'This fine victory achieved by the Revolution is envied by Europe.' I accept that this centralization is a fine victory and agree that Europe envies us for it but I maintain that it was not a victory achieved by the Revolution. On the contrary, it grew out of the Ancien Régime and I shall add that it was the only part of the political constitution of the old order which has survived the Revolution because it was the only one which could adapt to the new social state created by the Revolution. The reader with the patience to read this chapter carefully will find perhaps that I have fully justified my thesis.

I ask that I may be allowed to leave on one side what we called the Independent Provinces (*les pays d'état*): that is to say those provinces which governed themselves or appeared to do so to some extent.

These Independent Provinces at the furthest boundaries of the kingdom contained scarcely a quarter of the total population of France and among them only two enjoyed a regional freedom which was genuinely a living force. Later, I shall return to the

Independent Provinces and will show just how far the central government had subjected them to the common rules.

What I want principally to concentrate on is what were called in the official language of the time the Royal Provinces (*les pays d'élection*), although there were fewer elections in those areas than anywhere else. They surrounded Paris on all sides, formed a continuous group, making up the heart and most of the body of France.

When we first glance at the old administration of the kingdom, everything appears to be a diversity of rules and authorities – a tangle of powers. France was covered by governmental bodies or isolated officials who acted independently of each other and who took part in government by virtue of a right which they purchased and which could not be removed from them. Often their functions so overlapped and were so connected that they hampered each other's efficiency and clashed in identical spheres of business.

The courts of justice took part indirectly in the legislative process. They had the right to frame administrative rules which carried force within the scope of their jurisdiction. Sometimes they came into collision with the administration proper, loudly blaming its measures and issuing writs against its agents. Ordinary judges drew up police regulations in the towns and villages where they resided.

The towns had very diverse constitutions. Their magistrates bore different names or drew their powers from different sources. Here a mayor, there consuls, elsewhere receivers. Some were chosen by the king, some others by the former lord of the manor or by a prince with territorial rights. Some were elected for a year by their citizens and others had purchased the right to rule over the latter in perpetuity.

Such were the leftovers from former powers but gradually one comparatively new or transformed feature became established among them, which I have yet to describe.

At the heart of the kingdom an administrative body came into existence; it possessed an unusual power. At its centre, all other powers were united in a quite new way, namely the *Royal Council*.

Although it was of ancient origin, most of its functions were of recent date. It was everything at once. It was a supreme court, for it had the right to quash the judgements of all ordinary courts. It was the highest administrative court which issued all special jurisdictions in the last resort. As a government council it had, additionally, subject to the king's approval, legislative power; it could debate and propose most laws; it fixed and distributed taxes. As the highest administrative council, it was its duty to lay down the general rules which were to guide government agents. It decided all important business and supervised subordinate authorities. Everything ended up at its door and from it was derived the energy that activated everything. However, it had no jurisdiction of its own; it was the king who alone decided, even when the Council appeared to make public pronouncements. Even when it appeared to dispense justice, it was composed of only *simple advisers*, as the *parlement* expressed it in one of its remonstrances.

This council was not made up of great lords but of persons of middling or low birth, former Intendants and other people skilled in the practice of public affairs. All these men could be dismissed.

Normally it acted with discretion and quietly, always demonstrating less pretension than power. It did not display, therefore, any showiness, or, rather, it disappeared behind the splendour of the throne which was close by; it was so powerful that it affected everything, while being at the same time so obscure that history has scarcely noticed it.

Just as the whole administration of the country was directed by one single body, almost all the handling of internal affairs was entrusted to one single agent, the Controller-General.

If you open a yearbook of the Ancien Régime, you will find that every province has its own special minister. When, however, you study the administration in the public records, you soon realize that the minister for the province had only a few unimportant opportunities to act. The day-to-day course of events was led by the Controller-General who gradually attracted to himself all the business connected with money matters, which is to say almost the whole of the public administration. We see him act successively as Finance Minister, Minister of the Interior, Minister of Public Works and Minister of Trade.

In the same way as central government had actually only one agent in Paris, so it had only one in each province. In the eighteenth century, we still find great lords who bear the name of *Governor of the Province*. These were the old representatives of feudal royalty and they often held inherited offices. They were still granted honours but they no longer had any power. The Intendant controlled the government in reality.

The latter was a young man of humble birth, always an outsider in the province, who had his fortune to make. He did not exercise his powers by virtue of election, birth or purchase of office. He was chosen by the government from the lower orders of the Council of State and could always be dismissed. When away from this body, he was its representative, which is why in official parlance he was called *the detached commissioner*. Almost all the powers which the council possessed, he held too; he exercised all of them in the first instance. Just like the council he was both administrator and judge. The Intendant kept in contact with every minister; he was the sole agent in the province for all the decisions of government.

Beneath him, and appointed by him in each canton, was an official dismissible at his discretion called the sub-delegate. The Intendant was normally a recently ennobled official; the sub-delegate was always a commoner. Nonetheless, this man represented the whole government within the small area allotted to him, just as the Intendant did in the entire larger area. He was subordinate to the Intendant, as the latter was to the minister.

The Marquis d'Argenson tells the story in his Memoirs that one day John Law said to him: 'I would never have believed what I saw when I was Controller of Finance. You should know that this kingdom of France is ruled by thirty Intendants. You have neither Parlement, nor Estates, nor Governors. These men are masters of Requests, assigned to these provinces; upon them depends the unhappiness or happiness of these provinces along with their prosperity or poverty.'

These so very powerful functionaries were nevertheless outshone by the remnants of the old feudal aristocracy and virtually lost against the brilliant light which the latter still cast on society. That is why, even in their own time, they were scarcely visible, although their hands were already into everything. In society, the aristocrats enjoyed the advantage over them of rank, wealth and that reputation which always adheres to ancient things. In government, the nobles surrounded the king and made up his court; they commanded his fleets and controlled his armies; in a word, they caught everyone's eye and, too often, they focus the gaze of posterity. A noble lord would have been insulted, if invited to the appointment of Intendant; the poorest gentleman by birth would more often than not have looked down upon such an offer. The Intendants were, in his view, the representatives of an upstart, new men appointed to rule the middle classes and the peasants and, anyhow, not suitable to associate with. Nevertheless these men governed France as Law had said and as we shall see.

Let us make a start with the right of raising taxes which, in some ways, embodies all other rights.

We know that some taxes were farmed out. These were handled by the Royal Council, which dealt with the financial companies, fixed the terms of contract and set the method of collection. All other taxes, such as the *taille*, the capitation and the *vingtième* were set up and levied directly by the agents of the central administration or under their all-powerful control.

The Council it was which set annually by a decision in secret session the amount of the *taille*, of its countless subsidiary taxes and also how it should be shared out among the provinces. The *taille* had consequently been raised year upon year without there being any advance notice.

As the *taille* was an ancient tax, the terms and collection had been entrusted formerly to local agents, all more or less independent of the government since they exercised their authority by virtue of birth, election or offices bought. These were *the lord of the manor, the parish collector, the treasurers of France, the elected representatives*. These authorities still existed in the eighteenth century. Some, however, had completely stopped bothering with the *taille*, others dealt with it only in a very secondary and entirely subordinate manner. Even then, all the power lay with the Intendant and his agents. In reality, he alone shared out the *taille* between parishes, directed and supervised collectors, granted deferments or reprieves.

Other taxes, such as capitation, were of recent introduction, so the government was not hindered by the vestiges of old powers; it acted alone without any intervention from the governed. The Controller-General, the Intendant and the Council fixed the total amount of the assessment.

Let us move on from money to men. We are sometimes astonished that the French endured the burden of military conscription so patiently at the time of the Revolution and since. But we have to consider that they had long been subjected to it. Before conscription they had endured the heavier burden of service in the militia even though the numbers of men required were lower. From time to time lots were drawn among the youth of the country districts and a certain number of soldiers were taken into the ranks to form the regiments of the militia where they served for six years.

As the militia was a comparatively modern institution, the old feudal powers formed no part of it; the whole operation was entrusted to the central government agents alone. The Council fixed the number of men to be called up and how they would be shared out among the provinces. The Intendant settled the number of men conscripted in each parish; his sub-delegate took charge of the lottery, decided cases for exemption, indicated which men could stay at home, which were to leave and delivered the latter to the military authorities. There was no appeal except to the Intendant and the Royal Council.

Equally, it can be stated that, outside the Independent Estates, all public works, even those which had the most local interest, were decided upon and directed solely by the agents of the central power.

Certain local and independent authorities still existed, such as the lord of the manor, the finance officers and the district surveyors, which could participate in this part of public administration. Almost everywhere these ancient powers saw little or no action. A cursory glance at the administrative files of the time shows this to be the case. All the main highways, even the roads which linked town to town, were open and maintained by national tax contributions. The Council determined the plan and adjudicated contracts. The Intendant controlled the work of the engineers, the sub-delegate recruited the forced labour which was to carry out the works. Only work on minor roads, as these were impassable, was left to the old local authorities.

The chief agent of the central government with regard to public works was then, as now, the Highways Department. Despite the difference between then and now, there are astonishing points of similarity. The administration of roads and bridges had a council and a training school. It had inspectors who annually travelled all over France and engineers who lived on site. These men were responsible under orders from the Intendant to direct all the works. The institutions of the Ancien Régime which have been translated into our new society, in greater numbers than is supposed, have usually lost their titles in the transition while retaining the same structure. The Highways Department has preserved both – a rare event.

Central government, helped by its agents, took upon itself alone the maintenance of public order in the provinces. Mounted police in small brigades were scattered throughout the kingdom and stationed everywhere under the control of the Intendants. The Intendant, with the help of these soldiers and, whenever necessary, the army, countered all unforeseen dangers, arrested vagabonds, stamped on begging and snuffed out the riots which the price of corn endlessly caused. It never happened, as it had previously, that the governed were called upon to help the government in this part of its task, except in those towns which normally had an urban guard whose soldiers were chosen and officers appointed by the Intendant.

The judiciary had retained the right to make police regulations and often exploited that power. But these regulations applied only in one part of a region and most often in one single place. The Council could always overturn them, which it did constantly, whenever it was a matter of jurisdictions from lower courts. For its part, the Council was continually making regulations, which applied equally throughout the kingdom, whether with regard to matters other than those dealt with by the courts, or upon the same matters which the courts had dealt with in a different way. The number of these regulations, or Council decrees, as they were then called, was immense and increased in an endless stream at the approach of the Revolution. Almost no area of social economy or political organization was free from modification by these Council decrees for the forty years prior to the Revolution.

In the old feudal society, if the lord enjoyed powerful rights, he also had heavy responsibilities. He had to help the needy within his domains. We come across a last trace of this old European legislation in the Prussian code of 1795 which states: 'The lord must see to it that poor peasants receive education. He must, as far as possible, provide the means of livelihood for those of his vassals without land. He is duty-bound to come to the aid of anyone falling into want.'

No such law had existed in France for a long time. Since the lord had been relieved of his former powers, he had withdrawn from his former obligations. No local authority, no council, no provincial or parish association had taken its place. No one now had the legal duty of bothering with the poor in the countryside. The central government had taken the foolhardy step of alone providing for their needs.

Every year the Council assigned to each province out of the general taxation receipts certain funds which the Intendant distributed as relief among the parishes. The impoverished peasant had to apply to him. In times of food shortage, it was the Intendant who had grain or rice distributed to the people. The Council made annual decrees which ordered the setting up of charity workshops in certain places which it took care to choose itself. The poorest peasants could work there in return for a low wage.[14] It is easy for us to presume that charity exercised at such a distance was often blind or whimsical and always far from being sufficient.[15]

The central government did not merely come to the help of the peasants in their distress, it set out to teach them how to improve their lot, to help them to do so and, if need be, to force them to do so. With this in mind, it ordered its Intendants and their sub-delegates to distribute short pamphlets on the art of agriculture, founded agricultural societies, promised bonuses and went to great expense to maintain nurseries and to distribute their produce. It would seemingly have been more efficient to lighten the load and lessen the unfairness of the burdens which bore down on agriculture at that time. But that is something which does not appear ever to have occurred to them.

Sometimes the Council set out to force people to prosper come what may. The decrees restricting craftsmen to the use of particular methods or to the manufacture of particular products were innumerable.[16] As there were not enough Intendants to supervise the applying of all these rules, Inspectors-General of industry were there to tour the provinces to help out.

There were Council decrees which forbade the growing of certain crops on land declared unsuitable by the Council. Some ordered the uprooting of vines planted, according to the Council, in poor soil, which shows just how far the government had already moved from the role of sovereign to that of guardian.

CHAPTER 3

HOW WHAT IS NOW CALLED ADMINISTRATIVE CONTROL IS AN INSTITUTION OF THE ANCIEN RÉGIME

Municipal freedom in France survived feudalism. When the nobility had already ceased to administer the countryside, the towns still retained the right to self-government. Towards the end of the seventeenth century some towns still formed, in effect, small democratic republics where magistrates were freely elected by the whole population to whom they were answerable, where municipal life was public and energetic, where the town still exhibited pride in its rights and was very jealous of its independence

It was only in 1692 that elections were for the first time

generally abolished. Municipal functions were then transformed into offices, which is to say that the king sold to a few
inhabitants the right to govern all their fellow citizens forever.

This meant that the towns sacrificed their wellbeing along
with their freedom, for if this transformation of public functions
into offices often enjoyed advantages whenever it concerned the
courts – because the first requirement of a good justice system
is the complete independence of the judge – it never failed
to be a fatal disadvantage whenever it concerned government
proper where responsibility, obedience and enthusiasm were
necessary above all. The old monarchical government did not
make this mistake. It took great care not to exploit for its own
ends the regime it imposed upon the towns and it was at pains
not to put the offices of sub-delegates and Intendants up for sale.

The thing which deserves maximum contempt from history
is that this great revolution was achieved without any political
aim in mind. Louis XI had restricted municipal freedoms because their democratic character frightened him.[17] Louis XIV
destroyed them without any such fear; the proof of this is that
he restored those freedoms to the towns which were able to
buy them back. The reality was that he wished less to abolish
them than to make profits from them. If, in fact, he did abolish
them, it was, as it were, unconsciously, out of pure financial
expediency. And, oddly enough, this same game continued for
eighty years. Seven times over that period, the right to elect
their magistrates was sold to the towns and, just when the latter
had once more savoured the sweet taste of freedom, it was
whisked away from them, so that it could be sold back. The
motive of this device was always the same and was frequently
admitted. The preamble to the edict of 1722 stated, 'The necessities of our finances are forcing us to seek out the most reliable
means of relieving them.' The device was reliable but disastrous
for those on whom this bizarre tax descended. 'I am appalled
by the huge sums paid throughout the period to buy back
municipal offices,' writes an Intendant to the Controller-
General in 1764. 'The total sum of all that money, if used for
worthwhile projects, would have increased the profits of the
town which, as it is, has experienced only the burden of central

authority and of the privileges of the office holders.' In my view, no more shameful feature emerges from the face of the Ancien Régime.

Today it seems difficult to say exactly how towns in the eighteenth century were governed,[18] for, apart from the continuous shift in the source of their municipal powers, as has just been stated, every town still retained a few shreds of its former constitution and its own customs. No two towns in France resembled each other; yet, that very diversity is deceiving and conceals general similarities.

In 1764, the government attempted to frame a general law for the administration of towns. It ordered its Intendants to submit reports on the way in which things were enacted in each of the towns of that time. I have unearthed part of that inquiry and, in the end, I was convinced on reading it that municipal business almost everywhere was conducted in the same way. The differences were merely superficial and obvious; the reality was the same in each place.

More often than not the government of towns was entrusted to two assemblies. All main towns followed this pattern, as did most small ones.

The first assembly was made up of municipal officers, more or less numerous according to the location. This was the executive authority of the town, or the *town corporation* as it was called. Its members held power for a temporary period and were elected when the king had set up the election or when the town had managed to buy back its offices. When the king had restored the offices and succeeded in selling them – which did not always happen – they performed their duties for life on payment of a sum of money. Increasingly this kind of purchase became debased in value as municipal authority bowed further to the central government. In every case, these municipal officers received no salary but always enjoyed tax exemptions and privileges. There were no hierarchical divisions among these members and the administration was equally shared. No magistrate was obviously in special charge of the council, nor was responsible for it. The mayor was the president of the town corporation, not the administrator of the city.

The second assembly, called the General Assembly, elected the corporation wherever such an election took place and, everywhere, went on to take part in the chief business of the town.

In the fifteenth century, the General Assembly was often composed of all the citizens which *was a custom in harmony with the popular spirit of our ancestors*, as one of the inquiry reports expressed it. The populace as a whole elected its municipal officers at that time and was itself sometimes consulted and its officers were answerable to it. At the end of the seventeenth century, this still sometimes happened.

In the eighteenth century no longer did the populace itself, as a body, constitute the General Assembly. The latter was almost always a representative authority. But what we have to realize is that nowhere had it continued to be elected by the public as a whole, nor did it reflect the spirit of the community. In all places it was made up of notable citizens, some of whom were there by virtue of a right of their own, while others were sent by guilds or trade organizations and each man obeyed the binding instructions given him by his particular sponsor.

As the century progressed the number of the notable citizens, eligible by right, multiplied in the body of this assembly; those deputed by the trade guilds either became fewer or ceased to attend. From then on we meet only official town councillors; that is to say, the assembly was filled with the middle class alone with barely any tradesmen among its members. The people who were not taken in as easily as is imagined by a vain pretence of freedom from then on stopped taking an interest in local government and lived within their own walls like a stranger. Occasionally magistrates attempted, without success, to revive in them this local patriotism which had led to so many wonderful achievements in medieval times; they closed their ears. The most important concerns of the town seemed no longer to affect them. The wish was that they would vote wherever it was believed necessary to maintain the empty charade of a free election: they stubbornly kept away. History has no more common spectacle than this. Almost every ruler who has destroyed freedom sought at first to keep its outward form. This has been evident from Augustus down to the present day. Thus, these rulers flattered themselves that they would be able to add to the moral authority, which always stems from public consent, those advantages which absolute power can alone bestow. They have almost all failed in this endeavour and have soon realized that it was impossible to maintain for long those false appearances unsupported by reality.

In the eighteenth century, the government of towns had thus degenerated everywhere into a petty oligarchy. A few families controlled public affairs with their own special interests in mind, away from the public gaze and without any sense of responsibility towards the citizens. The entire French administration was struck down by this sickness. The Intendants all highlighted it but imagined that the only remedy was to increase the subordination of local powers to central government.

It was, however, difficult to better what had already been done. Quite apart from the official modifications to the administration of every town,[19] the laws peculiar to each town were often swept aside by arbitrary decrees of the central council, issued at the suggestion of the Intendant, with no advance inquiry and, sometimes, without the townsfolk themselves having any knowledge of it.

As the inhabitants of one town, which had been affected by such a decree, said, 'This measure has astonished citizens of all rank in the town since we were expecting nothing of the kind to happen.'

Towns were unable to institute a toll, nor levy a tax, nor mortgage, nor sell, nor plead their cause, nor lease their properties, nor administer them, nor enjoy the surplus of their income without the intrusion of a council decree issued after a report by the Intendant. All their public works were executed according to plans and estimates approved by council decree. These were adjudicated in the presence of the Intendant or his subdelegates and conducted usually by the state engineer or architect. All this will come as a big surprise to those who thought that what we now see enacted in France is new.

But the central government interferes much further still in

the administration of towns than even the above indicates. Its power was much more extensive than its rights.

I came across this in a circular addressed by the Controller-General to all Intendants about the middle of the century: 'You will pay particular attention to all that happens in municipal assemblies. You will make exact reports of what is done and must put all decisions taken on hold, in order to send them to me immediately, along with your opinion.'

In fact, from the Intendant's correspondence with his sub-delegates, we can see that the government had its fingers in all the business of towns, big or small. It was consulted upon everything; it expressed a firm opinion about everything; it even supervised public holidays. In some cases it issued orders for demonstrations of public rejoicing, for celebratory fires to be lit and houses to be decorated with lights. I came across one Intendant who imposed a 20 livres fine on members of the town watch who stayed away from a *Te Deum*.

Moreover, the municipal officials had a fitting sense of their unworthiness. 'We beg you very humbly, my lord,' some of them wrote to the Intendant, 'to grant us your goodwill and protection. We shall try to show ourselves worthy of it by our obedience to all Your Excellency's orders.'

'We have never stood against your wishes, my lord,' wrote others who still gave themselves the magnificent title of *Peers of the town*.

This is the way that the middle class prepared itself for governing and the people for liberty.

If only this strict dependence of the towns had at least safeguarded their finances! Nothing of the sort! It is suggested that without centralization towns would immediately have fallen into ruin; I don't know about that but it is certain that, in the eighteenth century, centralization did not prevent their ruin. The whole administrative history of that period is imbued with the chaos of their affairs.

If we turn from towns to villages, we encounter other powers, other methods but the same subordination.[20]

I see much evidence to support the view that, in the Middle Ages, the inhabitants of each village had formed a community independent of their lord. The latter exploited their services, supervised them, governed them but they had exclusive common ownership of certain property. They elected their leaders and administered their own affairs democratically.

You will see this old parish constitution in all those nations which had been feudal and in all those countries where nations had retained remnants of their legal systems. Traces of it are everywhere to be seen in England and it was still alive in Germany up to sixty years ago, as can be confirmed by reading the legislative code of Frederick the Great. Even in eighteenth-century France a few remains of it still existed.

I recall that, when first I was doing research in the archives of an intendancy to discover the nature of a parish in the Ancien Régime, I was taken aback to find in this exceedingly poor and subservient community several features which had struck me formerly in the rural townships of America and which I had wrongly thought must be peculiar to the New World. Neither had permanent representatives or a municipal council in the strict sense. Both of them were administered by officials operating independently under the control of the whole community. Both of them had from time to time general assemblies where all the inhabitants met in one single body, elected their magistrates and managed their important business. In a word, these two systems were as much like each other as the living can resemble the dead.

These two entities had in fact the same beginnings although their fates would be so different.

Transported at one stroke far from feudalism and in absolute control of itself, the rural medieval parish turned into the New England township. In France it was separated from the lord, locked into the powerful grip of the state and it turned into what I am about to describe.

In the eighteenth century the name and number of parish officials varied depending on the provinces. From the old documents it is clear that these officials had been more numerous when the life of the locality was more active; that number had declined as it had become sluggish. In most eighteenth-century parishes, they had been reduced to two: one called the collector, the other the syndic. Usually these municipal officers were still elected, or were supposed to have been. They had, however, everywhere, become tools of the state rather than representatives of the community. The collector raised the *taille* under the direct orders of the Intendant. The syndic, placed under the daily supervision of the Intendant's sub-delegate, represented him in every operation connected with public order or the government and the syndic was his chief agent with regard to the militia, state works and the implementation of all general laws.

As we have already seen, the lord remained outside all these details of government; he did not even supervise them or give any help. Furthermore, these responsibilities which once supported his power now seemed unworthy of his attention, as his power itself was being destroyed. Nowadays, his self-esteem would be wounded should one invite him to participate. He no longer governed but his very presence in the parish and his privileges hindered good parish government from establishing itself in his place. An individual, so independent, so privileged, so different from all the others, ruined or weakened the power of all the laws.

As I shall demonstrate later, the lord's presence had driven all those inhabitants who were comfortably off, or who had any education, into the towns one after another. As a result, he found around him only a swarm of ignorant and uncouth peasants incapable of administering the affairs of the community. 'A parish,' Turgot correctly judged, 'is an assembly of huts and of inhabitants just as inert as they are.'

The administrative documents of the eighteenth century are full of complaints arising from the incompetence, apathy and ignorance of the collectors and syndics in the parishes. Ministers, Intendants, sub-delegates, even nobles all continually condemned the fact but no one traced it back to its cause.

Until the Revolution, the country parish in France retained in its method of government something of that democratic element we had seen in the Middle Ages. Whenever municipal officials needed electing or some common business needed discussing, the village bell summoned the peasants to the church

porch where poor and rich alike had the right to attend. Once
they had gathered, there was no actual discussion or vote, it is
true, but everyone could express his opinion while a notary,
requested for the purpose and drawing up a deed in the open
air, collected the various statements and took minutes.

When one compares this empty show of liberty with the
genuine powerlessness which accompanied it, you can, on a
small scale, already see how the most absolute of governments
can co-exist with some of the most extreme features of democracy, to such an extent that to this oppression is added the
absurdity of being blind to its presence. This democratic parish
assembly was indeed able to voice its wishes but it had no more
right to implement its decision than the town council. It could
not even speak unless permission had been given for it to open
its mouth; for it was only after requesting the express approval
of the Intendant that it could meet *under his good pleasure*, as
the saying appropriately then went. Even though the assembly
was unanimous, it could neither raise taxes, nor sell, nor buy,
nor rent, nor sue without the assent of the Royal Council. A
decree had to be obtained from this council to repair recent
wind damage to the roof of the church or to rebuild the crumbling wall of the priest's house. The rural parish most distant
from Paris was as bound by this rule as was the closest. I
have seen parishes asking the Council for the right to spend
twenty-five livres.

It was normal for inhabitants to preserve the right to elect
their magistrates, it is true, but it frequently happened that the
Intendant sponsored one particular candidate who scarcely ever
failed to be appointed by the unanimous votes of this little
electoral body. At other times, he quashed the election of a
candidate elected on the council's own initiative and appointed
himself the collector and the syndic. He then postponed all
further elections indefinitely. I have seen a thousand examples
of this.

No more cruel fate could be imagined than that suffered by
these communal officials. The sub-delegate, the least important
agent of central government, made them obey his slightest
whim. He often condemned them to pay a fine, sometimes

had them locked up; for those guarantees which still defended citizens against arbitrary decisions no longer existed here. 'I have sent to jail,' said an Intendant in 1750, 'a few leading lights of those communities which were discontented and have imposed upon the latter the cost of the mounted police. This way, they have been easily tamed.' Therefore, these parish offices were considered less as honours than as burdens people sought to avoid by every trick possible.

And yet, these last remnants of the old form of government were still valued by the peasants and even today, of all public liberties, the only one they fully understand is that of the parish. The only business of a public nature that interests them is the parish. The same man who willingly left the government of the entire nation in the hands of one ruler jibbed at the idea that he could not have his say in the administration of his own village; so much importance still adhered to the hollowest of political forms.

What I have just said about towns and parishes must be extended to almost all bodies which had a separate existence and which owned shared property.

Under the Ancien Régime, just as it continues to be today, there was, in France, no city, town, village, no hamlet however small, no hospital, factory, convent or school which would have been able to enjoy an independent right to run its private affairs or to administer its own property as it pleased.[21] Then, as today, the administration kept, therefore, all Frenchmen under its own control and, if the insolence of this expression had not yet been coined, the reality of it at least already existed.

CHAPTER 4

HOW ADMINISTRATIVE JUSTICE AND THE IMMUNITY OF PUBLIC OFFICIALS ARE INSTITUTIONS OF THE ANCIEN RÉGIME

There was no European country where ordinary courts of law were less dependent on government than France; but there was hardly any country where more use was made of extraordinary courts. These two things were more closely related than might be imagined. Since the king could do nothing about the careers of judges, neither dismiss them, nor transfer them to other posts, nor even, in most cases, promote them, since, in short, he had no hold over them either through ambition or fear, he had soon felt irritated by their independence. This had led him, more than in any other sphere, to withhold from them information about matters which directly involved his own power and to create for his own special use, alongside the ordinary courts, a kind of more independent tribunal which would display to his subjects some semblance of justice without making him fearful about the reality.

In countries, such as certain parts of Germany, where the ordinary courts had never been so independent of government as the French courts of that period, similar precautions were not taken and administrative justice never existed. The ruler was sufficiently in control over judges never to need special commissioners.

If we read carefully the royal edicts and decrees published in the last century of the monarchy along with the decrees from the Royal Council of the same period, we will find few in which the government, having issued a regulation, has omitted to state that the challenges which might arise, and the lawsuits resulting from them, would be brought exclusively before the Intendants and the Council. 'His Majesty furthermore commands that all challenges arising from the implementation of this decree, its circumstances and dependent clauses, shall be brought before

the Intendant to be adjudicated by him except in the case of
an appeal to the council. We forbid our ordinary courts and
tribunals to take note of them.' That was the usual formula
of words.

In matters controlled by laws or customs of the past where
this precaution had not been taken, the Council continuously
interfered by issuing *evocations* to remove any case, which
involved the government, from ordinary judges and to bring it
under its own control. The Council registers are full of such
decrees of evocation. Gradually the exception became the general rule; the fact was transformed into theory. It was established, not in law, but in the minds of those who applied the
law, that, as a principle of the state, no trials which involved a
public interest, or which arose from the interpretation of a
government act, fell into the province of ordinary judges whose
sole function was to pronounce between private individuals. In
this matter we have done nothing but find the formula; it is to
the Ancien Régime that the idea belongs.

From that time on, the majority of legal disputes about
tax collection were exclusively the domain of the Intendant and
the Council. The same can be said for anything connected with
the regulation of traffic, with public transport, with highways,
river navigation, etc. In general terms, all lawsuits which
involved public authorities were siphoned off to government
courts.

Intendants saw to it with great care that this exceptional
jurisdiction should expand without hindrance. They alerted the
Controller-General and spurred on the Council. The reason
given by one of these magistrates for obtaining an evocation
deserves to be preserved: 'The ordinary judge,' he said, 'is
limited to fixed rules which oblige him to eliminate what is
against the law, whereas the Council is always able to depart
from the rules to achieve a useful purpose.'

According to this principle we often observe the Intendant
or the Council taking over lawsuits which had an almost invisible connection to public administration, or which quite
blatantly had no link at all. A gentleman, locked in a dispute
with his neighbour and unhappy about the procedure of his

judges, would ask the Council to *evoke* the case. The Intendant consulted replied: 'Although this case concerns only private laws belonging to the jurisdiction of the ordinary courts, His Majesty can always, when he sees fit, take jurisdiction over every category of suit without needing to be accountable for his reasons.'

Normally all those members of the public who happened to disturb civic order by some act of violence were tried by the Intendant or the Provost of the mounted police as a result of an evocation. Most riots caused by the rise in grain prices led to evocations of this type. Consequently the Intendant gathered around him a certain number of important citizens as a sort of improvised prefectural council, chosen by himself, and set himself up as a criminal judge. I have found decrees, created in this fashion, which condemned people to the galleys and even to death. Criminal trials judged by the Intendant were still frequent at the end of the seventeenth century.

Modern legal experts reassure us, with respect to administrative law, that great progress has been achieved since the Revolution: 'Formerly judicial and government powers were confused,' they said. 'We have untangled them since then and returned each to its proper sphere.' To appreciate fully the progress they refer to, we must not forget that if, on the one hand, judicial powers under the Ancien Régime grew endlessly more extensive, on the other hand, they never quite managed to fill the gap. Anyone viewing one of these facts without the other has only an incomplete and misleading picture of the subject. There were times when courts were allowed to make rules for public administration, which was clearly outside their remit; there were others when they were forbidden to judge cases within their proper competence, which meant exclusion from their legitimate sphere of action. It is true that we have banished judicial affairs from the administrative domain into which the Ancien Régime had allowed them to infiltrate quite improperly. But, at the same time, as we have seen, the government made endless invasions into the natural sphere of justice and we let it do so – as though this muddling of judicial powers was not as dangerous on this side as on the other or even worse.

For the intrusion of justice into administrative affairs harms only formal business, whereas the intrusion of the government into justice demoralizes men and tends to turn them into both revolutionaries and slaves.

Among the nine or ten constitutions which have been permanently established in France over the last sixty years, only one expressly states that no government official can be brought to trial in the ordinary courts unless this prosecution has been authorized in advance. This article of law seemed so well devised that, whenever the constitution which contained it was annulled, care was taken to rescue it from the ruins and it has always been scrupulously sheltered from revolutions. The administrators still have the habit of calling the privilege granted to them by this article one of the great victories of '89 but, in this matter, they are likewise deceived for, under the former monarchy, the government had scarcely less concern than nowadays to protect public servants from the unpleasantness of having to appear before the law like ordinary citizens. The only fundamental difference between these two eras is this: before the Revolution the government was unable to shield its representatives other than by having recourse to unlawful and arbitrary measures whereas, since then, it has been able to arrange for a violation of the law legally.

Whenever courts under the Ancien Régime intended to prosecute some representative or other from the central government, normally a Council decree intervened to remove the accused from his judges in order to direct him to appear before commissioners appointed by the Council; for, as a State Councillor wrote at that time, an administrator thus attacked would have encountered prejudice in the ordinary judges' minds and the king's authority would have been compromised. These kinds of evocations did not occur just on a few occasions but daily, not merely in reference to senior agents but also to minor ones. Your job needed only a thin thread of connection to the administration for you to have nothing to fear anywhere other than the government. A foreman in the Highways Department, in charge of the labour gang, was prosecuted by a peasant whom he had mistreated. The Council evoked the case and the

Chief Engineer, writing confidentially to the Intendant, said in connection to this case: 'It is true to say that the foreman is completely to blame but that is not a reason for allowing this matter to run its course for it is of the greatest importance for the working of the Highways administration that ordinary courts of law should not hear or receive complaints from the forced labourers against works foremen. If this set a precedent, these public works would be plagued by endless suits, stimulated by the public animosity which is aroused by these officials.'

In another situation, the Intendant himself sent a letter to the Controller-General about a State contractor who had taken materials from a neighbour's field which he had then used: 'I cannot impress upon you enough how much it would damage the interests of the administration to abandon its contractors to the judgement of the ordinary courts whose principles can never be reconciled with those of the government.'

These lines were penned exactly a century ago and it seems as though the administrators who wrote them might be our contemporaries.

CHAPTER 5

HOW CENTRALIZATION HAD BEEN SUCCESSFULLY INTRODUCED AT THE HEART OF THE OLD POWERS AND HAD SUPPLANTED THEM WITHOUT DESTROYING THEM

Let us now summarize what we have said in the three preceding chapters: one single body at the centre of the kingdom which regulates public administration throughout the country; the same minister directing almost all internal affairs; in every province, one sole agent in charge of every detail; no secondary administrative bodies which can act before first receiving authorization to go into action; extraordinary courts which preside over cases which involve the government and shield all its agents. What is this, if not the centralization that we know? Its make-up is less marked than today, its conduct less regimented, its existence more disturbed but it is the same animal. We have since needed neither to add nor to subtract anything essential; all that was necessary was to knock down everything that surrounded it for it to appear just as we see it now.[22]

Most of the institutions that I have just described have since been imitated in a hundred different places but at that time they were peculiar to France and we shall soon see how great an influence they exerted over the French Revolution and its aftermath.

But how had these modern institutions managed to establish themselves in France on the ruins of the feudal society?

It was a task requiring patience, skill and some length of time rather than strength and brute force. At the start of the Revolution almost nothing of the old administrative structure had been destroyed in France; a new framework had, as it were, been built beneath it.

There is nothing to indicate that the government of the Ancien Régime had pursued a thoroughly planned strategy laid down in advance in order to effect this difficult operation. It had simply surrendered to that inner feeling which carries any government towards its aim of running everything itself – a feeling which always remained the same despite the diversity of its agents. It had allowed the former government their antiquated names and honours while gradually removing their authority from them. It had not driven them out from their spheres of influence but had edged them out. Exploiting the inertia of some and the egoism of others, it had replaced them; taking advantage of all their faults and never trying to reform them, only supplanting them. It had in the end substituted for almost all of them one single agent, the Intendant, whose title did not even exist when they were born.

Judicial power alone had embarrassed the government in this undertaking but, even there, the latter had ended up by seizing the reality of power while leaving behind only the shadow to its opponents. The government had not eliminated the *parlements* from the realm of administration.[23] It had, step by step, spread to such a degree as to occupy all their space. When certain unusual and short-lived events happened – in times of food shortage, for instance – when people's feelings gave support to magistrates' ambitions, the central government allowed the *parlements* to govern briefly and to make a noise which has echoed down through history. But, soon enough, the government silently resumed its place and discreetly recovered its hold over everyone and everything.

Anyone wishing to look into the power struggle between the *parlements* and the king will discover that it is against a political not an administrative background that they clash. Normally these quarrels arose concerning a new tax, which means that their dispute was not about administrative but legislative power. Neither party had any more right of possession over this latter power than the other.

Increasingly this was the case as the Revolution drew near. As popular feelings began to ignite, the *parlement* became more involved in politics and, as the central power and its agents gained more experience and skill, this same *parlement* busied itself less and less with administration in its true sense; day by day it became less of an administrator and more of a demagogue.

Besides, time constantly opens up to central government new fields of action where the courts lack the flexibility to follow, for it was a question of new matters for which there were no precedents and which were alien to the *parlement*'s routine. The great advances of society created new needs at every turn, each of which was a fresh source of power, since central government was alone able to satisfy them. While the administrative scope of the courts remained static, that of the government was mobile and spread infinitely as civilization itself does.

The Revolution was drawing near and beginning to disturb the minds of the French, suggesting a thousand new ideas which the government alone could bring into being. The Revolution, before toppling this government, developed its powers. Like everything else, the government reached a high state of efficiency. This very striking fact emerges from a study of the archives. The Controller-General and the Intendant of 1770 no longer resembled those of 1740. The administration had been transformed. Its agents were the same but a different attitude motivated them and, as it spread its wings and covered more detail, it also became more systematic and more skilful. It took a moderate line in the way that it successfully took over everything; it was less oppressive but more dominant.

The first efforts of the Revolution destroyed the monarchy, that great institution; it was restored in 1800. As has been said so many times, in matters of administration it was not the principles of 1789 which triumphed at that time and thereafter but, quite on the contrary, those of the Ancien Régime which were all restored to their full vigour and which remained in place.

If you ask me how this part of the Ancien Régime could have been transformed in its entirety and been incorporated into the new society, my response is that, if centralization did not perish in the Revolution, it is because it represented itself as the beginning and as the emblem of the Revolution. I would add that, when a nation has destroyed the monarchy at its heart, it automatically hurtles towards centralization. Less effort is therefore needed to drive it down that slope than to hold it back. At their centre, all authorities by nature lean towards unity, since a great deal of skill is needed to succeed in keeping them apart.

The democratic revolution which had destroyed so many of the institutions of the Ancien Régime was bound to consolidate centralization and this settled so naturally into its own place in the society which the Revolution had shaped, that people could easily believe it to have been one of its achievements.

CHAPTER 6

ADMINISTRATIVE METHODS UNDER THE ANCIEN RÉGIME

It would be impossible to read the correspondence from an Intendant of the Ancien Régime to both his superiors and his subordinates without being struck how the similarity of institutions made the administrators of that era like those of our own day. They seem to reach out to each other across the chasm of the Revolution which separates them. I shall claim the same of the governed. Never did the power of legislation over men's minds manifest itself more clearly.

The minister had already conceived the desire to scrutinize personally the detail of every item of business and to decide everything himself in Paris. As time moved on and the administration improved, this passion increased. Towards the end of the eighteenth century not a single charity workshop was established in the depths of any far-off province without the Controller-General's insisting on supervising the expenditure himself, drawing up its regulations and deciding its location. Suppose that someone set up a poorhouse – he had to be told the names of the beggars who turned up, exactly when they went out and when they returned. From the middle of the century (1733), M. d'Argenson was writing: 'The details disclosed to ministers are immense. Nothing is done without them and nothing is done except through them. If their information is not as comprehensive as their powers, they are forced to leave everything to be accomplished by their clerks who turn into the real masters.'

A Controller-General asked not merely for reports on business affairs but also for snippets of information on individuals. The Intendant, in his turn, applied to his sub-delegates and virtually never failed to repeat word for word everything they told him, as if he knew it full well himself.

To succeed in directing everything and in knowing everything from Paris, a thousand methods of control had to be invented.

The reams of written material were already extensive and the delays in administrative procedures so long that I never even noticed when less than a year had gone by before a parish obtained permission to rebuild its bell tower or repair the priest's house; the norm was for two or three years to go by before such a request was granted.

The Council itself made notes in one of its decrees (29 March 1773) 'that administrative formalities cause endless delays in business matters and,' it adds, 'only too often stimulate quite justifiable complaints even though the formalities are entirely necessary.'

I had the idea that the taste for statistics was peculiar to administrators of today, but I was mistaken. Towards the end of the Ancien Régime, the Intendant was often sent small printed forms which he had merely to get filled out by his own sub-delegates and the parish syndics. The Controller-General commanded these reports to be prepared concerning the type of land, the crops grown, the kind and quantity of its produce, the number of animals, the work habits and customs of its inhabitants. Information thus obtained was hardly less detailed or more accurate than that which sub-prefects and mayors provide nowadays in similar cases. On these occasions the conclusions which the sub-delegates arrived at about those they governed were, in general, not at all favourable. They often reverted to the opinion that 'by nature the peasant is lazy and would not work if he had not been forced to do so in order to live'. That is economic dogma which appeared widespread among these administrators.

Even the official language of these two periods is strikingly similar. On both sides the style is equally colourless, smooth, vague and lifeless. The personality of each writer is removed and disappears into a common mediocrity. Were you to read a present-day prefect, you would be reading an Intendant.

Only towards the end of the century, when the language peculiar to Diderot and Rousseau had had the time to spread in diluted form into popular language, did the false sentimentality which filled the books of these two writers win over the administrators and infect even the accountants. The official style, with its normally dry tone, became after that sometimes unctuous and almost caring. A sub-delegate complained to the Paris Intendant, 'that, in the course of his duties, he often experiences a grief which is harrowing to a sensitive soul'.

The government used to distribute, as it does these days, certain charitable relief to the parishes on the condition that the inhabitants were themselves to make a certain contribution. When such a sum was sufficient, the Controller-General wrote in the margin of the distribution document: *Good, express satisfaction*; but when it was much more than sufficient he wrote: *Good, express satisfaction and heartfelt thanks.*

The government officials, almost all from the middle classes, already constituted a social class with its own peculiar spirit, traditions, virtues, code of honour and pride. This was the aristocracy of the new social order which was already established and active. It simply waited for the Revolution to open up a place for it.

What already typified French administration was the violent hatred it felt against all those nobles and middle-class citizens who wished to run their own affairs beyond the reach of the government. It was unnerved by the smallest independent body which appeared to want to come into being without its support. The most modest free association, whatever its aims, was irksome to the authorities, which sanctioned only those they had set up arbitrarily and had control over. The great trade guilds themselves were not to their liking. In a word, the government had no intention of allowing citizens to meddle in any way whatsoever in the scrutiny of their own business; they preferred stagnation to competition. But, since Frenchmen must always be allowed the sop of a little flexibility, to console them for their enslavement, the government allowed them to discuss very freely all kind of general and abstract theories in matters of religion, philosophy, ethics and even politics. It was quite willing to tolerate attacks against the fundamental principles upon which society then rested and even arguments about God Himself, provided that its most menial agents were not the subject of their ramblings. It felt that none of these topics had any relevance.

Although eighteenth-century newspapers, or, as they were then called, gazettes, contained more poetic verses than political wrangling, the administration was already casting a very envious eye over this small centre of power. It was relaxed about books but already very harsh about newspapers. Unable to get rid of them entirely, it undertook to turn them to its own use. In 1761, a circular addressed to all the king's Intendants announced that the king (Louis XV) had decided that, from then on, the *Gazette de France* should be written under the eye of the government: 'His Majesty wishes,' said the circular, 'to make this paper interesting and to confirm its superiority over all the others.' 'As a result,' adds the minister, 'you will kindly send me an account of anything happening in your area which might arouse the curiosity of the public, especially things relating to physical science, natural history, unusual or striking facts.' Attached to the circular was a prospectus announcing the new gazette which, although it would appear more often and contain more news than the paper it replaced, would cost subscribers much less.

Armed with these documents the Intendant wrote to his sub-delegates and set them to work; however, the latter began by replying that they knew nothing. Along came another letter from the minister complaining bitterly about the barrenness of the province. 'His Majesty commands me to inform you that he insists that you give very serious attention to this matter and issue the clearest possible orders to your agents.' The sub-delegates than went into action: one of them reported that a smuggler in salt had been hanged and had displayed great courage; another, that a woman of his district had given birth to triplet daughters; a third, that a terrible storm had raged without, it is true, causing any damage. One person declared that, in spite of all his efforts, he had found nothing worth reporting but that he had himself taken out a subscription to such a useful gazette and would invite all reputable citizens to follow his lead. So much effort, however, seemed ineffective for a new letter from the minister informs us that, 'the King who has the goodness to condescend to examine for himself all the details of the measures relating to the improvement of the gazette and who wishes to grant to this newspaper the superiority and reputation it deserves, has expressed considerable displeasure at seeing his plans so badly fulfilled.'

We see that history is a gallery of pictures of which few are originals and many are copies.

Moreover, we must recognize that in France the central government never imitated those governments in southern Europe which appeared to take over everything only to make it all sterile. It often displayed considerable intelligence in going about its task and often an extraordinary energy which, however, often achieved nothing and turned out to be damaging because, sometimes, it set out to do what was beyond its powers or beyond anyone's control.

It hardly ever undertook – or soon gave up – the most necessary of reforms which required a persistent effort for success to be achieved; rather it endlessly altered a few rules here and a few laws there. Nothing stayed still in its own place for an instant. New regulations succeeded one another with such an unusual speed that government agents under orders often found it difficult to sort out how to comply. Town officials complained to the Controller-General himself about the excessive fluidity of secondary legislation. 'The changes in financial regulations alone,' they stated, 'are such that they do not allow even a permanent town official to do anything but study the newly published regulations until they are forced to neglect their normal business.'

Even when the law had not altered, the way of applying it shifted from day to day. When one has not seen the administration of the Ancien Régime in operation, except by reading the secret records left to posterity, one cannot possibly imagine the contempt into which the law of the land had eventually fallen even in the minds of those implementing it, since neither political assemblies nor newspapers existed to check the government's capricious behaviour and to limit the arbitrary and changing attitudes of ministers and their staff.

Almost all Council decrees make reference to previous laws, often of recent origin, which had been passed but not executed. In actual fact, there was not a single edict, royal declaration or solemnly registered letters patent which did not sustain a thousand alterations in practice. Letters from Controllers-General and Intendants show that the government tolerated endless exceptions to its orders. It rarely broke the law but allowed it on a daily basis to be manipulated discreetly in all directions according to individual cases and to ease the general running of affairs.

An Intendant, writing to the minister about a city toll from which a public works contractor wished to be exempt, said: 'It is quite clear that, according to a strict interpretation of the edicts and decrees which I have just quoted, no man in the kingdom is exempt from these dues; those, however, who are expert in the knowledge of public business know full well that these authoritative regulations go the way of the penalties they entail and that, although such prohibitions are present in almost all the edicts, declarations and decrees which establish taxes, this has never prevented exceptions.'

There we can see the Ancien Régime in a nutshell: strict rules, lax implementation; such was its essential nature.

Anyone wishing to judge the government of that period through the collection of laws passed would fall into the most absurd errors. I found a royal declaration of 1757 which condemned to death all those who would compose or print written material antagonistic towards religion or the established order. The bookshop which sold them and the trader that peddled them were to suffer the same fate. Had we returned to the century of Saint Dominic? No, this is precisely the period of Voltaire's ascendancy.

We often complain that the French have contempt for the law. Alas, when might they have learned to respect it? It could be said that for the men living under the Ancien Régime, the place that the idea of law should occupy in the human mind was vacant. Every petitioner requested a departure from the established rules of law in his favour with as much insistence and as much authority as if he had asked for the actual law itself to be applied. In fact, the letter of the law was adhered to only when the authorities wished to turn him away. The submission of the people to authority was still complete but their obedience was more the result of habit than conviction for, were they by chance to be roused, the slightest excitement would lead them immediately to violence and, almost always, they would be put down not by appeal to the law but by a similar violent and arbitrary force.

The central power in eighteenth-century France had not yet acquired that healthy and robust constitution which we have observed since. Nevertheless, as it had already succeeded in destroying all the intermediate authorities and, since nothing but a huge and empty space had emerged, from a distance central government appeared to each citizen to be the only means of maintaining the social machine, the single, necessary agent of public life.

Nothing displays this more effectively than the writings of its detractors. When the long period of discontent leading up to the Revolution began to make itself felt, we saw all sorts of new systems of society and government hatched out. The aims recommended by the reformers were many and varied but their methods were the same. They wanted to borrow the strength of central government and use it to smash everything and rebuild according to a new plan of their own conception. Such a task could, they thought, be accomplished only by the central power. State power should, they said, have no limitations, just like its law. All that was needed was for them to persuade it to make suitable use of that power. Even Mirabeau the elder, that noble-man so enamoured of aristocratic rights that he called the Intendants by the blunt name of *intruders*, the man who declared that, if the election of magistrates was left solely to the government, the courts of justice would soon be mere packs of commissioners, even he felt confidence only in the power of central government to realize his dreams.

These ideas did not stay on the pages of books; they filtered down to all minds, fused with men's customs, entered social habits and spread everywhere, even affecting everyday life.

No one imagined that an important matter could be brought to a successful conclusion without the involvement of the state. Even farmers, normally people very antagonistic to in-struction, were inclined to believe that, when agriculture failed to improve, the fault lay mainly with the government which gave them neither enough advice nor help. One of them wrote to an Intendant in a frustrated tone which already anticipated the Revolution: 'Why doesn't the government appoint inspectors to tour the provinces once a year to inspect the state of crops, to teach farmers to make changes for the better, to tell them how to manage their animals, how to fatten them, raise them, sell them and the best market to use? These inspectors should be well remunerated. The farmer who could prove that his crops were the best would receive public recognition.'

Inspectors and medals! That's a strategy a Suffolk farmer would never have thought of!

Already by this time only the government could guarantee public order in the eyes of the majority. The ordinary people feared no one but the mounted police; the landowners had faith in them alone. For both, the mounted police officer was not only the defender of order, he was order itself. As the provincial assembly of Guyenne said:[24] 'No one has failed to observe just how much the sight of a mounted policeman is enough to bring to heel the most hostile of men.'

As a result, everyone wished to have a squad on his doorstep. The archives of Intendants' offices are full of such requests; no one seemed to suspect that behind the protector might lurk the master.

What most impressed émigrés arriving in England was the absence of this military police. It filled them with surprise and, sometimes, with contempt for the English. One of them, a man of worth but whose education had not prepared him for what he would see, wrote: 'It is quite true that any Englishman congratulates himself on having been robbed, with the words that at least his country does not have a mounted police force. Another, who is angry at everything that disturbs the peace, is consoled, however, when he sees rebels return to the bosom of society, thinking that the wording of the law is more important than any other consideration.' 'These misguided ideas,' he adds, 'are not absolutely in the minds of all, for there are some wise people who hold the opposite viewpoint and, in the long run, it is wisdom which must prevail.'

That these odd views of the English might have had some
connection with the freedoms they enjoyed did not enter his
head. He preferred to explain this phenomenon with scientific
reasoning: 'In a country where the dampness of the climate and
the mugginess in the circulating air give the temperament a
sombre hue, the people turn readily to serious questions. The
English are thus naturally inclined to take an interest in matters
of government, whereas the French stand at a distance from
them.'

Since the government had usurped the place of Providence,
it was natural for everyone to call upon the former for their
personal needs. Thus we see an immense number of petitions
which, while always based on the public interest, were nonetheless concerned only with small private interests.[25] The files in
which they are kept are possibly the only places where all the
social classes of the Ancien Régime mingle together. They make
melancholy reading: peasants ask to be compensated for the
loss of their cattle or their house; wealthy landowners ask for
help in making the best use of their estates; manufacturers
petition the Intendant for special advantages to protect them
from troublesome competition. We very frequently see manufacturers disclosing to the Intendant the poor state of their
businesses and asking him to obtain some help or a loan from
the Controller-General. It appears that such funds were available for this purpose.

The nobility themselves were sometimes great suppliants.
Their social status was never more apparent than when they
were begging in a very loud voice. The five per cent tax
(*vingtième*) was for many of them the main link of their dependence. Their share of this tax was fixed annually by the Council,
based on the Intendant's report; thus they usually had recourse
to him for postponements and exemptions. I have read a host
of such requests from nobles, almost all titled and often lords
of standing, submitted, they said, because of the inadequacy of
their revenues or the poor state of their affairs. In general, the
nobles never addressed the Intendant by any name other than
'Monsieur' but I have noticed that in these circumstances they
called him 'Monseigneur', as did the middle classes.

Sometimes in these petitions wretchedness ran hand in hand with pride in an amusing way. One of these men wrote to the Intendant: 'Your sensitive soul will never consent that a father of my rank should be taxed to the full five per cent as a lower-class father would be.'[26]

In times of food shortage – very frequent in the eighteenth century – the population of each district turned as one to the Intendant, seemingly expecting food supplies from him alone. It was true that everyone already blamed the government for all their hardships. The most unavoidable of these were its fault but even seasonal bad weather was laid at its door.

Let us cease to be surprised at the marvellous ease with which centralization was re-established in France at the beginning of this century. The men of '89 had overturned the building but its foundations had stayed in the very hearts of its destroyers and, upon these foundations, were they able to rebuild it, constructing it more stoutly than it had ever been before.

CHAPTER 7

HOW FRANCE WAS ALREADY OF ALL EUROPEAN COUNTRIES THE ONE WHERE THE CAPITAL HAD ACQUIRED THE GREATEST DOMINANCE OVER THE PROVINCES AND HAD ENVELOPED THE ENTIRE COUNTRY MOST EFFECTIVELY

Neither the situation, nor the size, nor the wealth of capital cities guarantees their political dominance over the rest of the country; it is, rather, the kind of government which exists.

London, which has a population the size of some kingdoms, has, as yet, exercised no sovereign influence over the destiny of Great Britain.

No American citizen imagines that the people of New York could decide the fate of the Union. Furthermore, no one in the state of New York itself imagines that the individual will of that city could by itself manage affairs. However, New York today contains as many people as Paris did at the outbreak of the Revolution.

Paris itself, during the wars of religion, was, compared with the rest of the kingdom, as populous as it was in 1789. Nonetheless, it had no power to take decisions. At the time of the Fronde, Paris was still merely the largest town in France. In 1789, it was already France itself.

In 1740 Montesquieu was writing to one of his friends: 'In France nothing exists but Paris and distant provinces because Paris has not yet had time to swallow them up.' In 1750 the Marquis de Mirabeau, a whimsical spirit, if occasionally profound, said, speaking of Paris without naming it: 'Capitals are necessary but, if the head becomes too big, then the body becomes apoplectic and dies. So, by abandoning the provinces to a kind of direct control which looks upon their inhabitants as second-class citizens, as it were, what will happen if, by removing all source of recognition and every path of ambition, any possible talent is drawn away to the capital?' He called this a form of silent revolution which drained the provinces of their leading lights, men of business and what we call intellectuals.

The reader carefully perusing these past chapters already knows the reasons for this phenomenon; it would be an abuse of his patience to refer to them once again.

This revolution did not escape the scrutiny of the government, which was struck only by the most tangible evidence, namely the growth of the city. It saw Paris growing daily and feared that it would become difficult to govern such a great city properly. The king issued a large number of rulings, mainly in the seventeenth and eighteenth centuries, which aimed at halting this growth. More and more, these kings concentrated the whole of French public life in Paris or at its gates and they set out to keep Paris small. The building of new houses was prohibited and people were forced to erect them on only the costliest scale in the least attractive localities designated in advance. True enough, each of these rulings stated that, despite the one before it, Paris had not stopped growing. Louis XVI at his most powerful tried six times during his reign to check growth in Paris but failed; the city increased continually regardless of these edicts. But its dominance expanded even more rapidly than its walls. The guarantee for this was less what was happening within its precincts than beyond them.

In fact, during the same period, local freedoms were increasingly disappearing all over the place. Everywhere the signs of an independent life ceased to exist; the very features of the various provinces were becoming blurred; the final traces of public life as it was before were being blotted out. Yet, it was not that the nation was sinking into indolence; on the contrary, there was general activity; simply the driving force was now in Paris alone. I shall cite only one example from a thousand. In the reports to the minister about the state of the book trade in the sixteenth and the beginning of the seventeenth century, I read that there had existed important printing works in provincial towns which now have no printers or else have nothing for printers to do. It is, however, indisputable that infinitely more written material of every kind was published at the end of the eighteenth century than in the sixteenth; it simply was that the flow of thought radiated now from the centre, as Paris had engulfed the provinces.

At the outbreak of the French Revolution this initial revolution had been fully completed.

Arthur Young, that famous traveller, left Paris shortly after the meeting of the Estates-General and not many days before the fall of the Bastille. The contrast he witnessed between what he had just seen in the city and what he found outside struck him with surprise. In Paris all was bustle and noise; a political pamphlet was produced every instant – up to ninety-two were published every week. 'Never,' he said, 'have I seen such a wave of publicity, even in London.' Outside Paris everything appeared unmoving and silent; few pamphlets and no newspapers were printed. Nevertheless, the provinces, though motionless, were in a disturbed state and ready to burst into motion. When citizens sometimes met together it was to be told the news they were expecting from Paris. In every town, Young inquired of the inhabitants what they were about to do. The reply was always the same, he said: 'We are only a provincial town; we must see what they are going to do in Paris.' 'These folk do not even dare to hold an opinion,' he added, 'until they know what Paris thinks.'

I am astonished at the surprising ease with which the Constituent Assembly was able to destroy at a stroke all the former French provinces, several of which were more ancient than the monarchy and then to divide methodically the kingdom into eighty-three distinct districts as if it was dealing with the virgin soil of the New World. Nothing surprised and even terrified the rest of Europe more, since it was not prepared for such a sight. 'It is the first time,' said Burke, 'that we have seen men tear their country into shreds in such a barbarous fashion.' In fact, while they seemed to be dismembering living bodies, they were only butchering dead flesh.

During the very time that Paris thus completed its acquisition of total power over the rest of France, at its centre another change was being accomplished which no less deserves to catch the attention of history. Instead of being only a city of trade, business, consumption and pleasure, Paris ended up as a city of industry and manufacturing. This second fact added a new and more formidable aspect to the first.

The outcome had its roots in the distant past. Apparently from the Middle Ages onwards, Paris was already the most industrialized town in the kingdom just as it was the biggest. This becomes clear as we approach modern times. Gradually, as all administrative affairs were drawn to Paris, industrial business rushed in too. As Paris became more and more the model and arbiter of taste, the only centre of power and the arts, the chief home of national activity, so the industrial life of the nation retreated and concentrated its forces there even more.

Although, generally speaking, the statistics of the Ancien Régime deserve little credibility, I think we can confidently state that, for the sixty years preceding the French Revolution, the number of working men more than doubled in Paris whereas, during the same period, the general population of the city increased by hardly a third.

Apart from the general reasons I have just described, there

were some very particular ones which drew working men from every part of France to Paris where, gradually, they gathered in certain suburbs, which ended up by being occupied by them alone. The hindrances that the fiscal legislation of the time were imposing on industry had been made less burdensome in Paris than anywhere else in France. Nowhere was it simpler to evade the shackles of the trade guilds. Certain districts such as Saint-Antoine and the Temple especially enjoyed very considerable privileges in this connection. Louis XVI widened these powers of the Saint-Antoine district still more and worked as hard as he could to amass a large working population there, 'wishing,' said this ill-fated king, in one of his decrees, 'to grant to the Saint-Antoine workers a new sign of our protection and to free them from the restrictions which are damaging to their interest as well as to the freedom of trade'.

The number of factories, workshops and blast furnaces had multiplied so rapidly in Paris as the Revolution drew near that, in the end, the government grew alarmed. The sight of this increase filled its mind with purely imaginary fears. One particular council decree of 1782 carried the statement that 'the King, fearing that the rapid increase of factories might result in a use of wood which would damage town supplies, henceforth forbids the erection of such establishments within a radius of fifteen leagues around the city'. As for the real danger posed by such a concentration, no one felt any anxiety.

Thus Paris had become the master of France and already an army was gathering which was to turn into the master of Paris.

As it seems to me, there is much agreement today that the administrative centralization and omnipotence of Paris have been very influential in the collapse of all the successive governments we have seen over the past forty years. I shall show quite easily how we must attribute to the same fact an important role in the sudden and violent ruin of the old monarchy and that we must rank this fact among the chief reasons for the first revolution which spawned all the others.

CHAPTER 8

HOW FRANCE WAS THE COUNTRY WHERE MEN HAD COME TO RESEMBLE EACH OTHER THE MOST

Anyone with an attentive eye on France under the Ancien Régime encounters two very contrasting aspects.

Seemingly all men living there, especially those occupying the middle and higher ranks of society – the only ones which could be observed – resembled each other exactly.

On the other hand, within this uniform crowd there was still an extraordinary collection of minor barriers which split it up into a large number of groups within each of which there existed, as it were, a particular social group that was involved with only its own concerns while not taking part in the life of the whole community.

When I think about this almost infinite division, I realize that, since nowhere were the citizens less prepared to act together or to lend each other support in a time of crisis, a great revolution was able in a flash to overturn such a society from top to bottom. I can imagine all those small barriers tipped over by this great upheaval. Immediately I can see a solid social body, more compact and homogeneous than any ever encountered in the world.

I have told how, in almost the entire kingdom, the individual life of the provinces had long since been obliterated, a fact which had very much helped to make all Frenchmen very similar to each other. Within these diverse elements, which still exist, the unity of the nation was already apparent as is clear from the uniformity of legislation. As we follow the advance of the eighteenth century, the number of edicts, royal declarations, orders of council increased visibly to apply the same rules and the same procedures to all parts of the kingdom. Not only the ruling class but also the governed entertained the idea of such a universal and uniform legislation, the same everywhere and for everyone. Two centuries before, the stuff of such ideas, if one can speak thus, would not have existed.

Not only did the provinces increasingly resemble each other but, in every one of them, men of different social class, at least those of higher status than the common people, became ever more alike despite the individual differences of rank.

Nothing highlights this more than the registers of grievances presented by the various orders in 1789. It is clear that the writers of these differed profoundly in their concerns but appear similar in all other respects.

A study of how things proceeded in the first Estates-General would show you a completely opposite picture: the middle class and the nobility had at that time many more shared concerns and common business; they displayed much less mutual dislike yet they still seemed to belong to two separate races.

Time which had maintained and, in many respects, aggravated the privileges dividing these two classes, had worked in a peculiar way to make them similar in everything else.

For several centuries, the French nobility had grown constantly poorer. 'Despite its privileges, the aristocracy is falling by the day into ruin and annihilation and the Third Estate is taking over its fortunes,' laments a nobleman in 1755. Yet the laws protecting the property of the nobles were the same and nothing in their economic position appeared to have changed. Nonetheless, they grew poorer everywhere in direct ratio to their loss of power.

One might say that, in human institutions, as in the case of man himself, leaving aside the organs which fulfil the various functions of life, a central and invisible force exists as the very principle of life. When that life-giving flame happens to die, it is useless for the organs to act as before; everything slows down and loses life. French noblemen still had land settlements (Burke even noted that, in his time, these were more frequent and more binding in France than in England); they had first-born inheritance, land fees on an indefinite basis and all those so-called useful rights. That very onerous obligation to wage war at their own expense had been withdrawn and yet immunity from tax had been preserved in much increased terms.

That meant that they retained the immunity while losing the inconvenience. They further benefited from several other financial advantages unavailable to their forefathers. Yet gradually they grew poor as the practice and instinct of government slipped away from them. It is to this gradual impoverishment that we must partly attribute this great division of land ownership which we have noted above.[27] The nobleman had ceded his land, piece by piece, to the peasant farmers, retaining for himself only his manorial dues which maintained the appearance rather than the reality of his former status. Several French provinces, such as Limousin, mentioned by Turgot, were populated by a small, impoverished nobility which owned almost no land and hardly survived except for manorial rights and land rents.

'In this region,' said an Intendant at the beginning of the century, 'the number of noble families still stands at several thousand but not fifteen of them have an income of twenty thousand livres.' I read in a kind of directive which another Intendant (from Franche-Comté) addressed to his successor in 1750, 'The nobles of this region are quite worthy but very poor and are as proud as they are poor. They are very humiliated in comparison with what they once were. It is not a bad policy to keep them in this state of poverty and to push them into serving us and needing our help. They form,' he adds, 'a fraternity into whose ranks are admitted only those who can give proof of four quarters on their coat of arms. This brotherhood is not officially recognized but simply tolerated and meets only once a year in the presence of the Intendant. Having dined and heard mass together, they return home, some on their old hacks, others on foot. You will see how comical this gathering is.'

This gradual impoverishment of the nobility is more or less evident, not merely in France but in every part of the Continent where the feudal system was finally disappearing like it was in France, without being replaced by any new form of aristocracy. Among the German people who lived along the Rhine this collapse was especially obvious and widely noted. The opposite was true only among the English where the ancient noble families still in existence had not only saved, but had much increased, their fortunes. They had remained leaders in wealth as well as in power. The new families which had risen up by their side had simply imitated their opulence without outstripping it.

In France, only the commoners seemed to inherit all the property lost by the nobles. They were on the increase, it might be said, only at the latter's expense. No law, however, existed to prevent the middle classes from courting ruin any more than to help them become wealthy. They never stopped, however, from growing rich and, in many cases, they had become as well off as the nobles, sometimes even more so. Moreover, their wealth was often of the same kind for, although they normally lived in the town, they often owned land in the country. Occasionally, they even purchased manorial estates.

Education and the way people lived had already created a thousand other shared features between these two classes. The middle classes were as educated as the aristocracy and, what we must not fail to notice, learning had been drawn from exactly the same source. Both were enlightened by the same sun. For both of them education had been equally theoretical and literary. Paris had become increasingly the sole instructor of France and, in the end, formed minds in the same mould and with a common attitude.

At the close of the eighteenth century, it was still possible, no doubt, to discern a difference between the manners of the nobility and those of the middle class, for nothing moved more slowly towards equality than that superficial behaviour which we call manners, but, deep down, all those men holding a position higher than the common people were alike – they had the same ideas, the same habits, they pursued the same tasks, indulged in the same pleasures, read the same books and spoke the same language. No longer did they differ except in relation to privileges.

I doubt that such a state of affairs existed to the same degree anywhere else, not even in England where the different classes, even though they were solidly united by common interests, often still differed in attitude and behaviour. For the political liberty, which possesses this admirable power to create vital links and common bonds of independence between all citizens, still does not make them similar for that reason. Only government by one man has, in the long run, the unavoidable effect of making men similar to each other and mutually indifferent to each other's fate.

CHAPTER 9

HOW SUCH SIMILAR MEN WERE MORE DIVIDED THAN EVER BEFORE INTO SMALL GROUPS, ALIEN AND INDIFFERENT TO EACH OTHER

Let us now consider another side of this picture to see how these same Frenchmen, who had so many similar features, were more isolated from each other than could be seen anywhere else or than had ever been seen in France previously.

It becomes very apparent that, when the feudal system became established in Europe, what we called from then on the nobility did not immediately constitute a caste but was composed at first of all the leading men of the nation and was thus, at the outset, simply an aristocracy. That is an issue I do not want to discuss here; all I need to note is that, from the Middle Ages, the nobility became a caste, whose distinguishing feature was birth.

Indeed it retained the one characteristic typical of an aristocracy, namely to be a body of citizens who govern. But birth alone decided who should be the leader of this body. Anyone not born noble was outside this peculiar and closed class and occupied a position more or less important in society but always subordinate in the state.

Wherever the feudal system was established in Europe, it ended up as a caste; in England it reverted to an aristocracy.

It has always astonished me that a fact which, in this respect, singles out England as special, and which alone may teach us an understanding of its laws, its mind, its history, has not caught the attention of philosophers and politicians more than it has – a fact that a long familiarity has made invisible, as it were, to the English themselves. It has often been partially seen and described but, it seems to me, never has it been clarified entirely. Montesquieu, on a visit to Great Britain in 1739, wrote shrewdly: 'I find myself in a country which barely resembles the rest of Europe', but he adds nothing further.

In fact, it was less its parliament, its freedom, its press, its jury system, which from then on made England so unlike the rest of Europe, than something still more peculiar and more influential. England was the only country where the caste system had been not so much modified as effectively destroyed. Nobles and commoners pursued the same activities, entered the same professions and, much more significantly, intermarried. The daughter of the greatest nobleman was already able to marry a self-made man without bringing shame on herself.

If you wish to know whether the caste system in a nation, with the ideas, habits and boundaries it has created, has been demolished for certain, just look at marriages. They will show you the decisive feature you seek. Even today, in France, after sixty years of democracy, you would often look for it in vain. The old and new families, which seem merged in everything, still avoid, as far as possible, any links in marriage.

It has often been said that the English upper class has been more prudent, more shrewd, more open than any other. What must be said is that, for a long time now, England has not, strictly speaking, had a noble class, if we use the word in the ancient and restricted sense it has retained everywhere else. This singular revolution is lost in the mists of time but one living testament still remains, namely the language. For several centuries the word 'gentleman' entirely changed its meaning in England and the word 'vassal' no longer exists. It would, already, have been impossible to translate literally into English this line of *Tartuffe* when Molière wrote it in 1664:

'And such as one sees him, he is indeed a gentleman.'

If you wish to make yet another application of linguistics to history, follow through time and space the fate of the word 'gentleman', which is born from the French word 'gentilhomme'. You will observe its meaning broaden in England as social classes draw together and close ranks. In each century it is used for men placed a little lower down the social scale. It moves across to America where it is employed to describe vaguely all citizens. Its history is the very history of democracy.

In France the word 'gentilhomme' has always remained closely tied to its original meaning; since the Revolution it has practically disappeared from use but that use has never changed. The word has been preserved intact to indicate the members of a caste because the caste itself has been preserved as separate from all other classes as it had ever been.

But I shall go much further and suggest that this caste has become much more than when the word was coined and that a course in quite the opposite direction has taken place from the course we have seen among the English.

If the man from the middle class and the nobleman were more alike, they had become, at the same time, more isolated from each other. These are two facts which it is so necessary not to confuse because the one often worsens rather than eases the difference.

In the Middle Ages, and so long as feudalism maintained its power, all those men who held land from the lord of the manor (men properly called vassals in feudal terms), many of whom were not nobles, had permanent links with the lord to serve the administration of the manor. This was indeed the chief condition of their tenure. Not only were they bound to follow their lord to war but, by virtue of their grant from him, they also had to spend a certain amount of time every year in his court to help him conduct legal affairs and govern the citizens. The lord's court was the main cog in the feudal government. It is evident in all the old law systems of Europe and I still currently come across visible traces of them in several parts of Germany. The feudal scholar Edme de Fréminville, who, thirty years before the French Revolution, took it into his head to write a substantial book on feudal rights and land tenure, tells us that he had seen in the 'title deeds of a number of manorial estates that the vassals were obliged to attend every two weeks at the lord's court when, once assembled, they would sit in judgement along with the lord or his judge-in-ordinary at the trials and disputes between citizens'. He adds 'that sometimes he found eighty, one hundred and fifty and even two hundred of these vassals in one manor. A great number of them were commoners.' I have quoted this not as a proof – there are a thousand more – but as an example of the way in which, from the outset and for a long time, the rural classes were closer to the nobles and, daily, joined with them in the conduct of the same affairs. What the manorial court did for the small country landowners, the Provincial Estates and later the Estates-General did for the inhabitants of towns.

It is impossible to study what remains today from the Estates-General of the fourteenth century and particularly from the provincial estates of the same period, without expressing surprise at the place in these assemblies held by the Third Estate and at the power the latter exercised.

The middle-class man in the fourteenth century, as an individual, was doubtless inferior to his counterpart in the eighteenth but the middle class as a body held at that time a higher and more established position in political society. Their right to take part in government is beyond dispute; the role they played in the political assemblies was always important and often dominant. The other classes felt the need to take account of them daily.

Above all, what is striking is the sight of the nobility and the Third Estate at that time finding it easier to run things together or to stand firm against things together than they have done ever since. We notice that not only in the Estates-General of the fourteenth century, several of which had a disorderly and revolutionary character caused by the misfortunes of the time, but also in the individual estates of the same period where nothing suggests that business did not follow orderly and regular procedures. Thus we see, in the Auvergne, the three orders taking shared responsibility for important measures which they implemented through commissioners chosen from all three. The same pattern is repeated in Champagne for the same period. Everyone knows the famous act by which the nobles and the middle classes in a great number of towns banded together at the beginning of this same century to defend the nation's freedoms and the privileges of the provinces against the encroachment of royal power.[28] At that period of our history, we come across several such episodes which look as if they were drawn from English history.[29] Such events no longer occurred in subsequent centuries.

In fact, as the government of the manor broke down, as the Estates-General finally met less frequently or eventually stopped altogether, and as general freedoms in the end collapsed, ruining local liberties alongside them, the middle classes and the nobles ceased to have contact in public life. Never again did they feel any need to draw closer to each other or to cooperate; every day saw the rift between them widen and they became estranged from each other. In the eighteenth century this revolution was complete. These two classes of men met only by chance in private life and then not only as rivals but as enemies.

And what seems entirely exclusive to France at the time when the order of nobility was losing its political powers, the individual nobleman was gaining several privileges he had never before possessed or was increasing those that were already his. You could say that the limbs of the body were growing rich from the remnants of the body itself. The nobility had a decreasing right to command but the nobles had an increasing and exclusive power to be the foremost servants of the ruler; it was easier for a commoner to become an officer under Louis XIV than under Louis XVI. Such a thing often occurred in Prussia while it was almost without precedent in France. Each of these privileges, once bestowed, was hereditary and unalienable. The more this noble order ceased to be an aristocracy, the more it apparently became a caste.

If we take the most hateful of all these privileges – the exemption from tax – it is easy to see that, from the fifteenth century right up to the French Revolution, this increased progressively as the march of public spending grew more rapidly. When only 1,200,000 livres of tax were raised under Charles VII, exemption was a minor privilege; when 80 millions were raised under Louis XVI, it meant a very great deal. When the *taille* was the only tax levied on commoners, this exemption was hardly noticeable. But when taxes of this kind had been multiplied under a thousand headings and in a thousand forms, when four other taxes had been amalgamated into the *taille* and when burdens unknown in the Middle Ages, such as forced labour applied by the crown to all public works and services, the army etc., had been tacked on to the *taille* and its accessories, imposed in an unequal fashion to boot, the exemption of the nobles appeared immense.[30] The unfairness, although great, was in truth much more apparent than real, for the nobleman, even if he escaped personally, was often affected through his tenant farmer who had to pay the tax imposed. But in this matter the apparent inequality did more harm than the actual.

Louis XIV, pressed by the financial burdens which overwhelmed him at the close of his reign, had created two universal taxes – the capitation and the *vingtième*. Yet, as if exemption from taxes was in itself so honourable that it had to be respected even when it was being attacked, care was taken to collect the tax in a different manner when it was universal. For some it remained harsh and humiliating; for others indulgent and respectful.[31]

Although inequality in the matter of taxation had been established throughout the European continent, there were very few countries where it had become so obvious and so consistently resented as in France.[32] In a great part of Germany most taxes were indirect. In relation to direct taxes, the nobleman's privilege consisted of a smaller contribution to the common payment. Furthermore, certain taxes impinged on the nobility alone and they were intended to replace the free military service which was no longer demanded.

Now, of all the ways of differentiating between men and underlining their social status, unevenness of taxation is the most pernicious and the one most likely to add isolation to inequality and, somehow, to make both of these incurable. For observe its effects: when the middle classes and the nobles are no longer subjected to the same tax, the annual assessment and collection of tax once again trace out in sharp and exact terms the divisions between classes. Every year each member of the privileged class feels a real and pressing incentive not to let himself be mixed up with the masses and he makes a fresh effort to keep himself apart.

As almost all public matters begin or end in a tax, from the moment the two classes were unequally subject to tax they had almost no reason ever to meet together again or any cause to have any shared needs or opinions. No one needed to keep them apart; the opportunity and desire to act in concert, in a sense, had been removed from them.

Burke, in the flattering picture he paints of the former French Constitution, cites in evidence for his support of the institution of our nobility the ease with which the middle classes obtained a noble title by procuring some office for themselves. That appeared to him a parallel to the open aristocracy of England. In fact, Louis XI had multiplied the number of titles he bestowed as a means of diminishing the status of the nobility. His successors were lavish with them to earn money. Necker tells us that, in his time, the number of offices that resulted in titles rose to four thousand. Nothing like that was found anywhere else in Europe; but the parallel Burke wished to establish between France and England could not have been more wrong.

If the English middle classes, far from waging war on the aristocracy, stayed so closely allied to it, this did not come about because the aristocracy was open but rather, as has been said, because its character was blurred and its boundaries unknown. It was less because you could enter its ranks than because you never knew when you had. The result was that anyone close to it was able to belong to it, join with its government and derive some reflected glory or some profit from its power.

But the barrier which separated the French nobility from the other classes, although very easy to cross, was always fixed and obvious. Striking and hateful signs always made it recognizable to those left outside its ranks. Having once crossed over, a man became separated from all those he had just abandoned by privileges which were for them a burden and a humiliation.

The system of bestowing titles, far from lessening the hatred felt by the commoner for the nobleman, on the contrary inflated it immeasurably. This feeling grew more bitter because of all the envy the newly created nobleman inspired in his former equals. This is the reason why the Third Estate in its grievances (*cahiers*) always displayed greater frustration against the newly ennobled than the old nobles and why, far from asking for the doorway leading to this ennoblement to be widened, always requested that it be narrowed.

At no period in our history had the title of nobleman been more easily obtained than in 1789 and never had the middle classes and the nobles been further apart. Not only did the nobles refuse to tolerate anything that smacked of the bourgeoisie in their electoral colleges but the middle classes pushed aside with the same concern everything which appeared to be noble. In certain provinces, the newly ennobled men were rejected on one side because they were judged not noble enough, on the other because they were already too much so. This, they say, is what happened in the famous Lavoisier episode.

Leaving the nobility aside, if we now consider this middle class, we shall see a quite similar picture: the bourgeois almost as separated from the common people as the nobleman from the bourgeois.

Almost the whole of the middle class in the Ancien Régime dwelt in the cities. There were two main reasons for this: the privileges enjoyed by the nobility and the taille. The lord living on his estates normally displayed a certain familiar friendliness towards the peasants, whereas his scorn for the middle class knew no limits. This had never stopped growing along with the lessening of his political power. On the one hand, with no governing to do, he no longer had any interest in showing consideration towards those who could assist him in his task and, on the other, as has been often noted, he was fond of consoling himself for the loss of his real power by an excessive use of his apparent rights. Even when he stayed away from his estates, instead of easing his neighbours' problems he aggravated their discomfort. Absenteeism did not even help in this matter, for privileges exercised by his legal representative were all the more unendurable.

Yet, I am wondering whether the *taille* and its associated taxes were not even more influential reasons.

I could, I think, explain relatively briefly why the *taille* and its associated taxes weighed much more heavily on the countryside than the towns but perhaps that will not be of much use to the reader. Sufficient, therefore, to say that the urban middle class, as a group, had a thousand ways of reducing the burden of the *taille* and often of escaping it altogether. None of them would have been able to do that individually if he had remained on his own land. Above all, in this way they avoided the obligation of collecting the *taille* which was dreaded even more still than the duty of paying it and justly so. For there never was in the Ancien Régime or, I think, under any regime, a worse position than that of the parish tax-collector. I shall have an opportunity to prove this later. However, no one in the village was able to evade this duty except the nobility. Rather than submit to it, the wealthy commoner rented out his property and withdrew to the nearest town. Turgot agrees with all the secret documents which I have managed to consult when he says that 'the collection of the *taille* transforms almost all rural landowners into town dwellers'. As an aside, this is one of the reasons that France had more towns, above all small towns, than most other European countries.

Thus confined within town walls, the wealthy commoner soon lost the taste and ways of the countryside; he became entirely alien to the work and business of those of his equals who had stayed behind. His life no longer had but one aim, so to speak – he wanted to become a public official of his adopted town.

It is a great mistake to think that the passion for office felt by almost all Frenchmen these days and, in particular by those of the middle class, originated during the Revolution; it was born several centuries before and, since that time, has never stopped growing thanks to the thousand new kinds of sustenance fed to it.

Public offices under the Ancien Régime were not like those of today but there were, I think, many more of them. The number of minor offices was almost limitless. From 1693 to 1709 alone, it was calculated that forty thousand posts were created, almost all within the reach of the lower middle class.

In a provincial town of moderate size in 1750 I counted up to one hundred and nine persons employed in the justice department and one hundred and twenty-six to execute their decrees – all people from the town. The enthusiasm of the middle class to fill these posts was really unrivalled. As soon as one of them felt he had a little capital, he immediately used it to buy a position, rather than using it in his business. This wretched ambition had a more damaging effect on the progress of agriculture and trade in France than the guilds and even the *taille*. Whenever official positions ran short, the imagination of the applicants set to work and soon invented new ones. A M. Lemberville published a paper in order to prove that it was perfectly in the public interest to create inspectors for a certain industry and he ended up by putting his own name forward for the post. Which of us has not encountered a Lemberville? In fact, a man with a little learning and some wealth did not think it becoming to die without having been a public official. As a contemporary expressed it, 'Every man according to his rank wishes to be something by royal appointment.'

The greatest difference in this respect between the era I am quoting and our own is that, at that time, the government sold official positions whereas today it gives them away. To obtain them, a man no longer offers money; he does better than that: he surrenders himself.

Divided from peasants by location and even more by style of life, the middle class was also more often than not separated from them by interest. There were justifiable complaints about aristocratic privileges in relation to tax; but what of those enjoyed by the middle class? Posts free from part or all of public dues could be counted in their thousands – here from service in the militia, there from forced labour, another from the *taille*. What parish is there, said someone in writing at the time, which does not include within it, aside from nobles and churchmen, several citizens who have purchased some tax exemption with the help of dues or commission? One of the reasons from time to time for the abolition of a certain number of posts intended for the middle class was the reduced tax receipts caused by the great number of exemptions from payment of the *taille*. I have no doubt that the number of people exempted was as great in the middle class as in the nobility, and often greater.

These wretched privileges filled those deprived of them with envy and those possessing them with selfish pride. Nothing was more obvious throughout the eighteenth century than the hostility of the urban middle class towards the peasants of the suburbs and the jealousy those suburbs felt for the town. 'Each of the towns,' said Turgot, 'wrapped up in its own private concerns is inclined to sacrifice the countryside and the villages of its neighbourhood to those concerns.' 'You have often been obliged,' he says elsewhere to his sub-delegates, 'to repress the encroaching and invasive tendency which symbolizes the behaviour of the towns towards the countryside and villages of their neighbourhood.'

Even the common people who lived with the middle class within the precincts of the town became estranged from them, almost hostile. Most of the local taxes which the middle class established were shaped so as to impinge primarily on the lower orders of society. I have had more than one chance to verify what this same Turgot states somewhere else in his writings, that the middle classes of the towns had discovered a way of managing the city tolls so that they did not feel the burden of them.

But what you observe especially in all the actions of the middle class is the fear of being confused with the common people and the passionate desire by every possible means to avoid being controlled by that class.

'If it pleased the King,' said the middle-class citizens of a town in a report to the Controller-General, 'to restore for election the position of mayor, it would be appropriate to force the voters to choose from only the leading citizens, in particular from those who were members of the presidial court.'

We have seen how the policy of our kings was directed towards the successive removal from townspeople of the use of their political rights. From Louis XI to Louis XV all their legislation illustrates this idea. Often middle-class townspeople went along with it, occasionally they recommended it.

At the time of the municipal reform of 1764, an Intendant

consulted the town officials of a small town on whether the right to elect magistrates should be retained for artisans and *other humble folk*. These officials replied that in reality, 'the common people have never abused this right and that it would certainly be a kindly act to leave them the consolation of choosing those who were to govern them. It is even more worth relying, for the maintenance of good order and public peace, upon the assembly of leading citizens.' The sub-delegate wrote back in his turn that he had summoned to his house for a secret meeting 'the six best citizens of the town'. These six best citizens came to the unanimous agreement that it would be preferable to entrust the election, not even to the assembly of leading citizens, as the municipal officials were suggesting, but to a certain number of deputies chosen from the different groups making up this assembly. The sub-delegate, more supportive of the people's liberties than these very middle-class citizens, added, while conveying their opinion, 'that it is nevertheless very harsh that these artisans should pay, with no power to regulate their use, sums of money imposed by those of their fellow citizens who are, perhaps, by reason of their privileged tax position, the least affected by the question'.

But let us finish the picture; let us now look at the middle class itself as distinct from the common people, just as we have considered the nobility as distinct from the middle class. We note the countless divisions in this small section of the nation when set apart from the rest. It appears as if the French nation resembled those so-called elementary bodies in which modern chemistry discovers new and distinct particles the more closely it looks. I have found no less than thirty-six groups among the leading lights of a small town. These different bodies, albeit very small, worked hard and constantly to become even smaller; daily they cleared out the alien parts they might contain in order to shrink to the basic elements. These fine efforts reduced some groups to three or four members, whose personality became all the more lively and temper all the more quarrelsome. They were all divided from each other by a few minor privileges, the least fair of which still carried signs of their status. Constant wranglings about seniority waged between them. The Intendant and the courts were deafened by the noise of their disputes. 'It has just been decided to give holy water to the members of the presidial court before the city council. The Parlement was unable to make up its mind, so the king raised the matter in his own Council and resolved it himself. It was high time; this affair was enraging the whole town.' If precedence was granted to one member of a group rather than another in the general assembly of leading citizens, then the latter stopped attending; he abandoned public life rather than seeing, as he said, his dignity lowered. The guild of wigmakers in the town of La Flèche decided that 'it would in this manner advertise the very real pain caused by precedence given to the bakers'. One group of notable citizens in one town pigheadedly refused to fulfil their office 'because,' said the Intendant, 'of the admission into the assembly of a few artisans with whom the leading bourgeois find it humiliating to be associated'. 'If the position of alderman,' said the Intendant of another province, 'is granted to a notary, that will disgust the other leading citizens since notaries here of low birth have not come from significant families and have all been clerks.' The six leading citizens I have already mentioned and who decided so readily that the common people should be deprived of their public rights, found themselves in a strange quandary when they came to look at who the leading citizens should be and what order of precedence should be established among them. In such a case they did nothing more than modestly express their misgivings, fearing, they said, 'to cause their fellow citizens too obvious a pain'.

That vanity natural to Frenchmen grew stronger and sharper in the unrelenting challenge to these small groups' self-respect and the citizen's legitimate pride was neglected. In the sixteenth century most of the corporate bodies I have just mentioned already existed but their members, once they had taken care among themselves of the business of their individual association, cooperated with all the other inhabitants to manage together the general concerns of the city. In the eighteenth century they had almost entirely withdrawn into themselves, for the activities of municipal life had become rare and were all implemented by authorized officials. Each of these small social groups lived just for themselves therefore, bothered simply about themselves and concerned themselves with only what affected them.

Our ancestors had no word for *individualism*, a word we have coined for our own use because, in their time, there was no individual who did not belong to a group or who could consider himself to be entirely alone. Yet of the thousand small groups constituting French society each thought only about itself. If I may express it in this way: this was a kind of collective individualism preparing itself for the real individualism which we know today.

What is more bizarre still is that all these men standing apart from each other had become so alike one to another that you would not have seen any recognizable difference if you had made them change places. Furthermore, if anyone could have plumbed the depths of their minds he would have discovered that these small barriers separating such similar people appeared to the men themselves as much opposed to the public interest as to common sense and that, in theory, they felt passionate about unity. Each of them felt attached to his individual social rank only because all the others based their own position on social rank. Yet they were all ready to blend into the same crowd as long as no one had anything which set him apart or rose above the common level.

CHAPTER 10

HOW THE DESTRUCTION OF POLITICAL LIBERTY AND THE SEPARATION OF CLASSES CAUSED ALMOST ALL THE ILLS WHICH RESULTED IN THE DEMISE OF THE ANCIEN RÉGIME

I have just described the most fatal of all the illnesses which attacked the constitution of the Ancien Régime, condemning it to death. Once more I wish to return to the source of so dangerous and strange a disease and show how other ills sprang from it.

If the English, after the Middle Ages, had lost all political liberty as we did and all the local freedoms which cannot exist for long without it, it is very likely that the various class groups in their aristocracy would have split apart, as had happened in France and in more or less the rest of the Continent, and would have separated themselves from the common people. But liberty forced them to stay within each other's reach in order to forge agreement when the need arose.

It is strange to observe how the English nobility, prompted by its own ambition, was able, when they thought it necessary, to mingle on familiar terms with its inferiors and to pretend to regard them as equals. Arthur Young, whom I have already quoted and whose book is one of the most informative works on the France of old, tells us that, when one day he found himself in the country on the Duke of Liancourt's estates, he expressed his wish to question some of the wealthiest and ablest farmers in the surrounding area. The Duke instructed his Intendant to introduce them to him. Whereupon the Englishman remarked, 'On an English lord's estate, three or four farmers would have been invited who would have dined with the family and in company of ladies of the highest rank. I have seen such a thing at least a hundred times in our islands. You would search in vain for its like in France from Calais to Bayonne.'

Certainly English aristocrats were, by nature, haughtier than their counterparts in France and less inclined to fraternize with their inferiors; but the necessities of their social condition forced them into doing so. They were prepared to do everything in order to govern. Over the ensuing centuries the only inequalities of taxation among the English were those successively introduced in favour of the poorer classes. Just look, I beg you, where the different political principles can lead nations so geographically close to one another. In the eighteenth century in England the poor enjoyed tax privileges; in France, it was the rich.[33] In the former, the aristocracy shouldered the heaviest public burdens in order to be allowed to govern; in France it preserved, to the last, the immunity from tax as a consolation for its loss of power.

In the fourteenth century, the maxim *Tax only with consent* seemed as sturdily established in France as in England itself. It was often quoted. To go against it always seemed an act of tyranny; to observe it, a return to legality. At that time, as I have said, there were many parallels between the political institutions of France and England. Then the destiny of the two nations went their different ways and continued to grow more dissimilar as time went by. They resembled two lines which, starting from nearby points but at a slightly different angle, are then forever diverging the longer they extend.

I venture to declare that, from the day when the French nation, wearied by the prolonged disorders which had accompanied King John's captivity and Charles VI's madness, let kings impose a general tax without its consent and when the nobles were mean enough to allow the Third Estate to be taxed so long as they were exempted, from that day was sown the seed of practically all the vices and abuses which plagued the Ancien Régime for the rest of its days and finally brought about its violent death. I admire the unusual wisdom of Commynes when he said: 'Charles VII, who won the argument over imposing the *taille* when he wished, without the agreement of the three Estates, laid a heavy burden on his own soul and upon that of his successors, inflicting a wound upon his kingdom which will bleed for a long time.'

Mark how, in reality, the wound has widened with the passing of time; follow the consequences of this act step by step.

Forbonnais in his learned *Researches into the Finances of France* rightly stated that, in the Middle Ages, kings generally lived off the revenues of their estates and he goes on: 'and as unexpected needs were met by extraordinary tax contributions, these fell equally upon clergy, nobles and commoners.'

Most general taxes voted by the three Orders during the fourteenth century were like that. Almost all taxes imposed at that time were *indirect*, which is to say that they were paid for by all consumers without distinction. Sometimes the tax was direct; it then fell not on property but on income. Nobles, churchmen and the townspeople were bound, for example, to surrender to the king over one year a tenth of their income. It ought to be understood that what I have just stated about taxes voted by the States-General applied equally to those taxes imposed during the same period by the various provincial assemblies in their districts.

It is true that, from that time on, the direct tax known as the *taille* never fell on the nobility. Their obligation to provide free military service cleared them from that tax but, as a general tax, the *taille* had a limited use because it was linked to the power of the manor rather than that of the king.

When the king for the first time undertook to raise taxes in the name of his own authority, he realized that his first task had to be to choose one which did not obviously hit the nobles directly; for the latter, who represented at that time a class that was a dangerous rival to the king, would never have tolerated an innovation which might have been so harmful to them. So he chose a tax from which they were exempt – he picked on the *taille*.

To all the inequalities that then existed he added thus one more universal one which intensified and supported all the others. From that moment on, as the needs of the public purse grew along with the functions of central government, the *taille* broadened and extended its application until, soon, it had multiplied ten-fold; all new taxes became *tailles*.[34] Year by year, inequality of taxation drove the classes apart and isolated men more profoundly than had ever been the case before. From the moment that taxation aimed not to affect those most able to pay but those least able to protect themselves, the monstrous consequence of sparing the rich and burdening the poor was inevitable. We are told that when Mazarin ran out of money, he took it into his head to impose a tax on the leading Parisian houses. Having encountered some resistance from those affected, he merely added the five millions he needed to the general warrant of the *taille*. His intention was to tax the most wealthy citizens; he had taxed the most wretched. The treasury lost nothing thereby.

The income from such badly distributed taxes had limits but the needs of the rulers no longer had any. However, they wished neither to summon the Estates in order to obtain grants nor to provoke the nobles, by taxing them, into seeking the convening of these assemblies.

This resulted in that fantastical and evil ingenuity of the financial mind in the Ancien Régime which has so strangely characterized the management of the public purse over the last centuries of the monarchy.

The administrative and financial history of the Ancien Régime needs a detailed study if we wish to understand how a benevolent government can be driven to violent and dishonest practices by the need for money, acting secretly and without accountability, once time has sanctified its power and has freed it from the fear of revolutions, which are the final safeguard of nations.

In these historical records we come across, page by page, royal property sold, then seized because it was not for sale; contracts violated and acquired rights ignored; creditors of the state losing out whenever a crisis arose; public confidence constantly deceived.

Privileges granted in perpetuity were perpetually taken away. If it was possible to feel sympathy for the unpleasantness caused by a foolish vanity, we would pity the fate of those luckless men, newly titled, who, throughout the course of the seventeenth and eighteenth centuries, were forced to repurchase from time to time those empty honours or those unfair privileges which they had already paid for several times over. Thus Louis XIV cancelled all the titles obtained over the previous ninety-two years, most of which had been granted by himself. These could be retained only by forwarding new payments, *since all these titles had been obtained by surprise* said the edict. This was a precedent that Louis XV did not fail to imitate eighty years later.[35]

The militiaman was forbidden to find a replacement for fear, it is said, that the state would have to increase its payment for recruits.

Towns, communities, hospitals were forced to fall short of their obligations in order to be in a position to lend money to the king. Parishes were prevented from undertaking useful works for fear that, by dividing their resources in this way, they paid their *taille* less punctually.

The story is told that M. Orry and M. de Trudaine, respectively the Controller-General and the Director-General of public highways, had thought up a plan to replace forced labour on the roads with a levy in money to be provided by the inhabitants of every district for the repair of their roads. The reason why these clever administrators had to abandon their plan is illuminating: they were afraid, so it is said, that the funds thus raised could not be stopped from being siphoned off into the public treasury for its own use, the result of which would mean that soon the taxpayers would have to tolerate both the new tax burden and the old forced labour. I am brave enough to say that no individual could have evaded the judgement of the courts if he had managed his own wealth as the mighty king in all his glory directed the public finances.

If you encounter some old medieval system which has been prolonged against the spirit of the time, with its defects growing worse, or some damaging innovation, you only have to dig to the root of this evil to find some financial short-term expedient which has grown into an institution. To pay off one day's debts you will see the creation of new powers which will last centuries.

In the far distant past, one particular tax called the right of *franc-fief* had been placed on commoners who owned noble lands. This right established the same distinction between land as existed between men and the one distinction was constantly worsened by the other. I think, perhaps, that the right of *franc-fief* has served more than all the rest to keep the common man separate from the nobleman because it prevented their coming together in the thing which most speedily and effectively unites men to each other, namely land ownership. Thus, from time to time, a gulf was re-opened between the noble landowner and his commoner neighbour. By contrast in England nothing has speeded up the unity of the two classes more than the abolition in the seventeenth century of all the marks which distinguished the noble fief from land held by commoners.

In the fourteenth century the feudal right of *franc-fief* was not onerous and was collected only at long intervals but, in the eighteenth, when feudalism was almost destroyed, it was demanded strictly every twenty years and was equal to a whole year's income. The son paid it on inheriting from his father. 'This right,' said the Agricultural Society of Tours in 1761, 'does infinite damage to the progress of the business of agriculture. Of all the burdens of tax imposed on the king's subjects, there is undoubtedly none more irritating or onerous in the country-side.' 'This tax,' says another contemporary voice, 'which at first was imposed once in a lifetime has by degrees since become a very harsh tax.'[36] Even the nobles would have wished it to be abolished for it prevented commoners from buying land but the needs of the treasury demanded its retention and increase.

It would be a mistake to accuse the Middle Ages of all the ills instigated by industrial corporations. All evidence shows that, in the beginning, the trade and craft guilds were merely means of binding together members of the same occupation and of creating within each industry a small free governing body whose task it was both to help the workers and to control them. Saint Louis apparently wished for nothing more than that.

It was only at the beginning of the sixteenth century, at the height of the Renaissance, that for the first time they imagined the right to work was tantamount to a privilege which the king could sell. Only then did each guild become a small, closed aristocracy and finally we saw the creation of those monopolies so damaging to any progress in the skilled professions and which so disgusted our ancestors. From Henry III, who, if he did not actually create this evil, at least brought it into general use, to Louis XVI who eliminated it, it can be said that the abuses of the craft guilds never stopped for an instant to increase and to spread at the very time when social progress made them more insufferable and public consciousness was more aware of them. Each year new professions lost their freedom; each year the privileges of the old ones were increased. Never was this evil pushed to greater extremes than during what we are used to calling the golden years of Louis XIV's reign because never had the want for money been greater nor the decision not to consult more firmly entrenched.

Letronne rightly said in 1775: 'The state has established the trade corporations simply to find resources, sometimes by the warrants it sells, sometimes through the new offices it creates and which the corporations are forced to buy back. The 1673 edict pushed the principles of Henry III to their logical conclusions by forcing all the guilds to take out letters of confirmation by payment of a sum of money. All the craftsmen were obliged to join a guild, if they were not already members. This wretched action brought in 300,000 livres.'

We have seen how the entire constitution of the towns was overturned not with any political view in mind but in the hope of collecting revenue for the treasury.

The sale of offices owed its existence to this same need for money along with the desire not to make requests to the Estates-General. It gradually turned into something so curious that the like had never been seen in the world. Thanks to this practice instigated by the mind of the fiscal authorities, the vanity of the Third Estate had been kept in suspense for three centuries and been directed solely towards the possession of public office. This universal passion for government jobs seeped into the very innards of the nation and became the combined cause of revolutions and slavery.

As financial embarrassments increased, new jobs were created which were all rewarded by exemptions from taxes or by privileges.[37] Since the decision to create these came from the needs of the public purse and not those of the administration, this was the way of instituting an almost unbelievable number of wholly useless or damaging offices.[38] In 1664, at the time of Colbert's inquiry, it was found that the capital involved in this wretched kind of ownership amounted to almost five hundred million livres. Richelieu, they say, abolished one hundred thousand posts which immediately sprang up under different names. For a small sum, the central authority lost the right to govern, control and to restrain its own agents. In this way was gradually constructed an administrative machine so huge, so intricate, so muddled, so inefficient that it had somehow to be left idling along while they had to construct around it an instrument of government that was simpler and easier to handle, by means of which all the tasks apparently done by public officials were actually performed.

We can state that not one of those hateful institutions could have lasted twenty years if people had been allowed to discuss them. Not one would have been established or allowed to grow worse, if the Estates had been consulted or if their grievances had been heard when it so happened that they met. The occasional Estates-General of recent centuries never stopped complaining about them. Several times these assemblies saw, as the origin of all these abuses, the power which the king usurped to raise taxes arbitrarily or, to imitate the very expressions used in the vigorous language of the fifteenth century, 'the right to grow rich off the substance of the people without the agreement or consultation of the three Estates'. They were concerned not only about their own rights but forcefully requested that the rights of the provinces and towns were respected; this they frequently managed to obtain. At every new meeting voices were raised in the body of the delegates against the inequality of taxes. On several occasions the Estates asked for the abolition of the guild system; they attacked through the centuries with a growing energy the selling of public offices. 'Whoever sells offices sells justice and that is a dishonourable thing to do,' they said. When the sale of offices was established, they continued to complain about the abuse made of them. Although they rose up against so many useless offices and dangerous privileges, it was always in vain. Those institutions had been set up precisely in opposition to them; they had been brought into existence from the wish not to summon the Estates and from the need to disguise from the gaze of the French the tax which no one dared to reveal in its true light.

And simply note that the best kings along with the worst had recourse to these practices. Louis XII finally established the sale of offices; Henry IV sold them as hereditary: the defects of the system are so much stronger than the virtue of the men operating it.

That very desire to bypass the control of the Estates-General made the kings entrust most of their political powers to the *parlements*. This entangled the power of law into the government in a way that was very damaging to the good order of public business. But it was necessary to appear to be providing some new guarantees in the place of those the king was removing. For the French, who quite patiently tolerate royal power as long as it is not oppressive, never like it when it is obvious and it is always prudent to erect some appearance of a barrier in front of power which at least hides it a little without the ability to block it.

Finally, it was this desire to stop the nation, from whom money was demanded, from reclaiming its freedom which constantly led the government to spare no efforts in keeping the classes apart from each other since that would prevent their gathering together or joining in a common resistance. Thus the government would never have to deal at any one time with more than a small number of isolated individuals. Throughout the whole course of our long history in which we see a succession of so many rulers, several noteworthy for their spirit, some for their genius and almost all for their courage, we come across not a single one making any attempt to unite or bring classes together other than to submit them all to an equal state of dependency. No, I am wrong: one man alone wanted to and even made heartfelt efforts to do so. That man – who could fathom the judgements of God! – was Louis XVI.

The separation of classes was the crime of the old monarchy

and further on it became its excuse. For, when all those belonging to the wealthy and educated groups in the nation could no longer combine or cooperate in the business of governing, the administration of the country by itself was virtually impossible and a master had to intervene.

'The nation,' said Turgot, sadly, in a secret report to the king, 'is a society made up from different, disunited orders and from a people whose citizens have only a small number of ties in common. As a result no one concerns himself with anything except his own private interests. Nowhere are any shared interests visible. The villages and the towns have no more mutual connections than the regions to which they belong. They cannot even agree among themselves about necessary public works. In this everlasting conflict of claims and undertakings, Your Majesty is obliged to make all the decisions independently or through your delegates. Your subjects wait for your special commands before they contribute to the public good or respect the rights of their neighbours or sometimes before exercising their own rights.'

It was no slight task to bring back together fellow citizens who had lived as strangers or enemies for centuries and to teach them how to conduct their own affairs in common. It had been much simpler to divide them than it was thereafter to reunite them. We have given the world a memorable example. When the different classes which took their place in the society of the France of old came back into contact sixty years ago, after being cut off by so many barriers for so long, they came into contact first over sensitive issues and then met only to tear each other to pieces. Even today their jealousies and hatreds survive them.

CHAPTER 11

THE FORM OF LIBERTY THAT EXISTED UNDER THE ANCIEN RÉGIME AND ITS INFLUENCE ON THE REVOLUTION

If the reader were to stop at this point in the book, he would have only a very incomplete picture of the government of the Ancien Régime and would have a poor understanding of the society which produced the Revolution.

When we see fellow citizens so divided and closed in upon themselves, a royal power so extensive and strong, we might conclude that the spirit of independence had disappeared along with public freedoms and that every Frenchman was equally bent double beneath the yoke. But it was not like that at all. The government already directed alone and despotically all the common public business but it was still far from being the overlord of every individual.

In the midst of many institutions already prepared for absolute rule, freedom still lived on, albeit a peculiar kind of freedom which we cannot easily grasp today; we must examine it at very close quarters to be able to understand the good and evil effects it has been able to cause.

While the central government was taking over all the powers at a local level and increasingly occupied the whole sphere of public authority, institutions it had left alone to survive or which it had created itself, old customs, former practices, even abuses still hindered its progress and fostered deep down in a large number of individuals the spirit of resistance while maintaining for many people their strength and shape.

This centralization already exhibited the same disposition, the same methods, the same aims as in our day but not yet the same power. The government, in its desire to make money and having put most public offices up for sale, had thus deprived itself of the advantage of giving them away and retrieving them at will. Thus one of its enthusiasms had greatly harmed the success of the other; its greed had counterbalanced its ambition. It was, therefore, endlessly reduced to act using tools it had never fashioned itself and which it could not destroy.[39] As a result, it often came to see its most determined wishes watered down in the implementation. This strange and faulty constitution of public functions took the place of a kind of political guarantee against the omnipotence of the central power. It was a sort of shapeless and badly constructed dyke which divided the central power's strength and muffled its impact.

Neither did the government have at its disposal that endless supply of favours, supports, honours and money which it is able to distribute these days; thus, it had many fewer means of inducing or compelling people.

Moreover, the government had a poor knowledge of exactly how limited its power was. None of its rights was consistently acknowledged or established on a sturdy footing. Its scope for action was extensive but it still moved forward with hesitant steps, as in a dark and unknown place. These frightening shadows which concealed at that time the limitation of all powers and surrounded all rights, were favourable to the king's undertakings and stood against the freedoms of his subjects but they also defended those freedoms.

The administration, feeling that it was recently created and of low birth, was always hesitant in its approach if it should meet any obstacle in its path. It is a picture that strikes the reader of correspondence from ministers and Intendants in the eighteenth century when he sees how this government, which was so intrusive and so imperious as long as obedience was not challenged, stood dumbfounded at the sight of the slightest resistance; how the mildest criticism embarrassed it, how the smallest noise startled it and how it then came to a standstill, hesitated, negotiated, felt its way and stayed well within the natural boundaries of its power. The gentle egoism of Louis XV and the good-heartedness of his successor lent themselves to this attitude. Besides, these rulers never imagined that anyone might think of dethroning them. They exhibited none of that worried and harsh nature which, since that time, fear has often brought to those in power. They trampled underfoot only those people they could not see.

Several of the privileges, prejudices and false ideas which were the strongest opposition to the creation of an ordered and benevolent freedom served to sustain in a great number of subjects that spirit of independence which inclined them to brace themselves against the abuses of authority.

The noble class utterly despised the so-called administration even though they occasionally applied to it. They retained, even while their former power was being washed away, something of their forefathers' pride, which was as hostile to enslavement as to law. They hardly bothered themselves with the general liberty of citizens and were willing to allow the hand of central power to weigh down on all around them but they had no intention that it should oppress themselves. To secure this aim, they were ready to run great risks, if need be. At the onset of the Revolution, the nobility, which was to fall away with the throne, still adopted an infinitely more arrogant and unrestrained attitude towards the king and especially towards his agents than towards the Third Estate, which would shortly overturn the monarchy.[40] Almost all the guarantees against the abuses of power which we obtained during the thirty-seven years of representative government were vigorously demanded by the nobility. Reading the register of their grievances we can sense, behind its prejudices and shortcomings, the spirit and some of the great qualities of the aristocracy. It must always be a matter of regret that, instead of bending the nobility to the rule of law, we cut it down to its roots. By this action the nation was deprived of a vital part of its substance and a wound was inflicted on liberty which will never be healed. This one class had been in the lead for centuries, had acquired in this long and unchallenged familiarity with greatness a clear proudness of heart, a natural trust in its own strength and a habit of being deferred to, which makes it the most resistant body in society. Not only did it possess manly habits, its example increased manly virtues in the other classes. By rooting it out, even its enemies were weakened. Nothing can completely replace it while, of itself, it could never be reborn; it can recover its titles and property but not the soul of its ancestors.

The priests, whom we have often seen since so slavishly submissive in civil matters to the temporal sovereign whoever he might be and this latter's most daring flatterers – provided he made it clear that he supported the Church – formed therefore in earlier times one of the most independent bodies of the nation and the only one whose special freedoms had to be respected.

The provinces had lost their free rights; the towns possessed only a shadow of theirs. Ten nobles could not meet together to discuss any matter at all without the express permission of the king. The French Church retained to the end its periodic assemblies.[41] At its heart, ecclesiastical power itself had respected boundaries. The lower ranks of clergy enjoyed serious guarantees against the tyranny of their superiors and were not ready to follow the unlimited decisions of the bishop into blind obedience of the king. I am not attempting a criticism of the old constitution of the Church, I am simply saying that it did not at all prepare the priest's soul for political servility.

Many clergymen, moreover, were of noble blood and brought into the Church the pride and intractability of people of their rank. Furthermore, they all enjoyed an elevated station in the state and possessed privileges. The use of these very feudal rights, fatal enough to the moral power of the Church, granted to each of its members a spirit of independence towards the civil power.

But what above all helped to give priests the ideas, needs, opinions and often the passions of the citizen was the ownership of land. I have had the patience to read most of the reports and debates which the former Independent Estates have bequeathed to us, especially those of Languedoc where the clergy were more than elsewhere involved in the details of public administration. I read too the minutes of the independent assemblies which were summoned to meet in 1779 and 1787. Since I brought to this reading the ideas of my own times, I was astonished to see bishops and abbots, several of whom were renowned as much for their saintliness as their learning, drawing up reports on the construction of a road or a canal, dealing with such matters from a position of considerable knowledge; discussing with extensive skill and art the best methods of improving agricultural produce; encouraging the wellbeing of the inhabitants and working towards the prosperity of industry. They were always equal and often superior to all those laymen, who, with them, managed the same business.[42]

Contrary to a generally held and firmly established opinion, I venture to think that those nations who deny Catholic clergy any share whatever in landownership and change all their incomes into salaries serve only the interests of the Vatican and the temporal power of kings and deprive themselves of a very important element of liberty.

A man who devotes the best part of himself to a foreign authority and in the country he inhabits cannot have a family is not, so to speak, rooted in the soil except by one solid tie, namely landownership. Cut that tie and he belongs nowhere in particular. In the place where chance has given him birth, he lives as a stranger in a civil society where almost none of its concerns touches him directly. For his conscience he depends only upon the Pope; for his living upon the ruler. His only homeland is the Church. In every political event he perceives only what serves the Church or harms it. As long as the Church is free and prosperous, what does the rest matter? The most natural attitude for him in politics is indifference – an excellent member of the Christian community; a poor citizen everywhere else. Such sentiments and similar ideas in a body of men who control children and guide their way of life cannot but weaken the soul of the entire nation as far as public life is concerned.

If we wish to have a fair idea of the revolutionary changes affecting men's minds as a consequence of alterations to their social condition, we must reread the registers of grievances presented by the clergy in 1789.[43]

In these the clergy often showed themselves as intolerant and sometimes as stubbornly attached to several of its former privileges but also as hostile to tyranny, as supportive of civil liberty and as much in favour of political liberty as the Third Estate or the nobility. It proclaimed that individual liberty had to be safeguarded not by promises but by a legal process similar to habeas corpus. They demanded the destruction of state prisons, the abolition of exceptional tribunals and of the practice of removing cases from lower to higher courts; they demanded the publicizing of all debates, the permanence of all judges, the eligibility of citizens to all public offices, which should be granted on merit alone; they demanded a less oppressive military recruitment, less humiliating for the lower classes and from which no one should have exemption; the redemption of feudal dues which resulted, they said, from the feudal system and which are hostile to liberty; unlimited freedom to work; the abolition of internal customs barriers; they recommended the increase of private schools – one for each parish and free of charge; lay charitable establishments throughout the country such as almshouses and workshops; every sort of encouragement for agriculture.

In politics proper, the clergy proclaimed more loudly than anyone that the nation had the absolute and inalienable right to assemble, to pass laws and to hold a free vote for taxation. No Frenchman, they affirmed, could be made to pay a tax he had not voted for either in person or through his representative. The clergy went on to demand that the Estates-General, freely elected, should meet annually to debate before the nation all important matters, to pass general laws which no custom or private privilege could oppose, to draw up the budget and control even the king's household, to insist that their deputies should be immune from arrest and that their ministers should always be answerable to them. They also expressed the wish that state assemblies should be established in all the provinces and municipal governments in all the towns. Of the divine right of kings, not a word.

Taking an overall view, and despite the startling failings of some of its members, I do not know whether there was ever in the world a more remarkable clergy than that of Catholic France at the hour when the Revolution took them by surprise, or more enlightened or more nationally minded or more public spirited or, at the same time, more loyal to the faith, as persecution subsequently demonstrated. I began my study of society as it was full of prejudice against the clergy but I ended up full of respect. Certainly they displayed the defects which are inherent in all corporate bodies whether political or religious, whenever they are closely knit and firmly constituted, namely the inclination to interfere, an intolerant attitude and an instinctive and sometimes blind attachment to the private rights of their group.

The middle classes of the Ancien Régime were similarly much better prepared to show a spirit of independence than they are today. Several of the very failings of their situation contributed to that end. We have observed that the offices they filled were even more numerous at that period than today and that the middle ranks showed as much enthusiasm to obtain them. But notice the difference in the times. Most of those situations, being neither given nor removed by the government, thus inflated the importance of the holder without placing him at the mercy of authority. In a word, those aspects, which today complete the subjection of so many people, were precisely what gave them then the most powerful weapon to achieve public respect.

All those kinds of immunity which caused such an unhappy division between middle and lower classes also turned the former into an imitation aristocracy which often showed the arrogance and the obstructive spirit of the real aristocracy. In each of those small private groups which divided the middle class into so many parts, the general welfare was willingly put aside while the concerns and rights of the lesser body was a constant preoccupation.[44] In that body they felt they had a common dignity and privileges to defend. No one could ever become hidden in the crowd or hide his cowardly servility. Each man stood on a very small stage, it is true, but the spotlight was upon him and before an audience which was always the same and always ready to applaud or hiss.

The art of stifling the sound of resistance was much less perfected than today. France had not yet become the deaf place we live in now; on the contrary, it reflected every sound and, despite the absence of political liberty, it was enough to raise its voice for the loud echoes to be heard afar off.

Above all, the feature which reassured the downtrodden of

that time that a way existed to have one's voice heard was the constitution of justice. We had become a country with an absolute government but through our judicial institutions we had remained a free nation. Justice in the Ancien Régime was complicated, cumbersome, slow and costly. These were great faults without a doubt, but you never came across that subservience in the face of power, which is one of the worst forms of corruption. This fundamental defect, which not only corrupts the judge but soon infects the whole nation, was entirely foreign to it. The magistrate could not be removed and did not seek promotion – two things equally necessary to his independence. For how does it matter that a magistrate cannot be forced to do something, if a thousand other ways of influencing him are available?

It is true that the power of the king had succeeded in concealing from the ordinary courts knowledge of almost all the dealings which concerned public authority but, even while robbing them of this, it still remained fearful of them. Even though it prevented them from hearing cases, it still did not dare to stop their receiving complaints and delivering their opinion. Since the language of the law at that time retained the style of old French which liked to give things their proper names, magistrates often crudely described the procedures of government as despotic and arbitrary acts.[45] The irregular interventions of the courts in the government, which often disturbed the efficient administration of business, thus served as a safeguard of men's freedom from time to time. This was a case of one great evil setting limits on an even greater one.

At the heart of these legal bodies and all round them the vigour of the old customs was still retained alongside new ideas. The *parlements* were doubtless more preoccupied with themselves than the public good but we must acknowledge that, as they defended their own independence and honour, they always showed themselves to be fearless and they communicated this spirit to all who approached them.

When in 1770 the Parlement of Paris was broken up, the magistrates who belonged to it suffered the loss of their position and their power without a single one of them being seen to yield to the royal will. More than that, courts of a different kind, such as the tax court, which were not directly attacked or threatened, voluntarily offered themselves to the same harsh treatment when that had become a certainty. Yet further still, the leading lawyers practising before the *parlement* of their own free will shared its fate, abandoning the path to prestige and wealth and condemning themselves to silence rather than appear before dishonoured magistrates. I know of nothing greater in the history of free nations than what took place on this occasion. Yet that happened in the eighteenth century alongside the court of Louis XV.

The ways of the law courts had become in many respects embedded in the ways of the nation. The idea that all cases were subject to discussion and that every verdict was subject to appeal, the custom of public scrutiny, the support for proper procedures, everything which was hostile to servitude, all came from the courts. That is the only area of the education of a free nation which the Ancien Régime has handed down to us. Even the administration had borrowed much of the language and practice of the law courts. The king always felt himself obliged to justify his edicts and to display his reasons before finally pronouncing them; the Royal Council issued decrees preceded by preambles; the Intendant issued his orders through a court usher. At the heart of all the administrative bodies of ancient origin such as, for example, the Treasurers of France or the elected officials, business was debated in public and decisions arrived at after appeals were heard. All these practices and structures acted as so many barriers to the whim of the king.

The lower classes, especially those in rural districts, were almost always in no position to resist oppression other than by violence.

Most of the methods of defence I have just underlined were effectively beyond their reach; in order to avail themselves of such methods they would need to have enjoyed a social position which enabled them to be seen and a voice which could have been heard. But outside the ranks of the common people, every Frenchman with the courage to do so could quibble over his obedience and resist even as he was bowing and scraping.

The king spoke to the nation as a leader rather than as a

master. 'We glory,' said Louis XVI at the outset of his reign in a preamble to one edict, 'in the fact that we command a free and generous nation.' One of his ancestors had expressed this idea before in more old-fashioned terms when he had thanked the Estates-General for the boldness of their remonstrances and had said, 'We prefer to talk to free men than to serfs.'

The men of the eighteenth century were hardly aware of that form of passion for material comfort which is tantamount to being the mother of servitude, a feeling, flabby yet tenacious and unchanging, which is ready to fuse and, as it were, entwine itself around several private virtues such as love of family, reliable customs, deference to religious beliefs and a lukewarm and regular practice of established Church ritual. While this supports integrity, it forbids heroism and excels in turning men into well-behaved but craven citizens. Those men were both better and worse.

The French of that time loved happiness and adored pleasure; they were perhaps more disorderly in their habits and more unbridled in their passions and ideas than the people of today but they were unaware of that moderate and decent sensuality which we see now. The upper classes were absorbed much more in elegant living than in personal comfort, more in building their reputation than their riches. Even in the middle classes a man did not let himself be wrapped up exclusively in a search for his own wellbeing; he often gave up its pursuit in favour of more refined and loftier pleasures; everywhere he invested in some other good beyond money. 'I know my nation,' a contemporary wrote in a curious style but one which did not lack pride, 'which, although skilled in melting and squandering precious metals, has not been shaped to honour these with the usual worship and would be quite ready to return to its ancient idols – courage, reputation and, I dare say, generosity.'

Besides, we must be careful not to estimate the meanness of men by the degree of their submission to the sovereign power; that would be to employ a false yardstick. However obedient men of the Ancien Régime were to the wishes of the king, one kind of compliance was quite unknown to them; they did not know what it was to bend the knee to an illegitimate or disputed power, one which was not respected, one which was often despised but one which you served willingly because it was useful or could do you harm. That demeaning form of servitude was always alien to them. The king inspired in them feelings which none of the most despotic rulers appearing since in the world has ever been able to evoke and which have even become almost incomprehensible to us because the Revolution has so uprooted them from our hearts. They felt for him both the tenderness one feels for a father and the respect one owes only to God. By submitting to his most arbitrary commands, they were yielding less to constraint than to love; thus they often kept complete freedom of soul even in the most extreme state of dependence. They thought the greatest evil of obedience was constraint; for us it is the least. For us, the worst evil stems from the slavish feeling which induces that obedience. Let us not despise our forefathers; we have not the right to do so. Would to God we could recover a little of their greatness along with their prejudices and failings![46]

We would, therefore, be quite wrong to think that the Ancien Régime was a period of servility and dependence.[47] Much more freedom existed then than nowadays although it was a kind of disjointed and spasmodic freedom, ever bound by narrow class distinctions, ever tied to the notion of exemption and privilege, which equally sanctioned the defying of the law and arbitrary decisions but which almost never went so far as to provide citizens with the most natural guarantees they needed. Though cramped and deformed, freedom was still fruitful. In times when centralization strove to equalize, mould and to spoil all characters, it was freedom which preserved in a great many individuals their inner originality, their colour and shape, nourished in their hearts a pride in themselves and, of all their enthusiasms, persuaded them to value that of personal reputation. Freedom shaped the strong hearts, the proud and courageous personalities which we would see make their appearance to turn the French Revolution simultaneously into an object of admiration and terror for the generations which followed on. It would indeed be strange if such manly virtues had been able to flourish in a soil where liberty no longer grew.

But if this form of disfigured and unhealthy liberty prepared the French to overturn despotism, it perhaps rendered them less qualified than any other nation to found in its place the peaceful and free authority of law.

CHAPTER 12

HOW THE CONDITION OF THE FRENCH PEASANT WAS SOMETIMES WORSE IN THE EIGHTEENTH CENTURY THAN IT HAD BEEN IN THE THIRTEENTH DESPITE THE PROGRESS OF CIVILIZATION

In the eighteenth century the French peasant could no longer be the victim of petty feudal tyrants; only rarely was he exposed to acts of violence on the part of the government; he enjoyed civil liberty and owned some land. But all the members of the other classes had moved away from him and he lived a more isolated life than perhaps had been seen anywhere in the world. This was a new and unusual form of oppression whose consequences deserve a very close scrutiny as a separate study.

From the beginning of the seventeenth century, Henry IV used to complain, according to Péréfix, that the nobles were deserting the countryside. In the middle of the eighteenth century, this desertion had become universal. All the records of the time noted and deplored the fact – Economists in their books, Intendants in their letters, agricultural societies in their reports. The definitive proof is found in the registers of the capitation tax, which was levied in the actual place of residence; the collection from the entire upper class and a part of the middle class was in Paris.

Almost the only noble left in the countryside was the one whose modest fortune prevented him from leaving.[48] He found himself, in relation to his neighbours the peasant farmers, in a position no wealthy landowner had ever occupied, I think.[49]

BOOK TWO, CHAPTER 12

Since he was no longer their leader he did not share the interest he had had previously in showing them consideration, in helping or guiding them. On the other hand, not being himself burdened by the same public dues as they were, he failed to experience any strong sympathy for their suffering since he neither shared nor associated himself with their grievances which were alien to him. These men were no longer his subjects; he was still not their fellow citizen – a unique fact of history.

This led to a form of absenteeism of the spirit, if I may put it that way; this was more common and more deep-seated than absenteeism properly so-called, the result of which was a nobleman living on his estate and often adopting the views and opinions which his steward would have held had he not been there himself. Like his steward he looked upon his tenants only as rent payers and he demanded from them everything strictly due to him according to law or custom. This sometimes made such a collection of former feudal dues harsher than when feudalism itself was in force.

Often burdened with debt and always in needy circumstances, the nobleman usually lived a very niggardly life in his chateau thinking only how to amass enough money for his winter expenses in town. The common people, who often pick the perfect word to express an idea, had given this petty squire the name of the smallest bird of prey – the hobby hawk.

Individual exceptions can doubtless be found to prove the opposite. I am speaking of classes as a whole who alone deserve the attention of history. Who can deny that during this time many rich landowners did concern themselves with the welfare of the peasants without needing to and without a shared interest? But these individuals fought successfully against the law of their new situation which, despite their best efforts, impelled them towards indifference just as it drove their former serfs towards hatred.

This abandonment of the countryside by the nobility has often been attributed to the particular influence of certain ministers or kings – some blame Richelieu, others Louis XIV. In fact it was an idea almost always pursued by rulers during the last three centuries of the monarchy, namely to separate the nobles from the common people and to draw them to the court and public office. That is an obvious feature of the seventeenth century when the nobility was still a source of fear to the king. Among questions asked of Intendants this one was still included: Do the nobles of your province choose to stay at home or to leave?

We possess one Intendant's letter replying on this theme: he complained that the nobles in his province were content to stay with their peasants instead of fulfilling their duties to the king. Now take note of this: they were talking about the province of Anjou, which was known as La Vendée later on. These nobles who refused, it was said, to do their duty to the king were the only men to have defended the monarchy in France, arms in hand, and were able to die fighting for it. They owed this glorious distinction solely to the fact that they had managed to keep about them the peasant farmers and they had been reproached for preferring to live among them.

Nevertheless we must guard against attributing to the direct influence of some of our kings the abandonment of the country-side by the class which formed the leadership of the nation. The chief and enduring cause of this phenomenon lay not in the decisions of certain men but in the slow and unceasing activity of institutions and the proof of that is that, when in the eigh-teenth century the government wished to counteract this evil, it could not even arrest its progress. As the nobility finally lost their political rights without acquiring new ones, and as local freedoms disappeared, this mass exit by the nobles increased; there was no longer any need to lure them from their homes; they did not care to stay there any more. Life in the country had become tasteless to them.

What I am saying here about noblemen should be understood of wealthy landowners in every country: if a country is cen-tralized, the land is emptied of wealthy and educated inhabitants. I could add: if a country is centralized, this means inefficient and humdrum agriculture. I could comment on that very profound saying by Montesquieu by clarifying his meaning: 'The land produces less by virtue of its fertility than the freedom of its inhabitants.' But I do not wish to exceed my brief.

We have observed elsewhere how the bourgeoisie left the countryside in their turn and looked out everywhere for a refuge in the towns. On no point do all the documents of the Ancien Régime agree more. They state that almost always all you saw in the countryside was a generation of wealthy peasant farmers. Should a farmer work hard and finally succeed in acquiring a small property, he immediately persuaded his son to drop the plough, sent him to the town and bought him a public position. From this period dates this sort of strange revulsion often manifested, even in our time, by the French farmer for the profession that made him rich. The effect has outlived the cause.

If truth be told, the only educated man, or, as the English say, the only *gentleman*, who resided permanently among the peasants in unbroken contact with them was the priest who would, therefore, have become the leader of the rural population, despite Voltaire, if he himself had not been so tightly and so obviously tied to the political hierarchy; by possessing several of the latter's privileges he had inspired some of the loathing these evoked.[50]

There we have the peasant farmer entirely cut off from the upper classes and far removed from those very members of his own class who would have been able to help and guide him. As they aspire to education or wealth, they abandon him while he remains behind, sifted out from the whole nation and shunted aside.

That treatment was not found to the same degree in any other of the great civilized countries of Europe and even in France it was a recent development. The fourteenth-century peasant was both more downtrodden and more cared for. The aristocracy sometimes treated him harshly but it never abandoned him.

In the eighteenth century a village was a community all of whose inhabitants were poor, uneducated and coarse. Its magistrates were as ill-educated and as despised as the rest; its syndic could not read; its tax collector could not, in his own hand, draw up the accounts upon which his own fortune and that of his neighbours depended. Not only did its former lord not have the right to govern it but he had reached the stage of seeing any contact with administration as a kind of humiliation. To assess the *taille*, call up the militia, control the forced labour gangs were servile tasks which belonged to the syndic. Only the central government concerned itself with the village and, since it was situated so far away and had nothing to fear from its inhabitants, its only motive was to make a profit from it.

Now come and see what becomes of an abandoned class no one wishes to tyrannize but which no one seeks either to educate or serve.

The heaviest taxes imposed on the country dweller by the feudal system were doubtless removed or lightened but other taxes, perhaps more burdensome than before, had been introduced instead – something not sufficiently researched. The peasant was not suffering all the evils endured by his forefathers but he was putting up with many miseries his forbears had never known.

We do know that the tenfold increase of the *taille* over two centuries was solely at the peasant's expense. We must at this point say something about the way in which this tax was raised from them to show what cruel laws can be established and maintained in civilized centuries when the most enlightened men of the nation have no personal interest in changing them.

I found, in a confidential letter written by the Controller-General himself in 1772 to Intendants, this description of the *taille*. It is a small masterpiece of precise and brief writing: 'The *taille*,' said this minister, 'is arbitrary in its imposition and binding jointly on all parties. It is levied on the individual and not on land owned. In most of France it is subject to all the annual changes in the fortune of those who pay it.' Everything is there in three sentences; it would be impossible to describe with greater skill the evil from which profit was made.

The total sum due from the parish was fixed each year, always varying, as the minister stated, so that no farmer could predict a year in advance what he would have to pay the following year. Within the parish each year a peasant was chosen at random and elected collector whose job was to divide up the burden of tax between all the others.

I promised to describe the position of this collector. Let us listen to the provincial assembly of Berry in 1779. It cannot be suspect since it was composed of privileged persons who did not pay the *taille* and were chosen by the king. 'As everyone wishes to avoid the responsibility of collector,' it said in 1779, 'every man must take the office in turn. The levying of the *taille* is, therefore, entrusted annually to a new collector without regard to his competence or honesty. Thus the composition of each tax roll reflects the character of the man completing it. The collector imprints on it his fears, weakness or failings. How else would he ever succeed in his task? He is acting in the dark. For who can exactly assess his neighbour's wealth and how this wealth compares with that of someone else? However, the collector's opinion alone must shape the decision and he is responsible for the receipts against his own property and person. Normally, for two years, he has to spend half his days chasing up those who have to pay. Those unable to read are forced to look for someone from the neighbourhood to stand in for them.'[51]

Turgot had already said of another province a little time before: 'This office brings about the despair and almost always the ruin of those who undertake it; thus year after year all the wealthy families of a village are reduced to wretchedness.'

Yet this hapless man was armed with unlimited power; he was almost as much a tyrant as he was a martyr. During this term of office, in which he ruined himself, he held in his hands everybody's ruin. It is again the provincial assembly which is speaking: 'Preferential treatment for his relatives, friends and neighbours, hatred and vengeance towards his opponents, the need for a protector, the fear of offending a wealthy citizen who can give him work – all these fight with the feelings of justice in his heart.' Terror often makes the collector merciless. There are parishes where the collector never steps out unless accompanied by bailiffs and constables. 'Whenever he goes out without bailiffs,' said an Intendant to the minister in 1764, 'the people are unwilling to pay.' 'In the district of Villefranche alone,' the provincial assembly of Guyenne again informs us, 'a hundred and six bearers of writs and other bailiffs' assistants are constantly on the road.'

To evade this violent and arbitrary taxation, the French peasant farmer in the middle of the eighteenth century acted the Jew of the Middle Ages. He put on a show of being unhappy when, in reality, he happened not to be. His very wealth made him justifiably apprehensive. I found a very clear proof in a document I took not from Guyenne but a hundred leagues away. The agricultural society of Maine announced in its 1761 report that it had conceived the idea of awarding animals as prizes and incentives. 'This has been stopped,' it says, 'because of the dangerous consequences which a crude jealousy might visit on the prizewinners and which might cause them trouble in the following years when the arbitrary imposition of the tax assessment made them suffer financially.'

In this tax system every taxpayer had, in effect, a direct and long-standing interest in spying upon his neighbours and in denouncing the increases of their wealth to the collector. They were all trained to be envious, to inform and to hate. You would surely say that this was happening in the domain of a Rajah of Hindustan![52]

Nevertheless there were areas at this same period in France where the tax was raised regularly and with kindness – these were certain Independent Provinces. It is true that these had been allowed the right to raise taxes themselves. In Languedoc, for example, the *taille* was applied only to property and did not vary with the wealth of the owner; a fixed and transparent land register, carefully compiled and renewed every thirty years, acted as a base for the tax and in it the land was divided into three categories according to its fertility. Each taxpayer knew in advance exactly what share of the tax he had to pay. Should he fail to pay, he alone or rather his land itself, was liable. Should he feel wronged in the allocated share he always had the right to demand that his assessment be compared with that of another citizen of the parish whom he chose himself. That is what we call the appeal to proportionate equality.

We can see that all these rules are exactly the ones we follow currently; they have hardly improved since then; they have simply been made universal. It is worth noting that, although we have borrowed from the Ancien Régime the same shape of our public administration, we have been careful not to imitate all the other features. It is not from the government that we have taken our best administrative practices but from the provincial assemblies. While adopting the machinery we have rejected what came out of it.

The habitual poverty of the lower rural classes had given rise to the sayings which were not likely to bring it to an end. Richelieu had written in his political testament: 'If the lower classes were well off, it would be difficult to keep them in line.' In the eighteenth century they did not go so far as that but they did still believe that the peasant would not work if he were not constantly spurred on by necessity. Poverty was apparently the only guarantee against idleness. That is precisely the theory I heard expressed on occasions with regard to the blacks in our colonies. This opinion was so widespread among the governing classes that almost all Economists have felt obliged to challenge it formally.

We know that the original object of the *taille* had been to allow the king to purchase soldiers to free the nobles and their vassals from military service. But in the seventeenth century the obligation of military service was once more imposed, as we have seen, under the name of the militia and this time it fell upon the common people alone and almost solely upon the peasant.

It is enough to consider the copious police reports which filled the Intendants' files, all connected with the pursuit of draft dodgers or deserters, to judge that the militia was not easy to raise. It appears, in fact, that no public tax burden was more intolerable to peasants than this one. To evade it they often fled to the woods where they were pursued with armed force. This is astonishing when you think how easy it is today to operate compulsory recruitment.

We must attribute the extreme loathing felt by the peasants of the Ancien Régime for military service less to the principle of the law itself than to the manner in which it was enforced. Above all, we must blame the years of uncertainty threatening those eligible (you could be called up at forty unless you were married), the arbitrary nature of the revision which rendered the advantage of a lucky number in the draw almost worthless, the prohibition against finding a stand-in and the revulsion of a harsh and hazardous profession where all hope for promotion was forbidden. But especially we must blame the feeling of such a mighty burden weighing down on them alone (upon the most wretched of them to boot) and the humiliation of their plight which made hardships more bitter.

I have had in my hands many transcripts of the draft lottery drawn up in 1769 in a great number of parishes. I saw listed the numbers of exempt persons in each parish: this man is a noble's servant; this one the warden of an abbey; a third is only the valet of a member of the middle class who, it is true, lived like a nobleman. Wealth alone brought exemption. Whenever a farmer was listed annually among those paying the most tax, his sons enjoyed the privilege of exemption from military service – that is what they called the fostering of agriculture. The Economists, normally great supporters of equality, were not affronted by that privilege; they simply asked for it to be extended to other cases, which meant that the burden on the poorest and least protected peasants became heavier. One of them said that, 'the low pay of the soldier, the manner he is billeted, clothed, fed and his complete dependence would make it too cruel to conscript any but a man of the very lowest class'.

Up to the end of Louis XIV's reign, the main roads were not maintained at all or were so at the expense of those who used them, namely the state or all the adjacent landowners. But about that time they began to repair them with the help of forced labour which meant at the expense of the peasants alone. This method of getting good roads without paying for them seemed such a happily conceived plan that in 1737 a circular from Orry, the Controller-General, applied it to the whole of France. The Intendants were armed with the right to imprison at will the defaulters or to send in the bailiff's men to fetch them.

From then on, every time commerce grew and the need and demand for good roads multiplied, the forced labour system spread to new routes and the tax went up.[53] In a report to the provincial assembly of Berry drawn up in 1779, we find that works carried out by forced labour in this poor province could have been valued at 700,000 livres per annum. In 1787, in lower Normandy, they were assessed at almost the same sum. Nothing could better demonstrate the sad lot of the rural classes; the social progress which was enriching all other classes drove them to despair. Civilization was turning against them alone.[54]

About the same period I read in the correspondence from Intendants that it was right to refuse to use the peasants for forced labour on the private roads in their village, seeing as they had to be used solely on the main roads or, as they were called then, *the king's highways*.[55] New though it was, this bizarre idea that it is right to have the money for roads paid by the poorest and those who least needed to travel on them took root so naturally in the minds of those benefiting from it that soon they no longer imagined things could have been otherwise. In 1776 the attempt was made to transform the forced labour into a local tax. Immediately inequality went hand in hand with this transformation and followed it into the new tax.

The forced labour system had moved from the manorial tax it had been to a royal tax and gradually had spread across all public works. In 1719 I see that forced labour served to build barracks![56] 'The parishes should send their best workmen,' says the order, 'and all other works should give way to this work.'[57] Forced labour transported convicts to the prison ships and beggars to workhouses. It carted the military equipment every time the troops moved – a very onerous burden at a time when every regiment was accompanied by a heavy baggage train. A great number of carts and oxen had to be assembled from a large area to pull them.[58] This kind of labour which started out as of little importance became one of the most burdensome when standing armies themselves grew in numbers. I came across state contractors loudly demanding forced labour to be allocated to them for the transportation of building wood from forests to naval dockyards. Usually the members of these gangs received a wage which was always low and arbitrarily fixed. The burden of such a badly imposed tax sometimes became so heavy that the collector of the *taille* expressed anxiety. One of them wrote in 1751, 'The expenses demanded from the peasants for the repairs of roads will soon place them in a position that makes it impossible for them to pay their *taille*.'

Could all these new oppressive measures have taken root if rich and enlightened men had stood alongside the peasant and had shown the inclination and the power, if not to protect him, at least to intercede for him with their common master who already held in his grasp the fortunes of both poor and wealthy?

I have read the letter of an important landowner written in 1774 to the Intendant of his province to urge him to open a road. According to this man this road was to bring prosperity to the village and he gave his reasons for thinking so. Then he moved on to the setting up of a fair which, he was sure, would double the money from produce. This worthy citizen added that, with the help of a small contribution, a school could be established to encourage more industrious subjects for the king. Until then he had not thought of these necessary improvements. Only after having being confined for two years in his chateau by orders from the king had they occurred to him. 'My two-year exile on my estate,' he says innocently, 'has convinced me of the exceeding usefulness of all these things.'

But it is above all in times of shortages that we perceive the ties of patronage and dependence which formerly bound together the country landowner and the peasants had been slackened or broken. In such moments of crisis the central government grows frightened at its isolation and weakness. At such a time it would like to have seen the regeneration of those individual influences or political groupings it had destroyed. It called them to its aid; no one came and it was usually surprised to see that those it had itself murdered were dead.

In such extreme times there were Intendants, such as Turgot, for example, who, in the most destitute provinces, issued illegal injunctions to force rich landowners to feed their tenant farmers until the following harvest. I found letters, dated 1770, from several priests who suggested to the Intendant that he tax the richest landowners in their parishes, both clergy and lay, 'who,' they said, 'own large estates where they do not reside and from which they draw huge revenues which they will consume elsewhere'.

Even in normal times, the villages were swarming with beggars because, said Letronne, the poor had help in the towns but, in the countryside in winter, begging was absolutely vital.

From time to time these wretched souls were dealt with in a very violent fashion. In 1767 the Duke of Choiseul wanted to rid France of begging once and for all. We can see in the correspondence of Intendants how vigorously he went about it. The mounted constables were ordered to arrest at one fell swoop all the beggars in the kingdom; we are assured that more than fifty thousand were seized in this way. Fully fit tramps were to be dispatched to the galleys; as for the others, more than forty workhouses were opened to house them. It would have been better to reopen the hearts of the rich.

This government under the Ancien Régime which was, as I have stated, so considerate and sometimes so hesitant, so devoted to formality, caution and deference when it was a matter of men ranked above the common people, was often harsh and always speedy when it dealt with the lower classes, especially the peasants. Among the documents which have passed under my gaze, not a single one witnesses to the arrest of a middle-class member by order of an Intendant; but the peasants were constantly arrested because of forced labour, military service, begging, criminal offences and a thousand other circumstances. One class had independent courts, long debates and the safety of publicity; the other had magistrates who gave summary judgement without appeal.

'The wide gap which stands between the common people and all the other classes,' wrote Necker in 1785, 'helps to divert our eyes from the way in which power can be used against all those lost in the crowd. Without the kindness and human feeling which characterize both the French people and the spirit of the century, it would be a constant source of sadness to all those who can feel pity for sufferings from which they themselves are free.'

Oppression was evident less from the evil done to these wretched people than from the good they were stopped from achieving for themselves. They were free and owned land but they stayed almost as uneducated and often more unhappy than their ancestors, the serfs. They remained outside industry while the arts wondrously advanced – uncivilized in a world sparkling with enlightenment. While retaining the intelligence and shrewdness peculiar to their race, they had not learned how to use them; they were not even able to succeed at agriculture which was their sole concern. 'I am gazing at an agricultural system from the tenth century,' said a famous English agriculturist. They excelled only in their calling as soldiers; at least in the army they had a natural and necessary contact with the other classes.

The peasant dwelt in this isolated and unhappy abyss; he hung there, sealed and out of reach. I have been surprised and almost frightened to see that, less than twenty years before the Catholic faith was abolished without resistance and the churches desecrated, the method sometimes adopted by the government to estimate the population of a district was thus: the priests counted the number of Easter communicants; they added to that number an estimated number of under-age children and sick people; that added up to the total number of inhabitants. Meanwhile, the ideas of the time were already creeping into these coarse minds from all directions, entering by roundabout and underground paths, and they assumed in these dark and narrow places peculiar shapes. The peasant's ways, habits and beliefs still appeared the same; he was obedient and even high-spirited.

But we must distrust the Frenchman's frequent display of good cheer in the face of his greatest sufferings; it simply underlines that, thinking his misfortunes unavoidable, he was trying to distract himself by not thinking about them. It was not that he did not feel them. Were you to have opened a way out of this unhappy state which seemed to bother him so slightly, he would have immediately shifted in that direction so violently that he would have trodden over your body without seeing you if you were in his way.

From our present standpoint we can see these things clearly but people at the time did not. Only with great difficulty did the upper classes ever succeed in perceiving clearly what was happening in the soul of the common people and in particular of the peasants. The peasants' education and way of life opened up to them insights on human affairs which, peculiar to them, remained closed to anyone else. But when the rich man and the poor man no longer have any shared interest, any shared grievances, any shared business, the shadows which conceal the mind of the one from that of the other become unfathomable and these two men could live side by side for ever without any contact between them. It is strange to see in what a bizarre state of security all those who occupied the upper and middle storeys of the social edifice were living at the very moment when the Revolution was beginning and to hear them discoursing cleverly among themselves on the virtues of the common people, on their gentleness, their devotion, their innocent pleasures, when '93 was already opening beneath their feet: what an absurd and terrible spectacle!

Let us pause at this point before going further and consider for a moment, amid all these detailed facts I have just described, one of the greatest laws of God in the governing of societies.

The French nobility persisted in remaining cut off from the other classes; noblemen in the end allowed themselves exemption from most of the public tax burdens. They imagined that they would preserve their high status by evading these dues and that appeared at first to be correct. But soon an inner sickness seemed to infect their position which gradually declined without anyone's interference. They grew poorer at the same pace as their immunities increased. By contrast, the middle classes, with whom they had been so frightened to join forces, grew richer and more educated alongside them, without their help and in opposition to them. They had not sought to have the bourgeoisie associate with them or be fellow citizens; they were to discover that they were their rivals, their enemies soon after and finally their masters. A power, external to themselves, had released them from the duty of governing, protecting and helping their vassals but, since at the same time it had left untouched their financial rights and honorary privileges, they judged that nothing had been lost. As they went on marching at the front, they thought they were still governing and indeed they continued to retain around them some men whom, in legal documents, they called their *subjects*; other men they named as their vassals, tenants and farmers. In reality no one was following them; they stood alone. When eventually an attack came along to overthrow them, the nobles' only recourse was to flee.

Although the fate of the upper and middle classes had been completely different in relation to each other, they did resemble one another in one respect: the bourgeoisie also ended up living as cut off from the lower class as the nobleman did himself. Far from drawing nearer to the peasants, he had run away from contact with their wretched state; instead of uniting closely with them to engage in a common struggle against a shared inequality, he had sought only to create new injustices for his own purposes. He had been as enthusiastic in obtaining exemptions as the nobleman had been in preserving his privileges. Those peasant ranks from which he had emerged had not only become strangers but were now totally unknown to him. It was only when he had issued arms to them that he realized he had aroused passions utterly beyond his experience which he was as powerless to control as to direct. Now he was going to be their victim after having been their supporter.

All ages will be astonished at the sight of the ruins of that great house of France which had seemed destined to spread throughout Europe. However, those who read carefully its history will readily understand its downfall. Almost all the failings, almost all the mistakes, almost all the prejudices, which I have just depicted, in fact owed either their beginnings or their duration or their development to the knack most French kings had of dividing men from each other the more completely to rule over them.

But when the middle classes had thus been isolated from the nobleman and the peasant from them both, when a similar process persisted at the heart of each class itself and small individual groupings had formed in the centre of each of them, almost as isolated from each other as the three classes were between themselves, then it was found that the whole nation was no longer anything more than one homogeneous mass whose parts were, however, no longer linked together. Nothing was arranged any longer to hinder the government any more than it was to shore it up. The result was that the whole structure of the king's greatness could collapse together and all at once, as soon as the society which served as its foundation started to tremble.

To sum up, this nation which apparently profited from the mistakes and errors of all its masters, has been unable, even though it effectively shook off their domination, to slip from beneath the yoke of the false ideas, of the misguided habits and of the evil tendencies they had given to it or allowed it to adopt. Sometimes we have seen this nation carry the inclinations of a slave across into the very exercise of its freedom, becoming as incapable of governing itself, as it had been intractable towards its teachers.

BOOK THREE

CHAPTER I

HOW AROUND THE MIDDLE OF THE EIGHTEENTH CENTURY MEN OF LETTERS BECAME THE LEADING POLITICAL FIGURES IN THE COUNTRY AND THE CONSEQUENCES OF THIS

I now leave behind the more remote and general facts which prepared the great Revolution I am trying to portray. I now come to the more particular and recent events which finally settled its place, its birth and its character.

For many years France had been the most literary of all the countries of Europe; nevertheless, men of letters had never displayed the attitudes they revealed towards the middle of the eighteenth century or assumed the place they then did. That had never been seen before in France or, I think, anywhere else.

They had not been involved in public affairs on a daily basis as in England; on the contrary, they had never lived more aloof from them. They were never invested with any authority at all, nor did they exercise any public office in a society already packed full with civil servants.

However, they did not remain, as did most of their counterparts in Germany, entirely foreign to politics and withdrawn into a world of pure philosophy or literature. They constantly spent time on matters connected with government; in fact, that was in reality their true occupation. Every day they were heard discussing the beginnings of societies and their primitive forms, the original rights of citizens and those in authority, the natural and man-made relations between people, the wrongs or rights of custom and the very principles of law. Thus, searching each day down to the foundations of the constitution of their time, they were curious enough to examine its structure and to criticize its general plan. It is true that not all of them made these great problems the object of special and profound research. Most of them touched upon them only *en passant* and as if toying with them, but they all dealt with them. These sorts of abstract and literary politics were scattered to an unequal degree in all the writings of those times and there was not a single work, from the ponderous treatise to the popular song, which did not contain some brief reference.

As for the political programmes of those writers, they varied so much that anyone wishing to reconcile them into one single theory of government would never reach the end of such a work.

Nevertheless, putting to one side the details in order to reach the master ideas, we easily discover that the authors of these different programmes at least agreed on one very general notion which each of them seemed equally to have thought of. This appears to have preceded in their minds all the individual ideas and to have provided their common source. However divided they might be along the rest of the way, they all clung to this same starting point: they all thought that it was right to replace the complex and traditional customs which guided the society of their time with simple and elementary rules borrowed from reason and natural law.

Looking closely, we will see that what we call political philosophy in the eighteenth century consisted, properly speaking, of this single notion.

Such an idea was not new; it had been passing backwards and forwards for three thousand years in the imaginations of men without coming to rest. How did it manage this time to take hold of all these writers' minds? Instead of stopping, as it had done often before, in the heads of a few philosophers, why had it filtered down to the crowd and why had it adopted the strength and heat of a political passion in such a way that general and abstract theories on the nature of society could be seen becoming the topic of the daily conversation of idlers, enthusing the imagination of even women and peasants? How did men of letters with neither status nor honours, nor wealth, nor responsibility, nor power become, in effect, the leading, if not the only, political figures of the time, since they alone had the authority, even though others did the actual work of government? I should like in a few words to show why and to make clear what an extraordinary and terrifying influence these facts, which seem to belong only to our literary history, had on the Revolution and even on our present times.

It was no accident that the philosophers of the eighteenth century had generally imagined notions so at variance with those which still served as a base for their society. Those ideas had naturally been suggested by the very society they all saw with their own eyes. The sight of so many excessive or absurd privileges, the burden of which was felt increasingly and the cause of which was less and less understood, nudged or rather precipitated everyone's mind towards the idea of a natural equality of social conditions. On seeing so many bizarre and disordered institutions – the offspring of other eras – which no one had tried to harmonize or to adjust to new needs and which seemed bound to live forever even when they had lost their value, they readily conceived a distaste for ancient ways and tradition and were naturally drawn to a desire to rebuild the society of their time following an entirely new plan which each of them traced by the light of his reason alone.

The social rank itself of these writers predisposed them to favour general and abstract theories of government[59] and to trust them blindly. In the almost total removal of their lives from the practical world, no direct experience came to modify the passions of their temperament. Nothing warned them about obstacles which existing conditions could bring to even the most desirable reforms. They had no idea of the dangers which always accompany the most necessary of revolutions. They did not even have the slightest inkling of them because the complete absence of all political freedom made the world of business not only unknown to them but also invisible. They had no

BOOK THREE, CHAPTER I
143

connection with that world nor could they see what others were
doing in it. They, therefore, lacked that obvious education
which the sight of a free society and the news of what is
happening give even to those who have the least contact with
government. Thus they grew much bolder in their novel suggestions, more addicted to universal ideas and systems, more con-
temptuous of ancient wisdom and still more inclined to trust
their own reason than is usually the case with the writers of
speculative books about politics.

The same ignorance brought the ears and hearts of the populace to them. If the French had still been taking part, as before,
in government through the Estates-General or even if they had
continued to be involved daily in the administration of the
country in their provincial assemblies, we could guarantee that
they would never have been fired, as they indeed were during
this time, by these writers' ideas. They would have kept hold
of a certain experience of public affairs which would have
warned against pure theory.

If, like the English, they had been able, without destroying
their former institutions, to change their ethos gradually in a
practical way, perhaps they would not have been so willing to
invent totally new ones. But each of them felt daily constricted
in his fortune, in his person, in his wellbeing or in his self-respect
by some old law, by some former political practice or by some
remnant of an old authority. He glimpsed no remedy within his
reach which he could himself apply to this particular evil. He
felt as if he had to endure everything or destroy everything in
the constitution of the country.

We had preserved, however, one freedom from the ruins of
all the others: we were able to philosophize almost without
restriction on the beginnings of societies, the fundamental
nature of governments and on the original rights of mankind.

All those men chafing from the daily practice of legislation
soon fell in love with this literary form of politics. The taste for
it affected even those whose nature and social position naturally
kept them as far away as possible from abstract speculations.
Not a single taxpayer bruised by the uneven distribution of the
taille was not warmed by the idea that all men should be

equal; any small landowner stripped bare by an aristocratic neighbour's rabbits was pleased to hear that every kind of privilege without exception was condemned by reason. Each public enthusiasm was thus cloaked in philosophy; public life was forced back into literature. Writers took hold of public opinion and found themselves for a time occupying the position which party leaders usually occupied in free countries.

No one was in a position to challenge this role of theirs.

In its heyday an aristocracy does not simply direct public business; it still controls opinions, creates a style for writers and lends authority to ideas. In the eighteenth century the French nobility had entirely lost this element of its supremacy; its reputation had gone the way of its power and the position it had occupied in the government of minds was empty and writers could spread into this world at their ease and fill it completely.

Furthermore, this aristocracy, whose position the writers were occupying, supported their project. The nobles had forgotten so completely how general theories, once they have been accepted, inevitably become transformed into political passions and actions. Doctrines entirely opposed to their own rights and even to their own existence looked to them like clever mind games. They willingly joined in to pass the time, enjoying calmly their immunities and privileges while serenely debating the ridiculousness of all established customs.

It is often astonishing to see the curious blindness with which the upper classes of the Ancien Régime themselves contributed to their own downfall. Yet where would they have found any enlightenment? Free institutions are no less vital to teach their leading citizens their dangers than to secure the lowest orders their rights. For more than a century since the final traces of public life had disappeared from our view, those people most intimately involved in the upkeep of the old constitution had been forewarned by no particular shock or any rumble that this ancient edifice was about to collapse. Since nothing on the outside had altered, they imagined that everything had remained exactly the same. Their minds had, therefore, stopped at the position held by their forefathers. In the 1789 register of grievances (*cahiers*) the nobility showed itself as preoccupied by the encroachments of the king's power as it might have been in those encroachments of the fifteenth century. On his side, the ill-fated Louis XVI, a short while before perishing in the flood tide of democracy (as Burke rightly noted) persisted in considering the aristocracy as the leading rival of royal power. He was as suspicious of it as if it was still the time of the Fronde. On the other hand, the middle and lower classes seemed to him, as to his ancestors, the most reliable support to the throne.

But what will appear stranger to us since we have witnessed the debris of so many revolutions is that the very notion of a violent revolution was not present in our fathers' minds. It was not discussed nor had it been imagined. The slight disturbances, which a state of public freedom constantly introduced in the most stable societies, serve to remind people of the daily possibility of upheavals and to maintain public caution in a state of alert. But in the eighteenth century, French society, about to tumble into the void, had had no warning that things were toppling.

I have carefully read the registers of grievances drawn up by the three orders before their meeting in 1789. I underline the three orders – the nobility, the clergy and the Third Estate. In one place a change of law is requested, in another a change of practice and I take note of these. Thus I continued my reading to the very end of this immense work. When I came to gather all the individual wishes, with a sense of terror I realized that their demands were for the wholesale and systematic abolition of all the laws and all the current practices in the country. Straightaway I saw that the issue here was one of the most extensive and dangerous revolutions ever observed in the world. Those who would be victims on the morrow knew nothing about it; they believed that the universal and abrupt transformation of such a complex and ancient society could be effected without a shock, with the help of reason and by its effectiveness alone. Poor fools! They had even forgotten this saying of their forefathers four hundred years before in the simple and vigorous French of those times: *a demand for too much freedom and liberty brings with it too much slavery.*

It is not surprising that the nobility and the middle class, having been excluded for so long from public life, should display this strange lack of experience. What is more astonishing is that the very men who directed affairs – ministers, magistrates, Intendants – hardly displayed any more foresight. Yet several were very skilled at their calling; they had a thorough grasp of all the details of the public administration of their time but, as for that great science of government which teaches an understanding of the universal shifts in society, judgement of what happens in the minds of the masses and anticipation of what will result from these, they were as completely naïve as the people themselves. In fact only the interplay of free institutions can really teach politicians this chief part of their art.

Such becomes clear from the report Turgot addressed to the king in 1775 where he advised him, among other things, to have a representative assembly freely elected by the whole nation which he would summon annually for six weeks in his own presence but to which he should grant no effective power. It would deal only with administration and never with government; it would offer suggestions rather than make demands and, if truth be told, it would be given the responsibility of debating laws without enacting them. 'In that way, the power of the king would be informed but not hindered,' he said, 'and public opinion would be appeased without risk. For such assemblies would possess no authority to oppose vital operations and if, by some miracle, they did not comply, Your Majesty would still remain in charge.' You could not more thoroughly misunderstand the influence of such a measure or the spirit of the times. It has often happened, it is true, towards the end of revolutions, that it has been possible to get away with what Turgot suggested and to grant the shadow of freedom without offering the real thing. Augustus tried it successfully. A nation tired of long debates is willing to agree to be tricked as long as it is given peace. History teaches us that all you need to please a nation is to gather together throughout the country a certain number of obscure or dependent men whom you force to play before it the role of a political assembly in return for pay. There have been several examples of this. But at the outset of a revolution these projects always fail and only ever serve to inflame the populace without satisfying it. The lowliest citizen of a free country knows that; Turgot, great administrator though he was, did not.

Now, when you think that this same French nation so alienated from its own affairs, so deprived of experience, so hindered by its institutions and so helpless to reform them was, at the same time, of all the nations on earth, the most literary and the most fond of intellectual things, you will easily realize how writers became a political influence at that time and ended by being the most important.

Whereas in England writers on government theory mingled with those who actually governed, the former introducing new theories into practice and the latter reshaping and restricting theories in the light of factual considerations, the political world in France remained divided into two separate provinces with no shared commerce between them. In the one group stood those who governed; the other established the abstract principles upon which all administration had to be founded. On this side the taking of particular measures prompted by everyday business; on the other the promulgation of universal laws with no thought for the means of applying them. One group directed the nation's affairs; the other guided the nation's minds.

Above and beyond the real society itself they saw that, with its ever traditional, muddled and unregulated constitution in which laws remained varied and contradictory, classes divided, social conditions set forever and tax burdens uneven, men's minds gradually constructed an imaginary society in which everything appeared simple and coordinated, uniform, just and in harmony with reason.

As time passed the imagination of the masses deserted the first to find refuge in the second. They lost interest in what existed, in order to dream of what might exist and, in the end, they came to live in that ideal city fashioned by writers.

Our revolution has often been attributed to that in America and indeed the latter exercised much influence on the French Revolution but it owed less to what was happening in the United States than to what was being thought at the same period in France itself. While in the rest of Europe the American Revolution was still only a novel and unusual event, in France it simply turned what we already knew into something more evident and striking. In Europe it evoked astonishment, in France it finally managed to convince. The Americans seemed merely to be putting into practice the ideas of our writers; they endowed what we were dreaming of with the solid achievement of reality. It was as if Fénélon had suddenly found himself in Salentum.

This situation – which was so new in history – where the whole political education of a great nation was conducted entirely by men of letters, was perhaps the main contribution to the particular genius of the French Revolution and to the resulting society which we now see.

The writers provided the nation not only with the ideas which brought the Revolution into being but also with its character and mood. Throughout the long years of instruction, the whole nation, in the absence of any other leadership and buried beneath the profound ignorance of practicalities in their lives, read these writers and ended up by adopting the instincts, the turn of mind, the inclinations and even the eccentricities characteristic of writers. The result was that, when the time came at last to act, the nation brought all the habits of literature into politics.

When we study the history of our Revolution, we realize that it was prompted by precisely the same outlook which inspired so many books on the theory of government. They reflected the same attractions for universal theories, comprehensive systems of legislation and an exact symmetry in the laws; the same contempt for existing facts; the same faith in theory; the same taste for the original; the ingenious and the novel in reshaping institutions; the same desire to reconstruct the entire constitution at one and the same time following the rule of logic and according to a single plan instead of seeking to reform it in its separate parts. A frightening spectacle! For what is a good quality in a writer is a failing in a politician and the very themes which have often produced fine books may lead to great upheavals.

Political language itself then adopted something of the language spoken by authors, packed with generalizations, abstract terms, pretentious vocabulary and literary turns of phrase. Fostered by the political passions which used it, this style infiltrated all three classes and moved with unusual rapidity even down to the lowest class. Well before the Revolution, the edicts of Louis XVI spoke often of natural law and the rights of man. I come across peasants who, in their petitions, called their neighbours fellow citizens; the Intendant, a respectable magistrate; the parish priest, the minister of the altars; God, the Supreme Being. All they needed to become quite second-rate writers was to be able to spell.

These new qualities have been so fully incorporated into the former mainspring of the French character that we have often attributed what simply stemmed from this particular education to our natural temperament. I have often heard stated that the liking, or rather the passion, we have displayed over the last sixty years for generalizations, systems and the high-flown language of political matters, took its beginnings from some unidentified characteristic of our race, from what we pompously called *the French spirit*. It was as if this so-called characteristic had managed to appear suddenly about the end of the last century, having been hidden throughout the rest of our history.

What is peculiar is that we have retained the habits derived from books while losing almost completely our former love of literature. I have often been astonished to see in the course of my public life people, who scarcely read any books from the eighteenth century or from any other and who thoroughly spurned authors, nevertheless preserving quite faithfully some of the chief defects which literature had displayed well before they were born.

CHAPTER 2

HOW IRRELIGION COULD HAVE TURNED INTO A UNIVERSAL AND DOMINANT PASSION FOR THE FRENCH OF THE EIGHTEENTH CENTURY AND WHAT KIND OF INFLUENCE IT HAD ON THE CHARACTER OF THE REVOLUTION

Ever since the great revolution of the sixteenth century, when the spirit of inquiry had attempted to distinguish the false from the true among the different Christian traditions, there had always been a continuous stream of more inquiring and bolder minds who had either challenged or rejected all these traditions. The same spirit which, in the time of Luther, had inspired several million Catholics to leave Catholicism at the same moment, also annually drove a few isolated Christians to leave Christianity itself. Non-belief had replaced heresy.

In general terms it can be said that in the eighteenth century Christianity had, over the whole continent of Europe, lost a great deal of its sway but, in most countries, people abandoned rather than violently attacked it; even those who abandoned it left it somewhat regretfully. Religious scepticism was widespread among rulers and intellectuals; it was not yet making its way into the middle and lower classes; it remained the whim of a few minds, not a commonly shared opinion. 'It is a prejudice widely held in Germany,' said Mirabeau in 1787, 'that the Prussian provinces are full of atheists. The truth is that, if a few freethinkers are to be found there, the lower classes are as attached to religion as in the most devout countries and that you can even count a great number of fanatics among them.' He adds that it was very regrettable that Frederick II did not ever sanction the marriage of Catholic priests and above all he refused to allow those who did marry to retain the income from their ecclesiastical livings. 'A measure,' he said, 'which we would be bold enough to believe worthy of that great man.'

Only in France had irreligion become a universal, enthusiastic, intolerant or oppressive passion.

One thing happened in France which had not been seen before. In other ages established religions had been violently attacked but the zeal shown against them had always taken root in the religious inspiration of new faiths. The false and hateful religions of antiquity themselves had many passionate opponents only when Christianity had arrived to supplant them. Until that point they gently died out without fuss, through doubt or indifference – such is the death of religion through old age. In France the Christian religion was attacked with a sort of madness with no attempt even to put another in its stead. The passionate and unrelenting effort to rid people of the faith which had settled there left their souls empty. A host of men fervently devoted themselves to this thankless task. Total disbelief in matters of religion, which is so alien to the natural feelings of man and places his soul in a dangerous state, appeared attractive to the masses. What had hitherto engendered only a kind of sickly torpor this time instigated the fanaticism and spirit of propaganda.

The coming together of several great writers inclined to the denial of Christian truths does not seem enough to account for such an extraordinary event. For why did all these writers turn their mind in this direction rather than any other? Why did we not see a single one of them who thought to choose the opposite thesis? And finally, why did they, more than any of those who came before them, find the ear of the masses so ready to hear them and minds so disposed to believe them? Only reasons very peculiar to the time and country of these writers can explain both this enterprise of theirs and its success. The spirit of Voltaire had been abroad in the world for a long while but he, himself, could hardly have been so dominant as in the eighteenth century and in France.

Let us firstly acknowledge that the Church was no more vulnerable to attack in France than elsewhere; the vices and abuses associated with it were, on the contrary, less prominent than in most Catholic countries. It was infinitely more tolerant than it had been up to that point and than it still was in other nations. Thus it is much less in the state of religion than in the state of society that we must seek the particular causes of this phenomenon.

To understand this we must never lose sight of what I stated in the last chapter, namely that all the spirit of political opposition aroused by the failings of government had taken refuge in literature since it could not thrive in public affairs. Writers had become the authentic leaders of that great gathering which leaned towards the total demolition of the social and political institutions of the country.

When that point has been fully grasped, the question changes direction. It is no longer a matter of knowing the sins of the Church of that time as a religious institution but the obstacles it was raising to the political revolution which was in preparation and the hindrances in particular it was to place before writers who were its chief proponents.

The Church, because of the very principles of its own government, opposed those principles the writers wished to see prevail in the civil government. The Church rested upon tradition whereas the writers expressed a deep contempt for all those institutions which were founded on respect for the past. While the Church recognized an authority above all human reason, they appealed to that same reason; the Church was based upon hierarchy, they preferred the merging of ranks. To reach an understanding with the Church both sides would have been obliged to acknowledge that religious and political societies, being in essence different by nature, could not be governed by similar principles. At that time such an idea was very distant and it seemed that, to attack successful state institutions, it was necessary to destroy those of the Church on which the former were founded and modelled.

Besides, the Church was itself the leading political power and the most loathed even though it was not the most oppressive. For it had come to join the political sphere without being called to do so either by vocation or nature. It often sanctified failings in politics which it condemned in other spheres, surrounded them with a sacred inviolability and seemed to want to immortalize them as it did itself. In the first place by attacking the

Church, the writers were sure to strike a chord with the passions of the masses.

However, beyond these general reasons, the writers had more particular and, in effect, personal reasons to be critical of the Church, which stood precisely for the nearest and most directly hostile arm of government. The other powers made their authority felt only occasionally but the Church, being specially responsible for supervising trends of thought and submitting written work for censorship, irritated them every day. By defending the universal freedoms of the human spirit against the Church, they were fighting their own battle and began by breaking the shackles which bound them most closely.

Furthermore, to them the Church seemed to be, and indeed turned out to be, the most vulnerable and least defended of the whole edifice they were attacking.[60] Its power had grown weaker as the power of earthly rulers grew stronger. Starting as their superior, then their equal, it had descended to the status of client; between rulers and Church a sort of reciprocal arrangement had been established; the rulers lent to the Church their material powers while receiving the latter's moral authority; they secured obedience for the Church's precepts while the latter ordered respect for its decisions – a dangerous negotiation when revolutionary times were looming and always a disadvantage to a power based not on constraint but upon belief.

Although our kings were still called the eldest sons of the Church, they were very slack in fulfilling their obligations towards it. They showed much less enthusiasm in protecting it than they expended in defending their own government. It is true they permitted no one to lay a finger on the Church but they allowed her to be pierced from afar with a thousand arrows.

These half-measures imposed upon the Church's enemies served to augment rather than lessen their power. There are times when the oppression of writers is successful in arresting the free exchange of thought; at other times it precipitates it. It always happened that the kind of policing of the press exercised at that time never failed to increase its power a hundredfold.

Authors were persecuted only enough to make them complain, not enough to make them tremble with fear. They suffered that kind of irritation which fires struggle, not that heavy yoke which crushes them. The attacks which were aimed at them, almost always slow, noisy and ineffectual, appeared to have the objective less of deterring works than to spur them on. Complete freedom of the press would have been less damaging to the Church.

'You believe our intolerance,' wrote Diderot to David Hume in 1768, 'is more favourable to the progress of the mind than your unlimited freedom; d'Holbach, Helvétius, Morellet [sic] and Suard do not share your opinion.' It was, however, the Scot who was right. Since he lived in a free country, he knew from experience: Diderot judged the matter as an author, Hume as a politician.

I stop the first American I meet, either in his own country or elsewhere, and I ask him whether he thinks religion useful to the stability of laws and good order in society. He answers without hesitation that a civilized society, especially a free one, cannot last without religion. Respect for religion, in his eyes, is the greatest guarantee of the state and of the security of individuals. Those least versed in the science of government at least know that. However, there is no country in the world where the boldest political doctrines of the eighteenth-century philosophers were more applied than in America; only their anti-religious doctrines have never managed to surface, even with the advantage of an unlimited freedom of the press.

I would say the same for the English.[61] Our anti-religious philosophy had been preached in England even before most of our philosophers were born. It was Bolingbroke who paved the way for Voltaire. Throughout the eighteenth century non-belief had its famous advocates in England. Skilled writers, deep thinkers espoused its cause but they could never enable it to triumph as in France because all those with something to fear from revolutions hurried to support established beliefs. Even those among the most involved in French society of that period and who did not judge the doctrines of our philosophers as false rejected them as dangerous. Great political parties, as always happens in free nations, found it to their advantage to unite their cause with that of the Church. We saw Bolingbroke allying himself with the bishops. The clergy itself, fired by these examples and sensing that it was never isolated, fought its own cause vigorously. The Church of England, despite the faults of its constitution and every sort of abuse which seethed within it, withstood the shock triumphantly. Writers and orators sprang from its ranks and zealously stood in defence of Christianity. Those theories which were hostile to the Church were debated and challenged, finally to be rejected by the efforts of society itself without any interference from government.

Yet why do we seek out examples elsewhere than in France? What Frenchman would take it into his head to write the books of Diderot or Helvétius? Who would wish to read them? I would almost ask, who knows their titles? The experience which we have gained over the last sixty years in public life, incomplete though it is, has been enough to cause a distaste for this dangerous literature. You can see how respect for religion has gradually recovered its influence in the different classes of the nation, as each estate gained this experience in the harsh school of revolutions. The nobility of old, which was the most irreligious class before 1789, became the most devout after 1793 – the first to be infected was the first to be converted. We saw the middle classes in their turn, when they felt under siege at the moment of their triumph, return to belief. Little by little, respect for religion permeated everywhere where men had anything to lose by popular upheavals; non-belief disappeared or at least hid away as the fear of revolutions came to the surface.

This was not how it was at the end of the Ancien Régime. We had so utterly lost the practice of great human affairs, and were so unaware of the role played by religion in the government of empires, that non-belief first lodged in the minds of those very people who had the most personal and the most urgent interest in maintaining order in the state and obedience in the lower classes. Not only did they welcome non-belief but, in their blindness, they fostered it in the lower orders and turned impiety into a kind of pastime in their indolent lives.

The French Church, so rich up to that point in great orators, went silent when it felt itself deserted in this way by all those who ought to have been associated with it in a common concern. For one instant we might have conjectured that it was ready to condemn its own beliefs as long as it was allowed to preserve its wealth and status.

With the voice of those denying Christianity raised high and the voice of believers still silent, there occurred what we have so often seen happen subsequently in France, not only in matters of religion but in every other concern: men who protected the old beliefs were fearful of being the only people to remain faithful and, dreading isolation more than heresy, joined forces with the mob while not sharing its opinions. What had been so far the feelings of only a single part of the nation thus looked like the opinion of everyone and from then on seemed irresistible even to those who gave it that false appearance.

The universal discredit into which all religious beliefs fell at the end of the last century exercised without any doubt the greatest possible influence upon our Revolution, giving it its distinctive character. Nothing contributed more to painting the terrifying features we saw upon its face.

When I seek to disentangle the different results caused by non-belief in the France of that time, I discover that it was the disorder in people's minds more than the degradation of their hearts or the corruption of their moral habits that brought men of that age to entertain such extraordinary excesses of behaviour.

When religion deserted men's souls, it did not leave them weakened or empty as so often happens; they briefly felt filled with sentiments and ideas which replaced it for a time and at first did not let them collapse completely.

If the French who conducted the Revolution were more sceptical than ourselves in matters of religion, they retained at least one admirable belief which we do not have: they had faith in themselves. They did not doubt the perfectibility and power of man; they readily and ardently pursued his glory and had belief in his goodness. They introduced into their own strength that arrogant confidence which often leads to error but without which a nation is incapable of anything except subservience. They had no doubt that they were called to transform society and to regenerate our human race. These opinions and these passions had become for them a kind of new religion which, while encouraging some of the important effects produced by religion, snatched them from selfish egoism and impelled them towards heroic action and devotion, often making them virtually unaware of all those small comforts which bring us solace.

I have spent much time studying history and I dare to state that I have never come across any revolution in which one could see at the start, in such a great number of men, a more heartfelt patriotism, a more selfless attitude and a more truthful greatness. The nation then displayed the chief failing but also the leading quality of youth, namely inexperience and generosity.

However, non-belief at that time perpetrated an immense public evil.

In most of the great political revolutions which had appeared before in the world, those which attacked the established legal system had respected religious beliefs and in most religious revolutions those who attacked religion had not attempted simultaneously to change the nature and order of all the nation's powers, or to abolish the complete foundation of the former government constitution. Therefore, there had always been one point of stability remaining after the great upheavals of society.

But in the French Revolution, since religious laws had been abolished at the same time as the civil laws had been overturned, the human mind entirely lost its bearings, no longer knowing what to cling to or where to stop. We saw an unknown type of revolutionary who pushed audacity to the point of madness, who was not taken unawares by any novelty, not slowed down by any scruple, never hesitating before the execution of any plan. And we should not believe that these new creatures were the isolated and transient invention of a passing moment, destined to disappear with it. They have since formed a race which has continued and spread to every civilized area of the earth; it has retained the same appearance, the same zeal, the same character. We found it in the world when we were born; it is still with us.

CHAPTER 3

HOW THE FRENCH SOUGHT REFORMS BEFORE FREEDOMS

One fact worth noting is that, of all the ideas and all the opinions which prepared the Revolution, the notion and desire for public freedom proper should have been the last to emerge just as they were the first to disappear.

For a long time the old structure of government had begun to shake and was already tottering while the question of freedom still did not feature. Voltaire hardly gave it a thought; his three-year stay in England had shown freedom to him without persuading him to like it. The sceptical philosophy freely preached in England delighted him but her political laws affected him little; he noted their failings more than their virtues. In his letters on the English – one of his masterpieces – he gives Parliament only the slightest mention. In reality, above all he envies the English their literary freedom but cares hardly a jot for their political freedom, as if the former could ever exist for long without the latter.

Around the middle of the century, there appeared a certain number of writers who dealt particularly with questions of public administration and who were given the common name of *Economists* or *Physiocrats* because of several similar principles they expressed. The Economists have made less of a splash in history than the philosophers; they perhaps contributed less than the philosophers to the coming of the Revolution. Nevertheless, I believe that above all we can best study its true character in their writings. The philosophers scarcely ever departed from very general and abstract ideas of government, whereas the Economists, without losing a grasp of theory, delved more closely into the facts. The former spoke of what could be imagined, the latter sometimes marked out what had to be done. All the institutions which the Revolution was to wipe out, never to return, were the particular object of their attacks; not one found favour in their eyes. On the other hand, all those institutions which could pass as the Revolution's own achievement had been heralded by them in advance and preached with enthusiasm. Hardly a single one could be quoted whose seed had not been sown in some of their writings. We find in the Economists all the most substantial of the Revolution's achievements.

In addition, we can already recognize in their books that revolutionary and democratic outlook which we know so well. Not only did they loathe certain privileges, diversity itself was odious. They worshipped equality even if it meant servitude. Whatever impeded them in promoting their plans was fit only for abolition. Contracts carried little respect; they had no regard for private rights, or rather there were for them no private rights strictly speaking but only public utility. Yet, in general, these were men of kindly and peaceful habits, men of substance, honourable magistrates, clever administrators; but the unique spirit in their work inspired them forward.

The past was, for the Economists, an object of boundless contempt. 'The nation has for centuries been governed by wrong principles; everything has been done at random,' said Letronne. With this idea as a starting point, they began their work. There was not a single institution, however old, however firm its foundations appeared in our history, whose abolition they did not demand, even if it hindered and damaged the symmetry of their plans. One of them suggested the removal of all former land boundaries and the changing of the names of the provinces forty years before the National Assembly actually did so.

They had already thought of all the social and administrative reforms achieved by the Revolution before the idea of free institutions had begun to surface in their minds. It is true that they were very favourably disposed to the free exchange of goods and to *laisser faire* or *laisser-passer* in trade and industry but, as far as political freedoms proper, they gave no thought to them and at first dismissed them whenever by chance they came into their minds. Most of them started out as firmly hostile to deliberative assemblies, to local and secondary powers and, generally speaking, to all those counterweights which have been established at different times in all free nations to check central power. 'The system of checks and balances,' said Quesnay, 'in government is a fatal idea.' 'Speculations which carry the idea of a system of checks and balances are the stuff of whimsy,' said a friend of Quesnay.

The only safeguard they invented against the abuse of power was public education for, as again Quesnay said, 'Tyranny is impossible if the nation is educated.' 'Struck down by the evils caused by the abuses of authority,' said one of his followers, 'men have invented a thousand completely useless measures while neglecting the only truly effective one, namely the universal and consistent education of the public in the essentials of the law and natural order.' With the help of this piffling literary rubbish, they intended to replace all political guarantees.

Letronne, who was so bitter in his condemnation of the government's neglect of the countryside, who describes it without roads, industry or education, never imagined that its affairs could indeed be conducted better in the hands of the inhabitants themselves.

Turgot, whose nobility of soul and exceptional qualities of character were to set him apart from all the others, did not have the taste for political freedoms any more than they did, or at least the taste for them came to him only late on when it was prompted by public opinion. As with most of the Economists, he felt that the chief political guarantee was some public education given by the state according to certain practices and with a certain ethos. The trust he displays in this sort of intellectual treatment or, as is said by one of his contemporaries, in the *mechanism of an education governed by sound principles*, was boundless. 'I am bold enough to answer, Sire,' he said in a report in which he suggests a plan of this kind to the king, 'that in ten years time your nation will no longer be recognizable and that, in education, in good manners, in devotion to your service and that of the country, it will be infinitely superior to all the other nations. Children now ten years old will then be men ready for state duties, attached to their country, obedient to authority not out of fear but reason, helpful towards their fellow citizens and accustomed to acknowledge and respect justice.'

It had been so long since political freedom had been destroyed that people had almost totally forgotten what its conditions and effects had been. Furthermore, the deformed remnants which were still in existence and the institutions built apparently to replace freedom made it suspect and often aroused prejudices against it. Most existing state assemblies still retained, along with outdated forms, the ethos of the Middle Ages and held the progress of society back rather than helping it forward. The *parlements*, alone responsible for taking the place of political bodies, were unable to halt the damage being caused by the government and often halted the good it intended.

The idea of completing the Revolution they were imagining with the help of this antiquated machinery appeared impracticable to the Economists; the thought of entrusting the execution of their plans to the nation, now its own master, pleased them very little. For how could they persuade a whole nation to adopt and follow a system of reform so huge and so strictly cohesive in its separate elements? They seemed to think it simpler and more convenient to make use of the royal administration itself to achieve their plans.

This new power had not issued from the institutions of the Middle Ages; it did not even bear their imprint; amid its errors, the Economists distinguished certain positive trends. Like them, it had a natural liking for equality of social conditions and uniformity of law. Just like themselves, it profoundly hated all the former powers which had been born of feudalism or which tended towards aristocracy. You would seek in vain in the rest of Europe a government as well set up, as great and as strong. The occurrence of such a government among us seemed to them a strangely fortunate situation. They would have called it providential had it been fashionable at that time, as it is today, to introduce Providence at every turn. 'The situation in France,' said Letronne, 'is infinitely better than in England, for here we can achieve reforms which change the state of the country in a flash whereas with the English such reforms can always be blocked by the party system.'

Therefore, it was not a question of destroying this absolute power but of converting it. 'The state must govern according to the rules of essential order,' said Mercier de la Rivière, 'and when it acts in that way, it must be omnipotent.' Another said, 'Once the state fully realizes its obligations, then it can be left free.' From Quesnay to Abbé Bodeau you will find everyone of the same temper.

They relied not only on the royal administration to bring about reforms in the society of their time but they borrowed from it in part the concept of the future government which they wished to establish. It was by looking at the one that they pictured the other.

According to the Economists, the state had not only to command the nation but to shape it in a certain way. It was up to the state to fashion citizens' minds according to a certain model they had predetermined; its duty was to fill their minds with certain ideas and their hearts with certain feelings considered necessary. In real terms, no boundaries were set to the state's rights nor to what it could enact; not merely did it reform men, it totally changed them. It would perhaps be up to the state alone to make different people out of them! 'The state makes men into whatever it wishes them to be,' said Bodeau. That saying sums up all the Economists' theories.

This unbounded social power conceived by the Economists was not only greater than any they could observe around them, it was also different in origin and character. It did not flow directly from God; it did not have ties to tradition; it was impersonal; no longer called the king but the state, no longer the inheritance of one family but the result and representative of all. The rights of each citizen had to yield to the will of all.

This particular form of tyranny, called democratic despotism, entirely unknown in the Middle Ages, was already familiar to the Economists – no social hierarchy, no distinct classes, or any fixed ranks. The nation would be composed of almost identical and totally equal individuals which turned this shapeless mass into the only legitimate sovereign power. It was, however, carefully deprived of all the capacities to enable it to control and even to supervise its own government itself. Above it was a single legal representative responsible for everything in its own name without the need for consultation. To control this authority there was public reason without any powers; to halt it, revolutions not laws were needed. Legally this was a subordinate agent; in actual fact it was a despot.

Since they were unable to find near at hand anything conforming to this ideal, they extended their search to the heart of Asia. It is no exaggeration to say that all of them without exception sang the boundless praises of China somewhere in their writings. At least that is what you can be sure to come across in reading the books they wrote; since China was still unknown, every kind of nonsense was conveyed to us about that country. That imbecilic and barbarous government, which a handful of Europeans manipulated at will, seemed to them the most complete model that all the nations of the world might copy. China became for them what later on England, and in the end America, would become for all Frenchmen. They felt moved and apparently entranced at the sight of a country where the absolute sovereign, free from prejudices, went ploughing once a year with his own hands to honour the practical arts, where all public offices were won through literary competitions, where philosophy was the only religion and men of letters the only aristocrats.

It is thought that the destructive theories described by the present-day name of *socialism* are of recent origin – that is a mistake. Those theories belong to the time of the first Economists. While the latter were using the all-powerful government of their dreams to change the structures of society, the socialists, in their imagination, were laying hold of the same power to destroy its foundations.

Read *The Code of Nature* by Morelly; there, alongside all the Economists' doctrines of the omnipotence of the state and its unlimited powers, you will find several political theories which have most terrified the France of recent times and which we reckon to have seen come into being – namely, shared ownership of land, the right to work, total equality, uniformity in all things, systematic control over individual movements, a regulated tyranny and the complete submerging of citizens' personalities in the body of society.

The first article of Morelly's code states: 'Nothing in society shall belong individually or as property to anyone. Property ownership is detestable and anyone attempting to re-establish it will be imprisoned for life as a raving lunatic and enemy of the human race.' Article number two states: 'Each citizen will be supported, maintained and employed at public expense.' 'Everything produced will be stored in public warehouses to be distributed to all citizens and to serve their needs of life. Towns will be built on identical lines; all buildings for personal use will be similar. At five, all children will be removed from their family and brought up communally at the state's expense in a uniform manner.' This book appears to have been written yesterday; it is one hundred years old. It was published in 1755 at the same time as Quesnay was founding his school. That is how true it is that centralization and socialism were the products of the same soil; relative to each other, these two are what the cultivated fruit is to the original wild stock.

Of all the men of their age, the Economists would appear the least out of their element in our time; their passion for equality was so entrenched and their taste for freedom so vague that they have a false air of being our contemporaries. When I read the speeches and writings of the men who led the Revolution, I feel immediately transported to a location and into a society I fail to recognize. But when I leaf through the books by the Economists, I seem to have lived with those men and I have just been debating with them.

About 1750, the nation as a whole would not have shown itself any more demanding in the matter of political liberty than the Economists themselves; it had lost the taste for freedom and even the concept because they had mislaid the thing itself. The nation longed for reforms more than rights and, had it found on the throne at that time a ruler of the stature and outlook of Frederick the Great, I am quite certain that he would have achieved several of the great changes made by the Revolution not only without losing his throne but also by greatly increasing his power. We are assured that M. de Machault, one of Louis XV's most capable ministers, glimpsed this idea and indicated as much to his master. But such projects are not the province of advice; no one is equipped to accomplish such plans unless they are capable of conceiving them.

Twenty years later the position was no longer the same; the image of political liberty had imprinted itself on Frenchmen's minds and was daily becoming increasingly attractive. Many signs allowed this to become evident. The provinces began anew to realize their desire for self-administration. The idea that the whole nation had the right to participate in government entered and took hold of people's minds. The memory of the former States-General was revived. The nation which loathed its own history recalled only that part of it with pleasure. This new current carried along the Economists themselves and forced them to add a few free institutions to their unitary system.

When in 1771 the Parlements were abolished, the same public, which had had to suffer because of their privileges, was profoundly moved at the sight of their downfall. With their collapse, the final barrier which might have restrained royal absolutism seemed to have gone with them.

This popular opposition astonished and annoyed Voltaire. He wrote to his friends, 'Almost the whole kingdom is bubbling in dismay; the ferment is as strong in the provinces as in Paris itself. The edict nevertheless seems to me full of useful reforms. Getting rid of the sale of offices, making justice free, taking away the need for litigants to come to Paris from the far ends of the kingdom simply to ruin themselves, the making of the king responsible for paying the expenses of the manorial courts – are these not important services to render to the nation? Besides, have these *parlements* not often been the sources of persecution and barbarity? In truth, I wonder at the ignoramuses taking the part of these insolent and undisciplined middle classes. As for me, I believe the king to be right and, since we must serve, I think it better to do so under a well-bred lion than two hundred rats of my own kind.' And he adds as a kind of excuse, 'You can imagine that I am obliged to be infinitely grateful for the favour shown by the king to all noble landowners in paying all their legal expenses.'

Having been away from Paris for a long time, Voltaire believed that public opinion had still stayed where he had left it. This was not at all the case. The French did not simply look for their affairs to be better directed; they were beginning to wish to manage their own affairs and it was evident that the great Revolution for which everything was preparing would take place, not only with the agreement of the people but also at their hands.

I think that from that moment this radical revolution, which was to join together in one and the same destruction of both what was worst and what was best in the Ancien Régime, was unavoidable. A nation so poorly prepared to act independently could not attempt total reform without total destruction. An absolute monarch would have been a less dangerous innovator. For myself, I observe that this same revolution, while it destroyed so many institutions, ideas and habits opposed to liberty, on the other hand it abolished so many others that freedom could hardly do without. Then I am inclined to believe that, had it been achieved by a despot, it might perhaps have left us less incompetent to become one day a free nation than one effected in the name of the sovereignty of the people and by their own hand.

We must never lose sight of the above if we wish to understand the history of our Revolution.

When the love of the French for political freedom awakened, they had already conceived a number of ideas in relation to government which not only failed to agree easily with the existence of free institutions but were almost hostile to them.

They had accepted as an ideal society a nation without an aristocracy other than that of public officials and one single, omnipotent administration which directed state business and protected individual citizens. While wishing to be free they had no intention of departing at all from this original idea; they simply attempted to reconcile it with the concept of liberty.

They undertook, therefore, to mould together a centralized administration without bounds and a dominant legislative body – administration by bureaucrats and government by voters. The nation as a body had all the rights of sovereignty; each citizen as an individual was gripped by the most restricted dependence. From the former was required the experience and virtues of a free people, from the latter the qualities of a good servant.

It is this ambition to introduce political liberty into institutions and ideas which were alien or hostile to it, but for which we had already caught the habit or conceived an advance inclination, that has produced for the last sixty years so many useless attempts at free government followed by deathly revolutions. Many Frenchmen finally reached the point when, exhausted from so much effort, discouraged by such heavy and sterile work, abandoning their second aim to return to their first, they were reduced to thinking that to live equal under one master still held, after all, a certain charm. Thus we find ourselves today much closer to the Economists of 1750 than to our forefathers in 1789.

I have often wondered where this passion for political liberty comes from – a passion which, throughout all ages, has inspired men to the greatest accomplishments of human kind – and what feelings feed and foster its roots.

I see quite clearly that, whenever nations are poorly governed, they are very ready to entertain the desire for governing themselves. But this kind of love for independence, which has its roots only in certain particular and passing evils brought on by despotism, never lasts long; it disappears along with the accidental circumstances which caused it. They seemed to love freedom; it turns out they simply hated the master. When nations are ready for freedom, what they hate is the evil of dependency itself.

Nor do I believe that the true love of liberty was ever born of the simple vision of material benefits it makes available, for this vision is often hidden from view. It is indeed true that, in the long term, freedom always brings with it, to those who are skilled enough to keep hold of it, personal comfort, wellbeing and often great wealth. But there are times when freedom briefly disturbs the enjoyment of such blessings; there are others when despotism alone can guarantee a fleeting exploitation of them. Men who value only those material advantages from freedom have never kept it long. What has tied the hearts of certain men to freedom throughout all history has been its own attractions, its intrinsic charm quite separate from its material advantages. It is the pleasure to be able to speak, act and breathe without restriction under the rule of God alone and the law. Whoever seeks anything from freedom but freedom itself is doomed to slavery.

Certain nations pursue freedom obstinately amid all kinds of danger and deprivation. It is not for the material comforts it brings them that they appreciate it; they look upon it as such a valuable and vital blessing that nothing else can console them for its loss and when they experience it they are consoled for all other losses. Other nations grow tired of freedom amid their prosperity, which they allow to be wrenched from their hands without a fight, for fear of compromising, by making an effort, the very wellbeing they owe to it. What is missing to keep such nations free? What? The very desire to be so. Do not ask me to analyse this lofty desire; it has to be experienced. It enters of itself into those great hearts which God has prepared to receive it. It fills and impassions them. We have to abandon any attempt to enlighten those second-rate souls who have never felt it.

CHAPTER 4

THAT LOUIS XVI'S REIGN WAS THE MOST PROSPEROUS PERIOD OF THE OLD MONARCHY AND HOW THAT VERY PROSPERITY HASTENED THE REVOLUTION

It cannot be doubted that the exhaustion of the kingdom under Louis XIV had begun at the very moment when that ruler was still triumphant throughout Europe. The first signs are to be found in the most glorious years of the reign. France was ruined well before it had finished defeating others. Everyone has read the frightening attempt in government statistics which Vauban has left us. The Intendants, in reports addressed to the Duke of Burgundy at the end of the seventeenth century and even before that unfortunate War of the Spanish Succession had begun, all alluded to the creeping decadence of the nation and did not refer to it as a recent event. One said, 'The population has been greatly diminishing in this district for some number of years.' Another said, 'This town, formerly wealthy and flourishing, is today without its industry.' One man writes, 'There were workshops in the province but they are abandoned now.' Another wrote, 'The inhabitants once obtained much more from the soil than they do now; agriculture was greatly more productive twenty years ago.' 'Population and production have declined by a fifth over about thirty years,' wrote the Intendant from Orléans during that same period. The reading of these reports should be recommended to individuals who prize absolute government and to rulers who love warfare.

Since these calamities had their source mainly in the failings of the constitution, Louis XIV's death and even peace itself did not revive public prosperity. It is a commonly held opinion among all those who wrote upon government and social economy in the first half of the eighteenth century that the provinces did not recover; many even thought they went on declining. As they said, Paris alone grew richer and more extensive. Intendants, former ministers and businessmen were in agreement on this point with men of letters.

I personally confess that I do not believe in this continuous falling away of France during the first half of the eighteenth century but such a universal opinion, shared by such well-informed people, at least proves that no obvious progress was then being made. All the administrative documents belonging to this period in our history and which have come to my notice describe in fact a sort of lethargy in society. The government did nothing much beyond continuing the round of old routines without creating anything new. Towns made almost no effort to make the life of their inhabitants more comfortable or healthy. Even individuals did not devote themselves to any enterprise of note.

About thirty or forty years before the outbreak of the Revolution, the scene began to change. It may be possible to observe, then, in all sections of society a kind of internal tremor not previously noticed. Only a close examination can begin to make it out, but gradually it became more characteristic and distinct. Every year this shift spread and accelerated. The nation finally shuddered throughout its boundaries and seemed to be reborn. Be careful! It was not its former spirit which was reviving it but a new life was stirring this great body; it brought it back from the dead for a short time before dissolving it.

Each citizen was worried and disturbed about his situation which he made an effort to alter; the search for something better was universal. It was, however, a restless and angry search which made men curse the past and imagine a state of things completely different from the position they saw before them.

Soon this wind of change affected the very heart of the government itself, transforming it from within without altering its external features; the laws were not changed but were exercised differently.

I have said elsewhere that the Controller-General and the Intendant of 1740 were quite unlike the Controller-General and Intendant of 1780. Administrative correspondence reveals this to be true in detail. The Intendant of 1780 had the same powers, agents and the same arbitrary authority as his predecessor but not the same aims. The former was scarcely concerned with anything but maintaining the obedience of his province, levying the militia and above all collecting the *taille*. The latter had many other tasks: his head was full of a thousand plans leading to the increase in public wealth. The roads, canals, workshops and trade were the chief objects of his consideration. Above all, agriculture held his attention. Sully became the fashion then among administrators.

It was at that time that the agricultural associations which I have already mentioned began to be formed along with the creation of competitions and the distribution of bonuses. The Controller-General sent circulars which were more like treatises on agricultural skills than business letters.

It is principally in the collection of all the taxes that we can best see the transformation visible in the minds of government officials. The legislation was still as unequal, as arbitrary and as harsh as in the past but all its defects were softened by the way they were enacted.

'When I began to study the fiscal laws,' said M. Mollien in his Memoirs, 'I was dismayed by what I found – fines, imprisonments, corporal punishments, all placed at the disposal of special tribunals to deal with simple omissions; farm stewards who held almost all estates and owners at the discretion of their oaths, etc. Fortunately I did not merely read the code by itself and I soon had reason to recognize that the same difference existed between the letter and administration of the law as between the practices of the old and the new financiers. The lawyers were always predisposed to mitigate offences and moderate punishments.'

'To how many abuses and annoyances can the collection of taxes give rise!' said the provincial assembly of Lower Normandy in 1787; 'however, we must pay heed to the leniency and consideration that have been practised for some years past.'

Examination of the documents gives ample justification to this assertion. Respect for men's life and liberty is often obvious. Above all, we can perceive a genuine preoccupation with the hardships of the poor which, before that time, we would have looked for in vain. The violent treatment by the treasury became rarer, remissions of tax more frequent and help more common. The king increased all the funds intended to set up charity workshops in rural areas or to help the destitute. Often he established new funds. I find that more than 80,000 livres were distributed by the state in this way in the district of Upper Guyenne alone in 1779; 40,000 in the Tours district in 1784; 48,000 in Normandy in 1787. Louis XVI did not wish to leave to his ministers alone this aspect of the government; occasionally he took charge of it himself. In 1776 when a Council decree set the compensation due to peasant farmers whose fields were being devastated by the king's game in the neighbourhood of the royal hunting seats and indicated simple and certain ways of issuing payment to them, the king himself drew up the legal preamble. Turgot tells us that this kindly and unfortunate prince gave him these documents written by his own hand with the words, 'You can see that I, too, do my share of the work.' If we described the Ancien Régime such as it was in the final years of its life, we would paint a very flattering but quite inaccurate picture.

As these changes took place in the minds of the governed and those in government, public prosperity was advancing at an unprecedented speed. Every sign revealed it: increase of population; an even quicker growth in wealth. The American war did not slow down this upward trend. The state was burdened with debt while individuals went on getting richer, becoming more hard working, more enterprising and inventive.

'Since 1774,' said an official of the time, 'the various branches of industry, as they have developed, have increased the bulk of consumer taxes.' In fact when, in the different periods of Louis XVI's reign, we compare the contracts enacted between the state and the finance companies responsible for the collecting of taxes, we see that the sum from farm rents never stopped rising at each renewal date with a growing rapidity. The lease of 1786 brought in 14 million more than that of 1780. 'We can guarantee that the total of all the consumer taxes will increase annually by two million,' said Necker in the 1781 balance sheet.

Arthur Young assures us that in 1788 Bordeaux conducted more trade than Liverpool and, he adds, 'In recent times the progress of maritime trade has been more rapid in France than in England itself; trade there has doubled over the last twenty years.'

If we wish to look closely at the difference between the two eras, we will be convinced that in none of the periods following the Revolution did public prosperity thrive more rapidly than during the preceding twenty years. Only the thirty-seven years of constitutional monarchy, which were for us times of peace and rapid progress, can be compared in this respect with the reign of Louis XVI.[62]

The sight of this prosperity, already so great and so flourishing, gives good grounds for astonishment if we think of all the defects still evident inside government and of all the obstacles still encountered by industry. It may even be that many politicians deny this fact because they cannot account for it, assuming, like Molière's doctor, that a patient cannot get better in the face of the rules. In fact, how can we believe that France could prosper and grow wealthy with inequality of taxation, differences of local practices, internal customs barriers, feudal rights, union guilds and sales of office, etc.? In spite of all that, France was, nevertheless, beginning to prosper and improve everywhere because, alongside all this badly built and badly geared machinery which appeared likely to slow down the social engine more than drive it forward, there were concealed two very strong and simple springs which were already enough to hold the entire mechanism together and to enable this whole to advance towards its aim of public prosperity: a still very powerful but no longer despotic government which maintained order everywhere; a nation whose upper classes were already the most enlightened and free on the continent of Europe and a nation in whose midst every individual was capable of growing wealthy in his own way and of keeping that fortune once acquired.

The king continued to speak in his role of master but, in reality, he was himself obedient to public opinion which daily encouraged or drove him on and which he endlessly consulted, feared and flattered. He was absolute in the letter of the law but constrained in the practice. In 1784, Necker reported in a public document what was in effect an undisputed fact: 'Most foreigners find it hard to have any idea how much authority is wielded in France by public opinion; they have difficulty in understanding the nature of this unseen power which even controls the royal palace. Yet that is how things are.'

Nothing is more superficial than to ascribe the greatness and power of a nation simply to the machinery of its laws for, in this matter, it is less the perfect workings of the instrument than the strength of the engines which produces the result. Just look at England. Even today its administrative laws appear more complicated, more diverse and more disorganized than ours.[63] Yet is there a single country in Europe where public wealth is greater, private property more widespread, secure or varied, society more stable and prosperous? All that stems not from moral integrity of particular laws but from the vitality which drives the whole of English legislation. In no way do the flaws in certain political organs hinder progress because their inner spirit remains powerful.

As the prosperity in France developed as I have just described, men's minds appeared meanwhile more anxious and more unsettled. Public disquiet sharpened; the loathing of all ancient institutions was on the increase. The nation was obviously marching towards a revolution.

Furthermore, the areas of France which were to be the leading homes of this revolution were precisely those where progress was most clearly observed. Studying what remains of the archives of the Île-de-France region, we can easily judge that it was in the regions bordering on Paris that the Ancien Régime was the soonest to undergo a profound reform. There the freedom and wealth of the peasant farmers were already more fully guaranteed than in any other of the state-run provinces. Well before 1789 the system of forced labour had disappeared. The collecting of the *taille* had become more organized, less harsh and fairer than in the rest of France. If one wishes to understand the power of the Intendant to increase either the wellbeing or the misery of a whole province at that time, the 1772 regulations to relax this tax should be read. As is seen in these regulations, this tax already assumed a quite different aspect. Government commissioners went to each parish yearly; the community met in their presence; the assessment of assets was established in public and the capacity of each citizen to pay was acknowledged after hearing both parties; the *taille* was finally calculated with the agreement of all those liable to pay it. No more arbitrary decisions by the syndics; no more pointless violence[64] – no doubt the *taille* still retained its inherent failings whatever the system of collection may have been. It weighed upon one class of taxpayers alone and hit industry as well as property. However, in everything else the tax in the Île-de-France was profoundly different from the tax carrying the same name in the neighbouring districts.

On the other hand, nowhere had the Ancien Régime been better preserved than along the Loire near its estuary, in the Poitou marshes and the Brittany moors. It was there precisely that the fire of civil war was ignited and fed and there that resistance to the Revolution was the most violent and long lasting. Consequently, it could be said that the French found their situation all the more intolerable the better it became.

Such a view is surprising but history is packed with such sights.

Going from bad to worse does not always mean a slide into revolution. More often than not, it occurs when a nation which has endured without complaint – almost without feeling them – the most burdensome laws rejects them with violence the moment the weight of them lightens. The regime destroyed by a revolution is almost always better than the one that immediately preceded it and experience teaches us that the most hazardous moment for a bad government is normally when it is beginning to reform. Only a great genius can save a ruler who is setting out to relieve his subjects' suffering after a long period of oppression. The evils, patiently endured as inevitable, seem unbearable as soon as the idea of escaping them is conceived. Then the removal of an abuse seems to cast a sharper light on those still left and makes people more painfully aware of them; the burden has become lighter, it is true, but the sensitivity more acute.[65] Feudalism at the height of its power had not inspired the French with as much loathing as when it was about to disappear. The slightest arbitrary decisions from Louis XVI seemed more difficult to tolerate than the whole of Louis XIV's despotic reign. Beaumarchais's short spell in prison stirred people in Paris more than the Dragonnades.

In 1780, no one was claiming any more that France was in decline; on the contrary it was said that there were no longer any barriers to its advancement. At that time the theory of continuous and indefinite improvement of man took root. Twenty years before, the future held no hope; now nothing was to be feared from it. Men's imaginations, in taking advance possession of this approaching and unheard-of happiness, made them unaware of the blessings they already enjoyed and hurtled them towards new things.

Apart from these general reasons there are other more specific and no less powerful ones for this state of affairs. Although government finances had improved like everything else, they retained the weaknesses which are characteristic of absolute power itself. Since they were secret and carried no safeguards, a few of the worst practices were still in force, as they had been under Louis XIV and Louis XV. The very effort by the government to extend public prosperity, the help and incentives which it distributed, the public works it instigated increased daily the outlay of money without increasing the revenues in the same proportion. Every day the king was thrown into still greater embarrassments than those of his predecessors. Like them he persistently left his creditors waiting; like them he borrowed with both hands, without transparency or competition, and his creditors were never certain of seeing any interest on their investments. Their capital itself was ever at the mercy of the monarch's good faith alone.

One witness we can trust, since he had seen with his own eyes and was better placed than anyone else to observe accurately, said in this connection: 'The French of that period encountered only risk in their contacts with their own government. Whenever they invested their capital in government loans, they could never count on a fixed date for interest payment; whenever they built ships, repaired roads, kitted out soldiers, they remained without guarantees for their advances, without a date for repayment, and were reduced to calculating the hazards of a contract with ministers as they would for a high risk loan.' And he added with good sense, 'At this time when industry was taking off and had developed in an increasing number of men the love of ownership along with the taste and need for wealth, those who had entrusted a part of their capital to the state tolerated more frustratingly the violation of the laws of contracts by the man who, of all debtors, should respect them the most.'

In fact, the abuses of the French administration criticized here were not new. What was new was the impression they made. The failings of the financial system had been even more glaring in earlier times but since that time changes had come about in government and society which made men infinitely more sensitive to them than previously.

For the last twenty years when the government had become
more energetic and had devoted efforts to every kind of project
which it would not have considered before, it had finally
become the leading consumer of industrial goods and the
leading contractor for public works in the kingdom. The
number of those who had financial arrangements with the state,
who were involved in state loans and who lived off its salaries
and speculated in its markets, had enormously increased. Never
had the prosperity of state and individuals been more inter-
woven. The poor management of finances, which had long been
a public evil, now became, for a host of families, a private
disaster. In 1789, the state thus owed almost 600 million to its
creditors, almost all of whom were themselves debtors. The
latter, in their complaints against the government, as a financial
expert of the time recounted, made common cause with all
those citizens also suffering from the state's poor payment
record. And take note that, as the number of discontented
people grew, the frustration also grew among them, for the
desire to speculate, the passion to grow rich, the taste for
personal comfort, expanding and increasing with the progress
of business, made such evils appear unbearable to the very men
who, thirty years before, would perhaps have suffered them
without complaint.

The result of all this was that the private investors, the
traders, the manufacturers and other businessmen or financiers
who, usually from that class of men most opposed to political
novelties and most sympathetic to the government of the day
whatever its complexion and the most obedient to laws (even
those they despise or detest), this time showed great impatience
and the greatest decisiveness in matters of reform. They called
loudly above all for a complete revolution throughout the whole
system of finances without thinking that a fundamental shift in
this area of government would lead to a collapse in all the
others.

How could they have avoided a catastrophe? On the one
hand, a nation, at whose heart lay the desire to make a fortune,
kept expanding every day; on the other a government, which
constantly aroused and disturbed this new passion, firing the

nation and disappointing it, was thus pushing from both sides towards its own ruin.

HOW THEY MANAGED TO STIR THE COMMON PEOPLE TO REVOLT WHILE INTENDING TO RELIEVE THEIR SITUATION

Since the common people had never for one moment, over the previous one hundred and forty years, made an appearance on the public stage, they had completely given up the belief that they could ever feature there; since they appeared insensitive, they were judged deaf. The result was that, when an interest began to be shown in their lot, we began to talk about them in their presence as if they were not there. The impression was that only the upper class should hear what was being said and that the only danger to fear was not being able to convey our message to them.

Those people, who had most to fear the anger of the lower classes, would converse out loud in their presence about the cruel injustices of which they had always been victims. They showed each other the monstrous failings of the institutions which were the most oppressive to the people; they exploited their rhetorical skills to paint their sufferings and their badly paid work; their attempts at bringing relief to the people merely filled them with rage. I do not mean to speak of writers but of the government, its principal officials and of the privileged themselves.

When the king, thirteen years before the Revolution, attempted to abolish the forced labour law, he said in his preamble: 'With the exception of the small number of Independent Provinces almost all the kingdom's roads have been constructed free of charge by the poorest group of our subjects. The entire burden has thus fallen upon those who have only their strength of arm and have only a very secondary interest in highways. The real involvement lies with the landowners, almost all of whom are privileged and whose property gains in value from the creation of roads. By forcing the poor man to maintain them and to give his time and effort without payment of a wage, we are depriving him of the only resource he has against suffering and hunger in order to be made to work for the profit of the wealthy.'

When, during the same period, attempts were made to eliminate the obstacles posed by the trade guilds system upon the workers, a proclamation was issued in the name of the king 'that the right to work is the most sacred of all possessions; that any law attacking that right violates natural law and should be considered null and void; that the existing trade guilds are in addition strange and tyrannical institutions, products of selfishness, greed and violence.' Such words were dangerous; what was even more so was to make an early pronouncement. A few months later the guilds and forced labour were re-established.

It is said that Turgot put such words into the mouth of the king. Most of his successors did not have the king speak differently. When in 1780 the king announced to his subjects that increases to the *taille* would from then on be subject to a public registration, he was careful to add as a gloss: 'Those paying the *taille*, already harassed by the annoying ways of collecting this tax, have been additionally exposed up until now to unexpected increases in such a manner that the payments of the poorest subjects in the population increased in a much greater proportion than those of all the others.' When the king, not yet daring to make all tax burdens equal, set out at least to establish an equal way of collecting those dues which were already levied on all, he said: 'His Majesty hopes that the wealthy will not feel wronged when, placed on an equal footing, they will be paying only that amount of tax which long since they ought to have been sharing more equally.'

But, above all, it was in times of scarcity that the aim appears to have been to inflame the passions of the lower classes much more than meeting their needs. One Intendant, attempting to arouse the charity of the wealthy, speaks at that time 'of the injustice and callousness of those landowners who owe to the poor man's efforts all that they own and who leave him to starve to death at the very moment he has reached the point of exhaustion from increasing the value of their property'. The king, on his side, said on a similar occasion: 'His Majesty wishes to defend the people against those tricky practices which make them vulnerable to shortages in the basic necessities of life by forcing them to offer their labour at a level of wage set at the whim of the wealthy. The king will not allow one group of his subjects to be sacrificed to the greed of another.'

Right to the end of monarchy the struggle between the different administrative powers gave rise to all kinds of events of this sort: the two opposing parties readily accused each other of causing the sufferings of the people. A good example of this can be seen in the notable quarrel which arose in 1772 between the Toulouse Parlement and the king about the transportation of grain. 'The government, through its badly conceived measures, is risking the starvation of the poor,' said that Parlement, to which the king retorts, 'The ambition of the Parlement and the greed of the wealthy are causing public distress.' Thus there was an effort on both sides to insert into people's minds the idea that blame for one's problems must always lie with one's superiors.

These things are not found in secret correspondence but in public documents which central government and *parlements* took care to publish themselves in their thousands. Incidentally, one day the king addressed to his predecessors and to himself some very harsh truths: 'The state treasury has been crippled by the extravagance of several reigns. Many of our inalienable domains have been given away cheaply.' 'The industrial guilds,' he was driven to say at another time with more justification than prudence, 'are above all the result of the king's fiscal greed.' 'If useless expenditure has often been incurred and if the *taille* has increased beyond moderation,' he noted further on, 'that was because finance ministers find increasing the *taille*, owing to its secrecy, their easiest resource; they resorted to that device when several others would have been less burdensome to our citizens.'[66]

All the above was aimed at the educated classes of the nation in order to convince them of the value of certain measures which special-interest groups were attacking. As for the lower classes, it was well understood that they were listening without understanding.

We have to recognize that a great reservoir of contempt lay within this benevolence towards these wretched people whose sufferings they sincerely wished to relieve. This recalls somewhat the feeling shown by Madame Duchâtelet who, according to Voltaire's secretary, found no difficulty in undressing before her servants since she could not be convinced that her lackeys were real men.

And let it not be thought that Louis XVI or his ministers were the only ones to entertain the dangerous language I have just reproduced; the privileged classes who were the closest object of the people's anger couched their remarks to the people in no different a manner. We have to acknowledge that the French upper classes in society began to concern themselves with the fate of the poor before the latter became a threat to them. They took an interest in the poor at a time when they did not yet think that their own ruin could emerge from these peoples' sufferings. That becomes clear above all in the ten years preceding '89. During that time the peasants were pitied and discussed endlessly; methods for relieving them were sought; a light was shone upon the chief abuses which caused them suffering and fiscal laws bringing them particular hardship were condemned. However, the upper classes, as is usual, expressed this newly found sympathy with as little forethought as they had shown in their previous long-felt callousness.

Read the minutes of the provincial assemblies which met in some parts of France in 1779 and later on throughout the kingdom. Study the other public documents left by them. You will be moved by the generous opinions you come across in them and taken aback by the unusual rashness of the language expressed.

'We have too often seen,' said the provincial assembly of Lower Normandy in 1787, 'the money allocated by the king to

roads used for the affluence of the rich while being of no use to
the common people. It has been frequently employed to ease the
approaches to a château instead of improving the access to a
town or village.' In this same assembly the orders of the nobility
and clergy, having outlined the failings of the forced labour
tax, offered of their own accord to devote 50,000 livres to the
improvement of the roads in order, they said, to make the roads
in the province passable without its costing anything more to
the people. It would perhaps have been less of a burden to these
privileged orders to substitute a general tax for the forced
labour scheme and then to pay their share of it, but, in giving
up willingly the advantage of tax inequality, they liked to preserve its appearance. Abandoning the useful part of their rights,
they carefully held on to the part which was hated.

Other assemblies composed entirely of landowners who were
free from paying the *taille*, and who intended to remain so,
nonetheless painted the sufferings which this *taille* inflicted on
the poor in the blackest of colours. They put together a frightening picture of all its abuses and were careful to make an endless
number of copies. What was most peculiar was that, to this
startling evidence of concern inspired by the common people,
now and then they added public expressions of contempt.
The common people had already become the object of their
sympathy without as yet ceasing to be the object of their disdain.

The provincial assembly of Upper Guyenne, speaking of these
peasants whose cause it was so warmly supporting, called them
*ignorant and coarse creatures, unruly beings and rough, undis-
ciplined characters*. Turgot, who had done so much for the
common people, speaks hardly any differently.[67]

These harsh expressions are found in documents which were
intended for the widest public attention and written to be seen
by the peasants themselves. You might have thought you lived
in those European countries such as Galicia where the upper
classes spoke a language different from that of the lower classes
and could not be understood by them. Feudal experts of the
eighteenth century, who often displayed towards their taxpayers and others owing feudal dues a spirit of kindness, moderation and justice not known to their predecessors, still spoke

on certain occasions of *worthless peasants*. It appears that, according to lawyers, these insults belonged to the style of the time.

As 1789 drew closer, this sympathy for the people's sufferings became more active and unwise. I have held in my hand circulars which several provincial assemblies addressed in the first days of 1788 to the inhabitants of different parishes in order to learn for themselves in detail all the grievances they might have reason to complain about.

One of these circulars was signed by a priest, a lord, three noblemen and a bourgeois – all members of the assembly and acting in its name. This commission ordered the syndic of each parish to summon all the peasants and to ask them what they had to say about the way the different taxes they paid were assessed and collected. 'We know,' they said, 'that in general terms most taxes, especially the salt tax and the *taille*, have calamitous consequences for the farmer but, in addition, we are keen to know about each abuse in particular.' The spirit of inquiry in the provincial assembly did not stop there; it wished to find out the number of people enjoying some tax privilege in the parish – noblemen, churchmen or commoners; what was the value of the property these exempted men owned; whether they resided or not on their estates; whether there were many Church lands (or, as they said at that time, lands which at death could not be passed on, which put them out of the market), and how valuable they were. All the above still did not satisfy their curiosity. They had to be told the level at which they had to estimate the taxes, *taille*, incidentals, capitation charge, forced labour dues which the privileged classes would have to pay, if taxation equality were to exist.

The effect of this was to inflame each individual citizen by listing his sufferings, to point out to him the authors of his distress, to give him courage at the sight of their small number and to reach his very heart in order to kindle greed, envy and hatred. They seem to have entirely overlooked the Jacquerie, the Maillotins and the Sixteen and to have been unaware that the French, the gentlest and even the kindest nation on the earth as long as they remain quiet in their normal state, become the most barbarous of men as soon as violent emotions drive them out of that state.

Unfortunately I have been unable to obtain all the reports sent in by the peasants in response to these deadly questions but I have recovered some which are enough to reveal the general attitude which dictated them.

In these diatribes, the name of every privileged person, noble or bourgeois was carefully noted; occasionally their way of life was described and always criticized. With great curiosity the value of their assets was investigated; the number and nature of their privileges were exposed at length and, above all, the wrongs they committed against all the other residents in the village. The bushels of corn which must be paid to them in feudal dues were counted; their income was calculated with an envious eye – income which profited no one, so it was said. The offerings to the priest, already called his salary, were exorbitant. It was bitterly noted that the Church had to be paid for everything and the poor man could not even have himself buried free of charge. As for taxes, they were all wrongly assessed and oppressive. Not one of them met approval in their eyes and they referred to all of them in intemperate language which verged on rage.

'Indirect taxes are hateful,' they said. 'No household is free from the exciseman's poking around; nothing is sacred in his eyes or in his hands. Stamp duty is crushing. The collector of the *taille* is a tyrant whose greed exploits every means of tormenting poor people. The bailiffs are no better than he is; not a single honest farmer is protected from their ferocity. The collectors are forced to ruin their neighbours so as not to expose themselves to the rapacity of these despots.'

The approach of the Revolution is heralded not only in this survey but is already present and speaking there in its own voice and showing its face full on.

Among all the differences between the religious revolution of the sixteenth century and the French Revolution, one difference is striking: in the sixteenth century most of the upper classes rushed to support the change of religion out of a calculated ambition or greed, whereas the common people embraced it

from conviction and without expectation of gain. In the eighteenth century, it was not the same: then unselfish beliefs and
warm-hearted sympathies motivated the educated classes and
led them to revolution whereas the bitter feeling of their grievances and the passion to change their social situation agitated
the common people. The enthusiasms of the former ended up
by inflaming and arming the latter's rage and cupidity.

CHAPTER 6

SOME PRACTICES WHICH HELPED THE GOVERNMENT TO COMPLETE THE REVOLUTIONARY EDUCATION OF THE COMMON PEOPLE

For a long time the government itself had tried hard to instil
and establish in the people's minds several of the ideas, since
named revolutionary, because they were hostile to the individual citizen and in opposition to private rights and the encouraging of violence.

The king was the first to show with what contempt the oldest
and apparently the most firmly established institutions could
be treated. Louis XV shook the monarchy and hastened on the
Revolution as much by his innovative ideas as by his failings,
by his energy as by his weakness. When the common people
saw the collapse and disappearance of the French Parlement –
an institution almost as old as royalty and which up until then
had seemed as unshakeable as royalty itself – they vaguely
understood that they were drawing near to those times of violence and uncertainty during which everything becomes possible
and there is scarcely anything so old that it needs to be respected
or so new that it cannot be tried out.

Louis XVI throughout his reign did nothing but speak about
reforms. There were few institutions whose imminent downfall
he did not predict before the Revolution came along to destroy
them in reality. Having removed several of the worst features

of the code of law, he soon replaced them: it could be said that he wished only to disturb their roots, leaving to others the bother of knocking them to the ground.

Among the reforms he had enacted himself, suddenly and without adequate preparation, some of them changed the ancient and respected habits and sometimes violated rights already in place. Thus, these reforms prepared the Revolution very much less obviously by knocking down what was standing in its way than by demonstrating to the common people how they might set about doing something themselves. What increased the evil was precisely the pure and unselfish intention which inspired the king and his ministers to action for there is no more dangerous example than violence motivated by goodness and exercised by people of goodwill.

A long time before, Louis XVI in his edicts had publicly proclaimed the theory that all the lands of the kingdom had originally been granted conditionally by the state, which was thus the only true landowner, while any other landowners were in possession under terms which remained disputable and under law which was defective. This doctrine had its roots in feudal law but was proclaimed in France only at the moment when feudalism was dying and had never been admired by courts of justice. The idea is the mother of modern socialism. It is odd to see it first taking root in royal despotism.

During the monarchies which followed Louis XIV, the government taught the common people everyday in a more practical way, well within their scope to understand, the contempt it was proper to feel for privately owned property. When, in the second half of the eighteenth century, the desire for public works and especially roads began to expand, the government did not find it at all difficult to seize all the land it needed and to tear down houses that obstructed it.[68] From then on the management of the Highways Department was besotted with the geometrical beauty of straight lines which we have seen since; it took great care to steer clear of existing roads if they appeared to curve ever so slightly; rather than making a short detour it carved a way through a thousand inheritances. Estates thus laid waste or destroyed were always compensated at an arbitrary rate, after an indefinite delay and frequently not at all.[69]

When the provincial assembly of Lower Normandy took over the administration from the Intendant, it recorded that the price of all the land officially seized for roads was still due to be paid. The debt thus contracted and not yet settled by the state in this small corner of France had risen to 250,000 livres. The number of major landowners affected in this way was limited whereas the number of small landowners hurt was large as the land was already sub-divided. Each one of them had learned from his own experience how little heed was paid to the rights of the individual whenever public interest needed them to be violated – a doctrine that they were careful not to overlook when it was a question of applying it to others for their own profit.

Formerly, in a very considerable number of parishes, charitable institutions had existed which, in the intentions of their founders, had had as their aim help for inhabitants in certain cases and in a way specified by the donor's will. Most of these institutions were destroyed in the last years of the monarchy or diverted from their original objectives by simple decrees of the Royal Council, which is to say by the purely arbitrary acts of government. Usually the sums thus given to the villages were seized to finance nearby hospitals. In its turn the ownership of these hospitals was transformed at about the same time for purposes never envisaged by the founder and which doubtless he would not have implemented. An edict of 1780 authorized all these establishments to sell the properties left them at different times, on condition of their enjoying permanent occupation and allowed them to forward the proceeds from the sale to the state which was obliged to pay interest upon the money. As was said, this was to make better use of their ancestors' charity than they had made themselves. It was forgotten that the best way to teach men to violate the individual rights of the living is to take no account of the wishes of the dead. The contempt expressed by the administration of the Ancien Régime towards the latter has not been surpassed by any of the governments which followed on. Above all, this revealed nothing of that rather detailed scrupulousness whereby the English lent each citizen the whole force of society to help him ensure the terms of his last testament and made them pay still more respect to his memory than to himself.

Compulsory purchase, the compulsory sale of commodities and setting maximum prices were government measures which had precedents in the Ancien Régime. In times of food shortage I have seen administrations fix in advance the price of produce which peasant farmers brought to market and, if the latter, out of fear of arrest, did not turn up, they issued orders to force attendance under threat of fines.

But nothing was more perniciously revealing than certain practices pursued by the criminal law when it came to dealing with the lower classes. The poor citizen was already better protected than one imagines against the onslaughts of a richer or more powerful citizen than himself but if he had dealings with the state all he encountered, as I have indicated elsewhere, were special courts, biased judges, a rapid or sham trial, executive decrees already decided and without appeal. 'The Provost and lieutenant of the mounted militia are appointed to recognize public disturbances and assemblies which might occur because of the grain supply; they are ordered to oversee the trial, judged by the Provost to its completion as a final court of appeal; his Majesty forbids any judicial courts from taking any jurisdiction over these courts.' This order in Council was in force throughout the eighteenth century. We can see from the mounted militia reports that, in such circumstances, suspect villages were surrounded at night, houses were invaded before daybreak, peasants informed against were arrested without any question of a warrant's being issued. The man arrested in this way often stayed a long while in prison before being able to talk to his counsel: edicts, nevertheless, laid down that anyone accused should be interrogated within twenty-four hours. This arrangement was neither less formal nor more respected than it is today.

So it transpired that a mild and well-established government gave daily instruction to the lower classes about the code of criminal law best suited to revolutionary times and most adapted to tyranny and this school was ever kept open. The

Ancien Régime gave the lower classes this dangerous education right to the end. In this matter, everyone, right up to Turgot himself, faithfully imitated his predecessors. When in 1775 his new legislation about the grain trade gave rise to resistance in the Parlement and riots in the countryside, he obtained a royal command which removed the jurisdiction from the ordinary courts and handed the rioters over to the Provost's court 'which is designed principally,' so it is said, 'to repress popular outbursts and when it is expedient for speedy examples to be made of them'. Furthermore, any peasant moving away from his parish without a certificate signed by the priest and the syndic was to be pursued, arrested and tried by the Provost's court as a tramp.

It is true to say that in this eighteenth-century monarchy, if the formal procedures were frightening, the punishments were almost always moderated. They preferred to frighten than to hurt or, rather, judges were arbitrary and violent out of habit and indifference. But the liking for this summary justice grew all the more popular. The lighter the punishment, the more easily people forgot the way it was pronounced. The mildness of the sentence concealed the horror of the procedure.

I venture to state, because I have the facts in my grasp, that a great number of the methods used by the revolutionary government had their precedents and models in the measures taken with respect to the lower classes during the last two centuries of the monarchy. The Ancien Régime provided the Revolution with several of its procedures; the latter simply added the savagery of its own personality.

CHAPTER 7

HOW A GREAT ADMINISTRATIVE REVOLUTION HAD PRECEDED THE POLITICAL REVOLUTION AND THE CONSEQUENCES THAT THIS HAD

Nothing had yet been changed in the structure of the government since already most of the secondary laws controlling the social conditions of individuals and the administration of affairs had been abolished or modified.

The destruction of the guilds and their partial and incomplete reinstatement had fundamentally altered the old relations between worker and master. Those relations had not only become different but uncertain and irksome. The manorial militia was in ruins; the protective role of the state was still not solidly established and the artisan, placed as he was in a constricted and ill-defined position between the government and the employer, was not too clear which of these two was able to look after him or should restrain him. This state of uneasiness and anarchy, in which the entire lower class in the towns had suddenly been placed, had important consequences as soon as the common people began to reappear on the political stage.

One year before the Revolution a royal edict had overturned the judicial system in its entirety, several new areas of law jurisdiction had been created, a host of others abolished and all the rules establishing legal competence changed. Now in France, as I have already remarked elsewhere, the number of those involved either as judges or in executing the rulings of judges was immense. If truth be told the entire middle class had more or less some connection with the courts. The effect of the law was, therefore, to disturb suddenly the position and prosperity of thousands of families and to give them a new and precarious status. This edict had inconvenienced litigants almost as much, for, placed in the middle of this legal revolution, they found it difficult to discover which law applied to their case or which court should judge it.

Above all, it was this root and branch reform which the so-called administration had to tolerate in 1787 that threw public affairs into disorder and finally upset every citizen even in his private life.

I have intimated that in the Royal Provinces (*pays d'élection*) – that is in three-quarters of France – the entire administration of the district was invested in a single individual, the Intendant, who acted not only without control but also without advice.

In 1787 a provincial assembly was placed at the Intendant's side to become the real administrator of the province. In each village an elected municipal body replaced both the former parish assemblies and in most cases the syndics.

A legislative system, so unlike the one that preceded it and which altered so completely both the manner of conducting public affairs and the relative status of individuals, was to be applied everywhere at the same time and in almost the same way with no regard to previous practice or the special circumstances of the individual provinces. This revealed how thoroughly the spirit of standardization of the Revolution had already permeated the old government which the Revolution was about to overturn.

Then we could see the influence of habit in the game of political institutions and how men can cope more easily with complicated and obscure laws which they have practised for so long than with simpler legislation which is new to them.

Under the Ancien Régime, there existed in France all kinds of powers infinitely varying from province to province, none of which had fixed or well-recognized boundaries and each of which had a field of action shared with several others. Nevertheless a regulated and relatively simple order had in the end been established in the conduct of affairs. By contrast, the new powers, smaller in number, carefully restricted and similar in form, collided and immediately became entangled with each other in the utmost confusion and often reduced each other to powerlessness.

The new system of law had, in addition, one great defect, one which would have been sufficient, especially at the beginning, to make its execution difficult: all the powers created were collective.[70]

Under the old monarchy only two methods of administration had ever been known. In the places where the administration had been entrusted to one single man, he had acted without the cooperation of any assembly. Where assemblies existed as in the Independent Provinces (*pays d'états*) or in the towns, the executive power was entrusted to no one in particular – the assembly not only directed and supervised the administration but conducted affairs itself or through temporary commissions it appointed.

Since only these two ways of acting were known, when one was abandoned the other was adopted. It is quite strange that, at the heart of such an enlightened society where public administration had already played such an important role, no one had ever considered joining the two systems together and separating, without divorcing them entirely, the executive power from the supervisory and directive power. This idea, though apparently so simple, never occurred nor is it found before this century. It is, so to speak, the only important discovery in matters of public administration which belongs to us. We shall see the consequences of the opposite practice: although the Ancien Régime was detested, they transported into politics its administrative ways, obeyed its traditions and adopted in the National Convention, the system which the provincial estates and the small urban municipalities had followed. And we shall see how, suddenly, the Terror emerged from what had been until then merely a source of administrative embarrassment.

Therefore, the provincial assemblies of 1787 were given the right to administer themselves in most of the spheres where the Intendant had hitherto acted alone. They were responsible under the aegis of central government for setting the *taille*, supervising its collection, deciding what public works should be undertaken and having them carried out. They had under their immediate control all the highways officials, from inspector to foreman. They had to lay down what they deemed appropriate, to report back about the service of these agents to the minister and to recommend to him the remuneration due to them. The guardianship of the villages was almost entirely placed in the hands of these assemblies who had to try in the first instance the major part of the disputes which had previously been tried before the Intendant, etc. Several of these functions sat awkwardly with a collective and irresponsible agency and besides would be exercised by people who were in administrative business for the first time.

The final cause of confusion was the fact that, while reducing the Intendant to impotence, they allowed him nevertheless to remain in post. Having stripped him of his absolute right to control everything, they burdened him with the duty of helping and supervising the assembly's business, as if a fallen civil servant could ever enter into the spirit of a legislative order which dispossessed him and help make it work!

What they had done to the Intendant they repeated for his sub-delegate. Alongside him and in the place he had just filled, they had set up a district assembly which was enjoined to act under the control of the provincial assembly and according to similar principles.[71]

All we know of the acts of these provincial assemblies created in 1787, and indeed their own records, tell us that right from their inception they were engaged in silent and often open warfare against the Intendants who used the superior experience they had gained simply to block the movements of their successors. In one place an assembly complained how it could seize from the Intendant the most necessary documents only with the greatest effort. Elsewhere, an Intendant accused the assembly members of wishing to usurp the functions which, according to him, the edicts had still left him. He appealed to the minister who often made no reply or who was in doubt, since the matter was as new and as obscure to him as to all the others. Sometimes the assembly considered that the Intendant had been guilty of maladministration and that the roads he had built were badly planned or maintained; that he had wrought ruin on the communities whose guardian he was. Often these assemblies dithered beneath the obscurities of such unfamiliar legislation. They consulted each other over a wide area and received an endless stream of advice. The Intendant from Auch claimed that he could oppose the decision of the provincial assembly which had authorized a village to set its own taxes. The assembly stated that henceforth the Intendant could give only advice not orders and it asked the provincial assembly of the Île-de-France for its opinion.

During these petty quarrels and consultations the progress of government often slowed down and sometimes came to a halt; public life was then suspended. 'The stagnation in public affairs is complete,' said the provincial assembly of Lorraine whose words are but an echo of several others. 'All reasonable citizens are distressed.'

At other times these new administrations fell down out of an overenthusiastic activity and self-confidence; they were quite overtaken by a disturbing and restless zeal which led them to want to change the old ways at one fell swoop and to correct hastily the most long-standing abuses. Under the pretext that from then on it was up to them to exercise guardianship of the towns, they undertook to manage communal business themselves. In a word, by wishing to improve everything, they ended up causing wholesale confusion.

If we now consider carefully the great position which public administration had already held for a long time in France, the countless interests daily affected and everything which depended upon it or whose support it needed, if we think that it was on public administration rather than upon themselves that individuals relied to guarantee the successful outcome of their own affairs, to support their industry, to lay out and maintain their roads, to preserve their peace and to safeguard their well-being, we will have an idea of the infinite number of people who were bound to find themselves personally harmed by the evil which they endured.

But it was above all in the villages that the failings of the new reorganization were experienced. The changes disturbed not only the regulation of powers but suddenly they altered the relative social status of citizens and brought every class into confrontation and conflict.

When in 1775 Turgot suggested that the king reform the administration of the countryside, the greatest obstacle he encountered – and he is the man who tells us of this – came from the unequal imposition of taxes. For how could people be encouraged to engage in communal action and shared discussion of parish affairs, such as, principally, self-assessment, collection and use of tax revenues, when they were not universally subject to paying them in the same way and when some were entirely exempt from their imposition? Every parish included nobles and clergy who paid no *taille* at all, peasant farmers who were partially exempt and others who paid the whole tax. There were virtually three distinct parishes each of which would have needed a separate administration. The difficulty had no solution.

In fact, nowhere was the difference in taxation more in evidence than in rural areas; nowhere was the population more obviously divided into different groups, often in a state of mutual hostility. To reach the position of granting to villages a universal administration and a small free government, it would first have been vital to subject everyone to identical taxes and to reduce the gap between classes.

That was not how they went about things when finally they undertook the 1787 reform. At the heart of the parish they retained the former division of classes and the inequality of taxation which was its principal sign but nevertheless they entrusted the whole administration to elected bodies, all of which led immediately to the most bizarre consequences.

If it was a question of the electoral assembly having to choose the municipal officers, the priest and the noble could not appear in it because, it was said, they belonged to the noble and ecclesiastical classes. It was mainly the Third Estate which had to elect its representatives in this case.

Once the municipal council was elected, the priest and the lord were contradictorily members by right, for it would not have seemed fitting to have excluded entirely two such notable inhabitants from the governing body. The lord even presided over those town councillors he had not helped to elect; yet it was important that he did not meddle in most of their dealings. For example, when they proceeded to the assessment and collection of the *taille*, the priest and the lord were unable to vote.

Were they not both exempt from paying this tax? On its side, the town council had nothing to do with the capitation tax which continued to be determined by the Intendant, following its special terms of reference.

Out of fear that this president, isolated as he was from the body he was supposed to direct, might still exercise an indirect influence against the interests of the social order he did not belong to, it was requested that the votes of his tenant farmers should not be counted. The provincial assemblies, when consulted on this matter, found this protest entirely fair and altogether in tune with principle. Any other nobles living in the parish could not belong to this same commoner body unless they had been elected by the peasants and, even then, as the rules were at pains to note, they no longer had the right to represent anyone outside the Third Estate.

The lord of the manor therefore appeared in the assembly only to be entirely subordinate to his former subjects who suddenly had become his masters. He was their prisoner rather than their leader.[72] By bringing men together in this way, they had apparently pursued the aim not so much of drawing them together as of making them see more clearly the differences between them and how their interests were hostile to each other.

Was the syndic still this discredited civil servant whose functions were fulfilled only when forced, or had his position been raised together with the community whose chief agent he still was? No one knew exactly. In the letter of a certain village bailiff in 1788 I read that he was insulted to have been elected to discharge the office of the syndic. 'That,' he said, 'is contrary to all the privileges of his office.' The Controller-General, in his reply, felt that this individual's ideas needed correcting and that 'he must be made to realize that he ought to consider it an honour to be chosen by his fellow citizens and that, besides, the new syndics are in no way like the officials previously bearing the same name and that they should expect more consideration from the government.'

On the other hand, we see important inhabitants in the parish and even noblemen suddenly drawing closer to the peasant class as soon as the latter became a power in the land. A lord, holding the post of high court judge in the outskirts of Paris, complained that the new edict forbade his taking part, *as a simple inhabitant,* in the dealings of the parish assembly. Others agreed, they said, 'out of devotion to the public good, to fulfil even the office of the syndic'.

It was too late. Even as men from the wealthier classes moved towards the common rural people and attempted to mix with them, the latter withdrew into the isolation which had been forced on them and defended their position. We come across parish assemblies refusing to welcome the lord into their midst; others engaged in every sort of trickery before admitting even commoners if they were rich. 'We have been informed,' said the provincial assembly of Lower Normandy, 'that several town assemblies have refused to welcome into their midst lower-class landowners of the parish if they do not dwell there even though there is no doubt that they have the right to belong. Other assemblies have even refused to welcome farmers who do not have properties within their boundaries.'

Therefore everything concerning secondary laws was novelty, obscurity and conflict even before the principal laws of state government had been touched. What still remained standing had been shaken and no longer did there exist a single regulation, so to speak, whose abolition or imminent modification had not been announced by central government itself.

This sudden and widespread remodelling of all the rules and administrative habits preceding the political revolution of our country and which we hardly mention today was nevertheless already one of the greatest upheavals ever encountered in the history of any great nation. This first revolution exercised an unimaginable influence over the second and it turned this latter into an event different from all those of a similar kind which had ever before taken place in the world or have occurred since.

The first English revolution which overturned the whole political constitution of that country and even abolished its royalty affected only superficially the secondary laws and changed almost nothing of customs or habits. The legal system and the administration kept their old structures and followed the same bad habits as in the past. At the height of the civil war, the twelve English judges continued, so it is said, to make the round of the Assizes twice a year. Thus not everything was shaken at the same time. The revolution was restricted in its effects and English society, although disturbed at its topmost level, remained firm at its base.

We have ourselves seen in France since '89 several revolutions which have transformed the structure of government from top to toe. Most have been very sudden and have been achieved by force in open violation of existing laws. Nonetheless, the disorder they caused has never lasted long nor been widespread. It was scarcely felt by the greater section of the population and sometimes went by unnoticed.

Since '89, the administrative constitution always remained standing amid the ruins of the political constitutions. The person of the ruler or the structures of central government were changed but the daily course of affairs was neither interrupted nor disturbed. Every citizen continued to remain obedient, in the minor business which interested him individually, to the rules and practices which he knew. He depended upon secondary powers which he had always had the habit of consulting. Usually he dealt with the same officials. For, if every revolution took off the head of the administration, its body remained intact and alive; the same functions were exercised by the same officials who transferred their spirit and methods across the diverse political rulings. They judged and administered first in the name of the king, then in that of the republic and finally in the name of the emperor. Then, as fortune's wheel turned once again full circle, they began once more to administer and judge for the king, for the republic and for the emperor, ever the same, ever in the same way. For what mattered the name of their master? Their business was less to be good citizens than good administrators and good judges. As soon as the first shock wave had passed by, it seemed as if nothing in the country had shifted.

At the outbreak of the Revolution, this section of government which, although subordinate, daily affected every citizen and intruded most persistently and effectively upon his wellbeing, had been completely overthrown. The public administration had suddenly replaced all its officials and recast all its principles. In the first instance the state appeared not to have undergone a great shock from this extensive reform but every Frenchman had experienced a small personal upheaval. Each citizen had been shaken in his social situation, disturbed in his habits or obstructed in his business. A certain normal orderliness continued to reign in the most important and the most general affairs of his life but by now no one knew any longer whom to obey, whom to consult, how to behave in those small matters of individual concern which make up the daily routine of social life.

Since the nation was no longer stable in any of its parts, one final blow could therefore set everything in motion and instigate the greatest upheaval and the most frightening confusion that had ever been.

CHAPTER 8

HOW THE REVOLUTION SPRANG INEVITABLY FROM WHAT PRECEDED IT

In conclusion, I wish to gather together some of the features already portrayed separately and to observe the Revolution springing naturally, as it were, from that Ancien Régime whose picture I have just painted.

If we consider that it was in France that the feudal system, without changing in it what could harm or irritate us, had most completely lost everything that could protect or serve us, we shall be less surprised that the Revolution which was violently to abolish this old constitution of Europe should have broken out in France rather than elsewhere.

If we note that the nobles, having lost their former political rights and having ceased, more than in any other country in federal Europe, administering and governing the inhabitants, had nonetheless not only retained but also greatly increased their financial exemptions and the advantages which their members enjoyed individually; if we note also that on becoming a subordinate class they had remained a privileged and closed estate, less and less, as I have stated elsewhere, an aristocracy and more and more a caste, we will no longer be astonished that their privileges appeared so inexplicable and loathsome to the French people and that, at the sight of all this, a democratic envy was ignited in their hearts to such a pitch that it burns there still.

Finally, if we reflect that this noble class, divided from the middle classes which it had driven from its midst and from the common people whose affections it had alienated, was in a state of complete isolation at the heart of the nation – the leader of an army in appearance, an officer corps without soldiers in reality – we shall realize how, after standing tall for a thousand years, it could have been overthrown in the space of one night.

I have shown the way in which the king's government, having abolished provincial freedoms and having itself taken the place of all local powers in three-quarters of France, had absorbed into itself all public affairs from the least to the most significant. I have furthermore shown how, as a necessary consequence, Paris had become the master of the country where previously it had been only the capital city or rather it had itself turned into the embodiment of the whole kingdom. These two facts which were peculiar to France would alone be enough to explain why a riot was able to destroy utterly a monarchy which had endured such violent onslaughts for so many centuries and which, on the eve of its downfall, still looked unshakeable even to those who were about to topple it.

Since France was one of the European countries where all political life had been the most entirely extinguished over the longest periods of time and where individuals had most profoundly lost touch with public affairs, the habit of reading the meaning of events, the experience of popular movements and almost the idea of being a nation, it is easy to imagine how all Frenchmen could have plunged simultaneously into a terrible revolution without seeing it. Those very men most threatened by it marched at its head and undertook to open up and widen the path which led to it.

Since there no longer existed any free institutions and consequently no political class, no living political bodies, no organized political parties with leaders and since, in the absence of all these organized forces, the guidance for public opinion when it happened to revive fell solely to the philosophers, we were bound to expect the Revolution, conducted less with a view to particular facts than following abstract principles and very general theories. We could anticipate that, instead of attacking individual bad laws, all laws would be under attack and that there would be a desire to substitute for the former French constitution a totally new system of government which these writers had imagined.

Since the Church was naturally connected to all the old institutions whose destruction was envisaged, there could be no doubt that this revolution was bound to shake religion at the same time as it overturned civil power. From then on it was impossible to say to what unheard-of acts of recklessness the minds of the innovators might be carried, freed as they were simultaneously from every obstacle placed upon men's imaginations by religion, customs and laws.

And anyone who might have studied the state of the country would readily have predicted that there was no reckless act so unheard-of that it could not be tried out nor any violent acts which should not be tolerated.

'What,' cried Burke in one of his eloquent pamphlets, 'is there not one single man who can reply on behalf of the smallest district? In addition, I do not see anyone who can speak on behalf of anyone else. Each man is arrested without resistance in his own home whether it is for royalism, moderantism or anything else.' Burke did not realize in what conditions this monarchy he regretted had left us to our new masters. The administration of the Ancien Régime had in advance removed from the French both the possibility of and the desire for mutual support. When the Revolution took place you would have searched in vain throughout the greater part of France for ten men who might have possessed the habit of acting in tandem on a well-organized basis or of looking after their own defence. The central government was supposed to take charge of these matters. The result was that the central power, having fallen from the hands of the king's administration into those of a sovereign and irresponsible assembly, from being good-natured to being terrible, saw nothing which could stop its progress nor even slow it down even briefly. The cause which so easily brought the monarchy low had made everything possible after its downfall.

Never had religious tolerance, leniency of rule, humanity and goodwill been more preached or seemingly more accepted than in the eighteenth century; the code of warfare, which is almost the final refuge of violence, had been restricted and softened. Yet from the heart of such gentle social customs was going to emerge the most inhuman revolution. Nevertheless, all this softening of customs was not a sham for, as soon as the fury of the Revolution had died down, this same softening of custom immediately spread throughout the law and permeated every political usage.

The contrast between the gentleness of theory and the violence of deeds, which has been one of the strangest features of the French Revolution, will surprise no one who observes that this revolution had been prepared by the most civilized classes in the nation and implemented by the most uneducated and coarse classes. Since the men of the former group had no established ties with each other, no familiarity with cooperation, no hold over the common people, it was the latter which almost immediately became the guiding power as soon as the former powers had been destroyed. Where they did not themselves hold the reins of government, they at least gave their complexion to the government. And if, on the other hand, we reflect upon the way the common people had lived under the Ancien Régime, we will have no trouble imagining what kind of government it would be.

The very peculiarities of the social conditions of the lower classes had given them several unusual virtues. Freed from early on and having long since owned a part of the land, in an isolated rather than dependent position, the people showed themselves moderate and proud; they were inured to hardship, indifferent to the delicacies of life, resigned under the worst of evils, stead-fast in danger, a simple and manly race which would fill the ranks of those powerful armies under whose efforts Europe would bend. But these features caused them to be a dangerous master. Since they had for centuries, and almost alone, carried the whole burden of abuse and since they had lived apart, feeding in silence upon their prejudices, jealousies and hatreds, they had become hardened because of the harshness of their fate and capable at once of enduring everything and of inflicting suffering.

It was in this condition that they placed their hands on government and undertook to finish themselves the work of the Revolution. Books had provided the theory, they took responsi-bility for the practice and adjusted the writers' ideas to their own rage.

Those who have given careful study, on reading this book, to eighteenth-century France have been able to perceive two main passions emerge and develop at its heart which were not at all contemporary with each other and have not always had the same aim in view.

The first, more deeply rooted and historically older, is the violent and inextinguishable hatred of inequality which had been inspired and nourished by the very sight of such inequality. It had been for a long time propelling the French, with a persist-ent and irresistible force, towards the destruction, to their very foundations, of all that remained of medieval institutions and, once the ground was cleared, towards the construction of a society in which men were as alike as human beings could envisage.

The second, of more recent origin and less deeply rooted, moved them to wish to live not only equal but free.

Towards the end of the Ancien Régime these two passions were as sincerely held and appeared as active as each other. At the start of the Revolution they came together; for a brief moment they joined forces and blended, gained the warmth from their mutual contact and finally inflamed at the same time the whole heart of France. It was '89, a time of inexperience certainly, but also of generosity, enthusiasm, manliness and grandeur, a time to be remembered forever, which the eyes of men will turn towards with wonderment when those who saw it and we ourselves have long since disappeared. Then the French were proud enough of their cause and of themselves to believe that they could achieve equality inside freedom. At the centre of democratic institutions, therefore, they placed free institutions at every point. Not only did they reduce to dust this outdated legislation which divided men into castes, guilds, classes and made their rights still more unequal than their social status but also they smashed at a stroke those other laws – a more recent result of royal power – which had removed from the nation its free enjoyment of itself and had placed alongside each Frenchman the government as tutor, guardian and, if needs be, oppressor. Along with absolute government centralization also collapsed.

But when that energetic generation which had instigated the Revolution had been destroyed or exhausted, as normally happens to any generation undertaking such enterprises, when the love of liberty, following the usual course of such events, had lost heart and languished in anarchy and popular tyranny and when the distraught nation began to search blindly for its leader, then absolute government found some amazingly simple ways of returning to life and reforming itself. These were easily discovered by the man of genius who was to be the one who would both continue and destroy the Revolution.

The Ancien Régime had possessed, in fact, a whole collection of modern institutions which were not hostile to equality, could sit easily in the new social structure and which, nevertheless, offered unusual ways of returning to despotism. These institutions were sought out in the wreckage of all the others and were located. Formerly they had created habits, passions and ideas which tended to keep men apart and obedient – these were revived and exploited. Centralization was recovered from its ruins and restored. Since, at the time of its restoration, all former checks upon its power were still destroyed, from the very entrails of a nation which had just overturned the monarchy, we saw the sudden appearance of a power, more extensive, more detailed and more absolute than had ever been exercised by any of our kings. This undertaking seemed one of extraordinary audacity and of unprecedented success simply because people were thinking only about what was immediately before their eyes and forgot what they had seen before. The despot fell but all the substantial elements of his achievements remained standing; his government perished but his administration went on thriving and, whenever we have wished since to do away with absolutism, we have simply placed the head of liberty upon the body of subjection.

On several occasions, from the start of the Revolution to our own times, we have seen the passion for freedom burn out, then come alive, then burn out once again to come alive once more. Accordingly, this will long be the case for a passion which is always untested and badly organized, easily discouraged, frightened and defeated, superficial and ephemeral. During this same period, the passion for equality has still occupied the depths of our hearts which it was the first to invade. There it clings to feelings most cherished by us. While the passion for freedom endlessly changes its appearance, growing smaller, greater, stronger, weaker according to events, that passion for equality remains always the same, always linked to the same aims, with the same obstinate and often blind zeal, ready to sacrifice all to those who allow it to thrive, ready to provide the government which it intends to support and to flatter the habits, ideas and laws which despotism needs in order to rule.

The French Revolution will seem as but a shadow to those who would restrict their view to that event alone. We must seek out the only light which can illuminate it in the times which led up to it. Without a clear idea of the former society, its laws, its failings, its prejudices, its sufferings and its greatness we will never grasp what the French have done during the sixty years which have followed its downfall. Yet this idea will not be enough unless we delve down into the intrinsic nature of our nation.

When I contemplate this nation in itself, I find it to be more extraordinary than any of the events in its history. Has there ever appeared on this earth a single nation so full of contrasts and so excessive in all its actions, guided more by emotions, less by principles; always achieving consequently either less or more than was expected of it, sometimes below the common level of humanity, sometimes well above; a people so constant in its basic instincts that we can still recognize it from portraits drawn two or three thousand years ago; at the same time so nimble in its day-to-day thinking and its tastes that it ends up becoming a spectacle surprising to itself and often it remains as astonished as foreigners at the sight of what it has just enacted; the most stay-at-home and the most humdrum nation of all when left to itself yet, once uprooted involuntarily from its home and routines, ready to go to the ends of the earth and to risk all; unruly by temperament yet better suited to the arbitrary and even violent authority of a king than to the free and orderly government by leading citizens; today the declared enemy of all obedience, tomorrow devoting to servitude a kind of passion which nations best suited to slavery cannot manage; led by a thread as long as no resistance is offered; ungovernable as soon as an example of such resistance appears somewhere; thus always tricking its masters who fear it either too much or too little; never so free that one need despair of enslaving it nor so enslaved that it cannot still break its yoke; fitted for everything but excelling only in warfare; in love with chance, force, success, fame and rumour more than true reputation; more capable of the heroic than the virtuous, of genius than common sense; better suited to imagine vast plans than to complete great projects; the most brilliant and the most dangerous of European nations and the best shaped to become an object, by turns, of admiration, loathing, pity and terror but never of indifference?

This nation alone could have given birth to such a precipitate revolution, so radical, so impetuous in its progress, yet so full of retreats, of contradictory events and contrasting examples. Without the reasons I have stated the French would never have achieved it, but we must acknowledge that all these reasons together would not have managed to explain such a revolution elsewhere than in France.

Here I am at the threshold of this memorable revolution. On

this occasion I shall not enter the gate; perhaps I shall be able to do so in the future. I shall then no longer look at its causes; I shall examine it in itself and I shall finally judge the social order which has emerged from it.[73]

APPENDIX:
INDEPENDENT PROVINCES
AND ESPECIALLY LANGUEDOC

It is not my intention to make a detailed inquiry into the way that things were conducted in each of the Independent Provinces which still existed at the time of the Revolution.

I simply wish to register their number, to indicate the ones which still retained an active local life, to show what their relations were with the royal administration, how far they diverged from the general rules I have previously described and how far they conformed and, finally, using one of their number as an example, to illustrate what they might all have easily become.

Estates had existed in most French provinces. Each one of them had been administered, under the government of the king, by the *people of the three Estates*, as was then said, by which we must understand an assembly composed of representatives from clergy, nobility and commoners. This provincial constitution, like other political institutions of the Middle Ages, exhibited the same features in almost every civilized region of Europe, at least in all those where Germanic customs and ideas had permeated. In many Germanic provinces Estates had lasted right up to the French Revolution. Where they had been abolished they had disappeared only in the course of the seventeenth and eighteenth centuries. For two centuries rulers everywhere had waged war against them, sometimes hidden, sometimes openly but without interruption. Nowhere had rulers sought to improve the institution in accordance with the progress of the times but simply to destroy or to disfigure it when the opportunity had arisen or when they could not do anything worse.

In France in 1789 there existed Estates of any significant size in only five provinces and in a few small unimportant districts. Real provincial freedom subsisted only in two of them, namely Brittany and Languedoc. Everywhere else the institution had completely lost its lifeblood and was merely an empty sham.

I shall move Languedoc away from the rest in order to use it as a subject of a special analysis.

Languedoc was the most extensive and most densely populated of all the Independent Provinces; it included more than two thousand townships, or *communities* as they were called then, and reckoned more than two million inhabitants. Furthermore, it was the most efficiently regulated and prosperous of all these provinces, as well as the biggest. Thus Languedoc is the best example to illustrate what provincial freedom could be under the Ancien Régime and to what degree this freedom had been subordinate to the king's rule, even in the regions where it seemed to thrive the most.

In Languedoc the Estates could meet only on the direct order of the king and after a writ of summons addressed by him annually to every individual member who was to sit in the assembly. This inspired the statement by one contemporary discontent: 'Of the three bodies which make up our Estates, the first, the clergy, is nominated by the king since he appoints incumbents to bishoprics and parish livings. The other two are considered to be in the same position since an order from the court can prevent any member he likes from attending without needing to exile him or to take him to the law. All he needs to do is not to summon him.'

The Estates had not only to meet but also to recess on certain dates set by the king. The normal length of these sittings had been fixed at forty days by an order of the Royal Council. The king was represented by commissioners who always had access at their own request and who were charged with presenting the government's wishes. The Estates were, in addition, tightly supervised. They were unable to pass a resolution of any importance or determine any financial measure of any kind unless their decision had been approved by a Royal Council decree.

For a tax, a loan or a lawsuit they required the express permission of the king. All their general regulations, even one governing the holding of their sittings, had to be authorized before coming into force. The total of their receipts and their expenditure (their budget as we would call it today) was annually subjected to the same control.

Furthermore, the central power exercised in Languedoc the same political rights which were acknowledged as belonging to it everywhere else; the laws that it thought good to pass, the endless general regulations it issued, the general measures it took were applicable there as in the Royal Provinces. The central power exercised there in the same manner all the natural functions of government. It set up the same police and the same officials; from time to time it created, there like everywhere else, a host of new civil servants whose offices the province was obliged to repurchase at a high price.

Languedoc was governed as in the other provinces by an Intendant who had, in every district, sub-delegates who corresponded with heads of communities and directed them. The Intendant fulfilled an administrative role as guardian in exactly the same way as in the Royal Provinces. The smallest village hidden in the Cevennes gorges was unable to incur the slightest expense without there being a decree from the Royal Council authorizing it. That area of the justice system, which we today call administrative legal departments was no less extensive in Languedoc than in the remainder of France; it was even more so. The Intendant acted as the first court for deciding all matters relating to public highways; he judged all lawsuits dealing with roads and in general pronounced upon all affairs where the government was involved or thought it was. The government, no less than elsewhere, shielded all its agents against injudicious prosecutions by citizens injured by them.

What peculiar features, then, did Languedoc have to distinguish it from the other provinces and to make it the object of their envy? Three things were enough to make it entirely different from the rest of France.

1) An assembly composed of important men, esteemed by the population, respected by the royal power, in which no government servant – or according to the language of the time, *no officer of the king* – could take part and an assembly where annually a free and serious discussion dealt with the special concerns of the province. That the royal administration stood alongside this house of enlightenment was enough to persuade it to exercise its own powers in quite a different manner and, though using the same officers and the same instincts, to behave quite otherwise than in all other parts of France.

2) In Languedoc many public projects were carried through at the king's expense and using his officials; there were others for which central government supplied a share of the cost and directed to a large degree their execution. But the greatest number were executed solely at the expense of the province. Once the king had approved the plans and sanctioned expenditure on them, they were executed by officials chosen by the Estates and inspected by commissioners from among their number.

3) Lastly, the province had the right to levy by itself, and following its preferred procedures, a proportion of the royal taxes as well as those it was allowed to establish to cover its own needs.

We shall see the advantages gained by Languedoc from these privileges. It is worth the trouble of taking a closer look.

The most striking feature of the Independent Provinces is the almost complete absence of local taxes. The general taxes were often oppressive but the province spent almost nothing on itself. In Languedoc, on the contrary, the sums expended annually by the province on public works were enormous; in 1780 they exceeded 2,000,000 livres every year.

The central government was occasionally perturbed at the sight of such a great outlay; it was afraid that the province would be drained of money by such efforts and thus unable to settle its share of the tax burden due to itself. It criticized the

Estates for not exercising moderation. I have read a report in which the assembly replied to these criticisms. The extracts from the text I am about to quote will draw a more effective picture than I could describe of the spirit which fired this small-scale government.

In this report there was an acknowledgment that in fact the province had undertaken and was pursuing still extensive public works but, far from making excuses, it announced that, if the king did not object, it would increasingly embark upon this course. It had already improved or straightened the course of the main rivers crossing its territory and was busy extending the Languedoc canal, dug by Louis XIV and no longer adequate, to traverse Lower Languedoc in its journey via Cette and Agde to the Rhône. It had developed the commercial role of the port at Cette as well as maintaining it at great expense. It was noted that all these expenses were more national than provincial in character; nevertheless this province which benefited more than any other had borne the responsibility for them. It was similarly engaged in the draining of the marshes at Aigues-Mortes and restoring them to agricultural use. But it wished above all to concern itself with the roads: it had opened or put into good condition all the roads which crossed the province to connect with the rest of the kingdom. Even those which joined villages to towns in Languedoc alone had been repaired. All these different thoroughfares were excellent even in winter, in perfect contrast with the bumpy, badly maintained highways found in most of the neighbouring provinces such as Dauphiné, Quercy and the Bordeaux region (all Royal Provinces it is to be noted). On this point, the province was right to rely upon the opinion of traders and visitors, for Arthur Young, travelling through the country ten years later, wrote in his notes: 'Languedoc, independent estate, good roads constructed without forced labour.'

The report goes on to say that, if the king would allow, the Estates would not stop at this; they would undertake to improve the community roads (the local roads) which were just as important as the others. 'For if,' they further remark, 'the produce cannot leave the landowners' granary to go to a local market, what does it matter that it can be transported from there to a distant market?' Again they note: 'The principle adopted by the Estates as far as public works were concerned had always been that the size of the projects should be considered as less important than their usefulness.' Rivers, canals, roads which add value to all the products of the land and industry by allowing them to be transported in all weathers and at low cost to wherever they are needed and by means of which trade can reach every part of the province, increase the wealth of the country whatever the cost. Furthermore such projects, undertaken at one and the same time at a judicious level throughout various parts of the territory in a manner more or less equal, maintain the level of wages everywhere and support the poorer classes. 'The king has no need to set up almshouses at his own expense in Languedoc as he had in the rest of France,' concluded the province with justifiable pride. 'We do not seek such favours; the useful public works we undertake annually take their place and provide everyone with productive work.'

The more I study the general rules and regulations issued by the Estates of Languedoc with the king's permission but usually without his initiative concerning that part of public administration still left to them, the more I admire the wisdom, justice and humanity I see shown in them and the more the methods of this local government seem to me to be superior to everything I have just seen in those regions administered by the king alone.

The province was divided into *communities* (towns and villages), into administrative districts called *dioceses*, and, lastly, into three big departments overseen by Seneschals. Each of these divisions had a distinct system of representation and a small, separate government acting under the control either of the Estates or the king. If the issue was public works whose objective concerned one of these minor bodies, the latter's request was all that was required for the work to be undertaken. If the work of a community could bring some benefit to the diocese then the latter had to cooperate in the payment to some degree. Were the Seneschalsy to be involved, it had in its turn to provide help. Finally, the diocese, the Seneschalsy and the province were bound to come to the aid of the community even if the matter was of special interest only to the latter provided that the work was vital and was beyond its power. For, as the Estates never failed to declare, 'the fundamental principle of our constitution is that all parts of Languedoc are entirely supportive of each other and must all help each other by turns'.

The works carried out by the province should be planned long beforehand and first of all be submitted to the scrutiny of all secondary agencies which had to agree. They could be undertaken only for cash payments; forced labour was unknown. I have stated that in the Royal Provinces the land taken from landowners for public use had been poorly or belatedly paid for or often not at all. This was one of the greatest grievances raised by the provincial assemblies when they gathered in 1787. I have seen it remarked that they had even been deprived of the possibility of clearing debts incurred in this manner because the acquisition had been destroyed or spoiled before valuation had been established. In Languedoc every plot of land taken from the landowner had to be carefully assessed before the start of work *and paid for during the first year of construction.*

The rules applied by the Estates relating to different public works, from which I have taken these details, appeared to central government so excellently framed that it admired them without copying them. The Royal Council, after sanctioning their being put into operation, had them printed by the royal press and ordered that they should be sent to all Intendants as a consultative document.

What I have said about public works was even more aptly applicable to that other no less important element of provincial administration which dealt with the raising of taxes. It is in that sphere of influence above all that, passing from kingdom to province, one has real difficulty in believing that one is still in the realm.

I have elsewhere had the chance to show how the procedures followed in Languedoc to set and collect the *taille* were to some extent those we now follow ourselves for the levying of taxes.

I shall not return to that point here; suffice it to add that the province appreciated the superiority of its methods so much that, every time the king created new taxes, the Estates never hesitated to buy at a premium the right to raise them in their own way and using only their own officials.

Despite all the expenses I have successively listed, affairs in Languedoc were nonetheless in such good order and to its credit so well established that central government often had recourse to the province, borrowing in the province's name money which would not have been lent on such good terms from its own coffers. I found that Languedoc had borrowed with guarantees from itself for the king's account 73,000,000 livres in the final years for which it stood itself as guarantor.

The government and its ministers viewed with an albeit jaundiced eye these special freedoms. At first Richelieu cut them down and then abolished them. The weak and indolent Louis XIII, who loved nothing, detested them; he displayed such a horror for all provincial privileges, said Boulainvilliers, that his anger flared up simply at hearing their name. One never quite appreciates the great energy feeble souls expend on hating anything which drives them to make an effort. Their last remaining signs of virility are used for that effort and they almost always show themselves strong on these occasions however weak on all others. Good fortune dictated that the old constitution of Languedoc should be reinstated during the childhood of Louis XIV who respected it because he considered it as his own work. Louis XV suspended its operation for two years but allowed its restoration after that.

The creation of municipal offices exposed the province to dangers which, though less direct, were just as great. This obnoxious practice had not only the effect of destroying the constitution of the towns but also the tendency to disfigure that of the provinces. I do not know whether the deputies of the Third Estate in the provincial assemblies had ever been elected for this purpose but, for a long while back, they had not been. The municipal officers of the town were the only rightful representatives of the middle and lower classes in the assemblies.

This absence of a special authority, granted with the concerns of the time in mind, was hardly noticed as long as the towns themselves elected their magistrates in a free universal vote and more often than not for a very short period. The mayor, consul or syndic also represented at the heart of the Estates the decisions of the population in whose name he spoke as faithfully as if he had been chosen expressly by it for that purpose. We realize that this was not the case for the man who had used money to buy the right to administer his fellow citizens. Such a man represented only himself or at best minor concerns or the petty bigotries of his circle. However, this magistrate-by-purchase was able to retain rights which elected magistrates had deployed. That immediately changed the whole character of the institution. The nobility and clergy, instead of finding at their side or in front of them in the provincial assembly the representatives of the people, only found there a few lone middle-class members, diffident and powerless. The Third Estate became increasingly more overlooked in the government at the very time it was becoming richer and stronger in society. This was not the case at all in Languedoc because the province had always taken care to purchase offices back from the king whenever he put them up. The loans contracted for this purpose in 1773 alone rose to more than 4,000,000 livres.

Other more powerful reasons had contributed to spread the new spirit in these old institutions and gave to the Estates of Languedoc an indisputable superiority over all the others.

In this province, as in a large part of the south, the *taille* was a tax on real estate not on income, namely based on the value of property not on the social status of the owner. It is true that there were some estates which benefited from the privilege of non-payment. These had formerly been owned by the nobility but, with the progress of time and industry, some of these properties had happened to fall into commoners' hands. On the other hand, nobles had become owners of many properties subject to the *taille*. Privilege thus transferred from persons to things was doubtless more irrational but it was much less keenly felt because, though still irksome, it no longer caused humili-

ation. Since it was no longer linked indissolubly to the idea of
class and since it did not create for anyone completely alien or
hostile concerns, nothing stood in the way of the participation
of everyone in government business. In fact, in Languedoc more
than anywhere else, all citizens cooperated and stood together
on a footing of perfect equality.

In Brittany, all nobles had the right to appear in person in
the Estates; this often turned these into quasi-Polish diets. In
Languedoc, noblemen participated in the Estates only through
representatives, twenty-three of whom stood for all the others.
The clergy took its place in the persons of twenty-three bishops
of the province and, what we must especially note, the towns
had as many votes as the two senior orders.

Since the assembly was the only chamber and debates were not
conducted on a class basis but by individuals, the Third Estate
naturally gained a great importance; gradually its particular
ideology spread throughout the whole body. Furthermore the
three magistrates who under the title of Syndics-General were
responsible, in the Estates' name, for the day-to-day conduct
of business, were always lawyers – that is commoners. The
nobility, strong enough to safeguard its status, was no longer
strong enough to rule alone. From its position, the clergy,
although mostly made up from noblemen, lived in perfect understanding with the Third Estate. They joined forces enthusiastically in most of the latter's projects; they worked in harmony to
increase the material wealth of all citizens and to support their
trade and industry, often placing at the disposal of the people
their knowledge of men and their own rare skill of handling
affairs. It was almost always a member of the Church who was
chosen to negotiate at Versailles with ministers on questions of
dispute which pitted the king's authority against that of the
Estates. It can be said that during the whole of the eighteenth
century Languedoc was administered by the Third Estate,
controlled by the nobility and supported by the bishops.

Thanks to the particular constitution of Languedoc, the spirit
of the new age could spread peacefully through this old institution modifying everything without destroying anything in it.

It could have been like that everywhere else. A part of the persistence and effort exerted by rulers to abolish or damage the Provincial Estates would have been enough to improve them in this way and to adapt them all to the needs of modern civilization, if only these princes had ever had another ambition than becoming and remaining masters.

NOTES

(These are Tocqueville's own notes to his text.)

1. (p. 9) In particular, I have used the archives of some large intendancies, especially those of Tours, which are very full and are connected to an extensive region, situated in the centre of France and with a million inhabitants. At this point I owe my thanks to the clever young keeper of the record room, M. Grandmaison. Other regions (among others those of the Île-de-France) have shown me that events in most of the kingdom followed a similar pattern.

2. (p. 29) THE POWER OF ROMAN LAW IN GERMANY – THE WAY IT HAD REPLACED GERMANIC LAW

    At the end of the Middle Ages, Roman law became the chief and almost the only study of German jurists, most of whom pursued their education, at that time, outside Germany at Italian universities. These jurists, although they were not leaders of political society, were charged with clarifying and applying its laws. If they were unable to abolish Germanic law, they at least distorted it so as to make it fit the framework of Roman law. They applied Roman laws to everything in Germanic institutions that appeared to possess any remote parallel with Justinian's law code. Thus, they inserted a new spirit and new practices into the national legislation, which was gradually transformed in such a way that it became unrecognizable. In the seventeenth century, for example, it had lost its original shape, so to speak, and was replaced by something which was still vaguely Germanic in name but Roman in fact.

    I have reason to believe that, in the work of the jurists, many social conditions of the old Germanic society grew worse, notably those of the peasant farmers; several of these men, who had succeeded in retaining until then all or part of their freedom or possessions, lost them because of pedantic parallels to Roman slaves or hereditary tenants.

This gradual transformation of national law and the useless efforts expended to oppose it are very evident in the history of Württemberg.

From the birth of the county of that name in 1250 up to the creation of the Duchy in 1495, its legal system was entirely home grown. It was composed of customs, of local laws promulgated by towns or by manorial courts and of statutes formulated by estates. Only ecclesiastical matters were governed by foreign, that is to say, canon law.

From 1495, the character of the legal system alters: Roman law begins to intrude. The *Doctors*, as they were called, who had studied law in foreign schools, entered government and took over the management of the higher courts. Throughout the early part of the fifteenth century and through to the middle years, political society was seen to wage the same struggle against them as was taking place in the England of the same period but with quite a different outcome. In the Diet of Tübingen in 1514 and in those succeeding it, the representatives of feudalism and town deputies raised all manner of objections to what was happening. They attacked the jurists who were bursting into all the courts and changing the spirit or letter of every custom and every law. At first, they appeared to be holding the advantage; they obtained a promise from the government that from that time forward appointments to the higher courts should come from honourable and enlightened people chosen from the nobility and the Estates of the Duchy, not from the Doctors, and that a commission, comprising government agents and state representatives, should draw up a code of law which could stand as a guide throughout the country. What fruitless efforts! In the end, Roman law soon expelled entirely national law from a great area of legislation and planted its own roots on the very ground where it let this national legislation subsist.

This triumph of foreign law over home-grown law has been attributed to two causes by several German historians: firstly, to the movement which drew all minds at that time towards the languages and literature of the ancient world together with the contempt which that evoked for the intellectual achievements of the national genius; secondly, to the idea which had always preoccupied the whole German Middle Ages and which had surfaced in the law-making of that time, namely that the Holy Roman Empire was the continuation of the Roman Empire and that the legislation of the latter was inherited by the former.

However, these causes are not enough to make us understand how this same law should be introduced simultaneously throughout the whole continent of Europe. I believe that this resulted from the fact that the absolute power of rulers was being solidly established everywhere on the ruins of the old European freedoms along with the arrival of Roman law – a law of servitude – which wonderfully coincided with their own views.

Roman law, which improved civil society everywhere, has tended to degrade political society because it has been mainly the work of a very civilized and very subservient nation. Thus kings adopted it with enthusiasm and established it everywhere they were the masters. Those who interpreted this law became throughout Europe their ministers or their chief agents. Lawyers provided them, whenever the need arose, with legal support against the law itself. They have often done so since. Alongside a ruler bent upon abusing the law, it is seldom that a lawyer has not appeared on the scene to give assurances that nothing could be more lawful and to provide learned proof that the abuse was just and that the victims of oppression were in the wrong.

3.   (p. 30) THE TRANSITION FROM FEUDAL TO DEMOCRATIC
MONARCHY
Since monarchies had become absolute at about the same time, this change in the constitution hardly appears likely to have resulted from some particular circumstance present by accident in each state at the same moment and we can suppose that all these similar and simultaneous events must have been instigated by a universal cause in action everywhere equally and at once.

This universal cause was the transition from one social state to another, from feudal inequality to democratic equality. The nobles had already been knocked to the ground and the common people had not yet risen up; the former were too low, the latter not high enough to interfere with the activities of power. One hundred and fifty years had already passed as a golden age for kings during which they enjoyed both stability and complete power, things which usually cancel each other out. These kings were as sacred as the hereditary heads of a feudal monarchy and as absolute as the master of a democratic society.

4.   (p. 31) DECLINE OF FREE CITIES IN GERMANY – THE
IMPERIAL CITIES (REICHSSTÄDTE)
According to German historians these cities enjoyed the greatest period of brilliance during the fourteenth and fifteenth centuries. At that time, they were sanctuaries of wealth, the arts and

learning, the masters of European trade and the most powerful centres of civilization. Above all, in the north and south of Germany, they eventually formed independent confederations with the surrounding nobles, as the Swiss towns had done with the peasant farmers.

In the sixteenth century, they still retained their prosperity but the era of their decline had arrived. The Thirty Years War hastened on their final ruin. Scarcely a single town escaped destruction or ruin during this period.

However, the Treaty of Westphalia names them specifically and preserves their status as 'immediate states', that is to say, states dependent upon the emperor alone. But the rulers along their borders, on the one hand, and the emperor himself, on the other (whose power since the Thirty Years War could hardly be exercised except over these small imperial vassals), restricted their sovereignty within very narrow boundaries as the days went by. In the eighteenth century, they still numbered fifty-one and occupied two benches in the Diet and they had a separate vote; but in fact they no longer wielded any power over the management of general affairs.

Within their own ranks they were riddled with debts which came in part from the burden of tax by the Empire which they continued to pay according to their former splendour, in part from their poor management. And what is more remarkable is that this bad management seems to have been derived from a secret sickness that they all shared, whatever the shape of their constitution. Whether aristocratic or democratic, it gave rise to complaints which, if not similar, were at least equally virulent. Aristocracies, so it was said, had become the club of a small number of families in which patronage and private interests controlled everything.

Democracies were filled with intrigue and bribery. In both cases complaints were levelled at governments for the lack of honesty and selflessness. The emperor was constantly obliged to intervene in their affairs to try and restore order. They lost their populations and fell into poverty. They were no longer centres of German civilization; the arts abandoned them to shine in the new towns which were created by sovereigns and represented the new era. Trade shunned them; their former energy and patriotic strength disappeared. Hamburg, almost alone, remained a great centre of wealth and enlightenment but for reasons peculiar to itself.

5. (p. 36) DATE OF ABOLITION OF SERFDOM IN GERMANY
It will be clear from the following list that the abolition of serfdom in most German regions is very recent. Serfdom was
abolished in:
1. Baden only in 1783;
2. Hohenzollern in 1789;
3. Schleswig and Holstein in 1804;
4. Nassau in 1808;
5. Prussia. Frederick-William I had rid his domains of serfdom
    from 1717. Frederick the Great's own law code, as we have
    seen, claimed to have abolished it throughout his kingdom
    but, in reality, he removed only its harshest form, *Leibeigen-
    schaft*, while he kept its milder form, *Erbunterthänigkeit*.
    Only in 1809 did it completely cease to exist;
6. Bavaria, serfdom disappeared in 1808;
7. The Grand Duchy of Berg and in various other small terri-
    tories such as Erfurt, Bayreuth, etc., where a decree of
    Napoleon, dated Madrid 1808, abolished it.
8. The Kingdom of Westphalia, its destruction dates from
    1808–9;
9. The principality of Lippe-Detmolt, from 1809;
10. Schaumburg-Lippe, from 1810;
11. Swedish Pomerania from 1810 as well;
12. Hessen-Darmstadt from 1809 and from 1811;
13. Württemberg from 1817;
14. Mecklenburg from 1820;
15. Oldenburg from 1814;
16. Saxony, Lusatia, from 1832;
17. Hohenzollern-Sigmaringen from 1833 only;
18. Austria from 1811. In 1782 Joseph II had eliminated *Leib-
    eigenschaft*; but serfdom in its milder form – *Erbunter-
    thänigkeit* – lasted until 1811.
    There are some regions presently German, such as Branden-
burg, Old Prussia and Silesia, which were originally peopled by
Slavs and which have been conquered and partly occupied by
Germans. In these regions, serfdom always displayed a much
harsher aspect than in Germany and it left still greater marks
there at the close of the eighteenth century.
6. (p. 37) FREDERICK THE GREAT'S LAW CODE
Among Frederick the Great's works, the least known, even in his
own country, and the least brilliant, is the code drawn up on his
orders and promulgated by his successor. Yet I do not know

whether any other work casts more light upon the man himself and upon his times or better shows the reciprocal influence of the one upon the other.

This code is a real constitution in the sense granted to this term. Not only does it aim to regulate relations between citizens but also the relations of citizens and the state. It is a civil code, a criminal code and a charter all in one.

It rests, or appears to rest, upon a certain number of general principles, couched in a very philosophic and very abstract form, looking in many respects like those which fill the Declaration of the Rights of Man in the 1791 Constitution.

This code proclaims that the welfare of the state and its inhabitants is the aim of society and the limit of the law; that law can restrict the freedom and rights of citizens only in pursuit of the common good; that each member of the state should work for the general welfare in accordance with his position and his means; that the rights of individuals should yield to the good of all.

Nowhere is there any question of the hereditary rights of the ruler or his family, or even of individual rights which would be separate from the rights of the state. The name of the state is already the only one used to indicate the power of the king.

On the contrary, there is discussion of the universal rights of men. The universal rights of men are founded on the natural liberty to pursue one's own welfare without harming another's rights. All actions which natural law or positive state law do not prohibit are allowed. Each state citizen can demand that the state defend his person and his property; he has the right to defend himself by force if the state fails to come to his aid.

Having highlighted the lofty principles, the lawgiver, instead of drawing from them, as in the 1791 constitution, the dogma of the sovereignty of the people and the organization of a popular government inside a free society, turns sharply round and arrives at another conclusion equally democratic but not liberal. He considers the ruler to be the sole representative of the state and grants him all the rights which had just been seen as belonging to society. By this code, the sovereign is no longer the representative of God; he is only the representative of society, its agent, its servant, as Frederick signed himself for all to read in his works. But he represents it by himself and by himself he exercises all his powers. The chief of state, as it says in the introduction, who has the obligation to foster the good of all – which is the sole aim of society – is authorized to control and regulate all acts by individuals towards this goal.

Among the principle duties of this all-powerful agent of society, I find the following: to maintain public peace and security at home and to safeguard everyone from violence. Externally he possesses the right to make peace and war. He alone should create laws and establish general police regulations. He alone holds the right to pardon and to annul criminal prosecutions.

All associations which exist in the state, all public establishments, are under his scrutiny and control in the interest of peace and general security. So that the head of state may fulfil his obligations, he has to have certain revenues and useful rights. Therefore he has the power to establish taxes on private wealth, on individuals, on their professions, on their trade, on their produce or on their consumption. The orders of public officials acting in his name have to be obeyed as his own would in all matters within the scope of their functions.

From beneath this totally modern head we shall now see the appearance of a quite gothic body: what Frederick has removed is everything which might hinder the action of his own personal power. The whole document will take the shape of a monstrous creature which appears to be a compromise between two creations. In this strange production Frederick displays as much contempt for logic as concern for his power and a desire to avoid creating any useless difficulties by attacking anything with enough strength to defend itself.

The inhabitants of the countryside, with the exception of a few districts and certain localities, are placed in an hereditary enslavement which is not restricted simply to forced labour and those services attached to the ownership of certain lands but extends to the owner himself, as we have seen.

Most of the landowners' privileges are once again sanctified by the code or, it might even be said, in opposition to the code. For it is stated that, whenever the local customs and the new legislation are in conflict, it should be the former that are followed. It is formally declared that the state cannot destroy any of these privileges except by purchase or by the adoption of legal forms.

It is true that the code confirms that serfdom as properly understood (*Leibeigenschaft*), insofar as it establishes personal slavery, is abolished, but the hereditary subjection which replaces it (*Erbunterthänigkeit*) is still a kind of slavery, as we have been able to judge from reading the text.

In this same code the bourgeois remains assiduously separate from the peasant. Between the middle class and the nobility we can observe a sort of intermediate class, composed of high-ranking officials (who are not from the nobility), of churchmen, of professors of higher education, gymnasia and universities.

Furthermore, to remain apart from the middle class, these bourgeois were not, however, to be confused with the nobility in relation to whom, on the contrary, they stayed in an inferior position. In general, they could not purchase noble lands, nor obtain the highest posts in the civil service. Nor were they *hoffähig*, that is they could not be presented at court, except in rare cases, and never with their families.

As in France, this inferior position hurt all the more because the class was becoming more educated and influential and because these bourgeois state officials, while not holding the most illustrious posts, already occupied those where most of the work – and the most valuable at that – was transacted. The frustration felt against the privileges of the nobility which in France was to contribute so much to the Revolution, in Germany prepared the approval with which the Revolution was first welcomed. The chief author of the code was, however, a bourgeois. No doubt he was following his master's orders.

The old European constitution, despite the contempt Frederick felt for it, was not in a state of sufficient decay in this part of Germany for him to believe that it was yet time to sweep away the remnants. In general, he merely removed from the nobility their right to assemble and govern themselves as a body and he did not touch each individual's privileges; he simply restricted and regulated their use. Thus it turned out that this code, drawn up by the orders of a pupil of our French philosophers and implemented after the outbreak of the French Revolution, is the most authentic and the most recent legislative document to give lawful grounds for those same feudal inequalities which the Revolution was about to abolish throughout Europe.

The nobility is declared to be the first body in the state; noble-men were to be appointed by preference, so it states, to all honourable posts when they are capable of filling them. They alone may own noble lands, create entailments, enjoy hunting rights and legal rights belonging to noble property, as well as rights of patronage over churches. They alone may take the name of the estate that they own. Those members of the middle class who are allowed, by special exception, to own noble lands can enjoy the rights and honours attached to the ownership of such property only within the precise limits of this permission. Even if a bourgeois becomes the owner of noble land, he cannot bequeath it to a bourgeois heir unless he is heir in the first degree. Whenever he does not have such heirs or other noble heirs, the property has to be sold.

One of the most characteristic sections of Frederick's code is its criminal provisions for political offences, which is appended to it.

Frederick the Great's successor, Frederick-William II, despite the feudal and absolutist part of the legislation I have just portrayed, thought he could perceive in this work of his uncle revolutionary tendencies and suspended its publication until 1794. It was said that he was heartened only by considering the excellent measures in the code by help of which the worst principles it contained could be corrected. Never, in fact, have we seen since anything more comprehensive in this kind of writing. Not only are revolts and conspiracies punished with the greatest severity but any disrespectful criticisms of government acts are equally very harshly repressed. The purchase and distribution of dangerous writings are carefully prohibited – the printer, publisher and distributor are responsible for the author's work. Public balls, masquerades and other amusements are declared public meetings to be authorized by the police. It is the same even for public banquets. Freedom of the press and freedom of speech are narrowly subject to arbitrary supervision. It is forbidden to carry firearms.

Finally, throughout this work, half-borrowed from the Middle Ages, appear provisions whose extreme centralizing spirit borders on socialism. Thus it declares that it is incumbent on the state to see to the feeding, employing and paying of all those who cannot support themselves and who have neither rights to the lord's assistance nor to the help of the community; they must be assured of work appropriate to their fitness and competence. The state must provide establishments for relieving the poverty of the citizens. The state, in addition, is authorized to destroy those charitable foundations which tend to encourage laziness and itself to distribute to the poor the money these establishments possess.

The boldness and novelty in theory and the fearfulness in practice which characterize this work by Frederick the Great are evident everywhere. On the one hand the code proclaims the great principle of modern society that everyone should be equally subject to taxation; on the other, it allows the provincial laws to contain exemptions to this rule. It states that all lawsuits between a subject and the sovereign shall be judged according to due process and following the rules laid down for all other cases; in practice this rule was never followed whenever the interests or the passions of the king were opposed to it. The Mill of Sans-Souci was ostentatiously displayed but in several other circumstances justice was made to bend unnoticed.

The fact which proves how this code apparently conveyed so much innovation and in reality conveyed so little, and the fact which consequently makes it such a curious document to study in seeking to understand fully the true state of society in this part of Germany at the close of the eighteenth century, is that the Prussian nation appeared hardly to have noticed its publication. Only lawyers studied it and in our day a great number of educated people have never read it.

7.   (p. 39) PEASANT PROPERTY IN GERMANY
Among the peasants there were found families who were not only free and landowners but whose property constituted a type of permanent entail. The land owned by such people was indivisible and passed to one son only who was normally the youngest, as in certain English customs. He had only to pay a dowry to his brothers and sisters.

Hereditary estates of the peasant farmers were more or less to be found throughout the whole of Germany, for not all the land was obviously swallowed up by the feudal system. In Silesia, where the nobles have maintained up to our own day extensive estates to which most villages belonged, one would nevertheless come across villages owned entirely by the inhabitants and wholly free. In certain parts of Germany, such as the Tyrol and Frisia, the peasant farmers owned the land mainly on an hereditary basis.

But in the majority of German districts this kind of ownership was simply a more or less common exception to the rule. In those villages where this took place, the small landowners of this kind represented a sort of aristocracy among the peasantry.

8.   (p. 39) THE POSITION OF THE NOBILITY AND THE DIVISION
OF LAND ALONG THE RHINE
From information gathered on the spot and from people who had lived under the old regime, in the electorate of Cologne, for

example, the following can be established: there were a large number of villages without lords and administered by royal agents; in places where the nobility existed, its administrative powers were very limited; its position was rather more showy than powerful (at least, individually); it possessed many honours and took on the ruler's service but did not exercise real or direct power over the people. Moreover, I have become convinced that, in this same electorate, ownership was very much divided and that a large number of peasants became owners of land. This is attributed in particular to the state of penury and semi-poverty in which already a great many of the noble families had for a long time lived. These financial difficulties and needs forced them all the time to sell off a few small parcels of land to be acquired by peasants either for rent or for ready cash. I have had in my hands a list of the population of the bishopric of Cologne at the beginning of the eighteenth century in which the state of the land of that time is itemized. I have seen that from that time on a third of the land belonged to the peasants. From this state of affairs was born a collection of opinions and ideas which brought populations much nearer to revolution than those people who lived in other parts of Germany where these particular conditions had not yet been seen.

9. (p. 39) HOW THE LAW ON CHARGING INTEREST ON LOANS HAD ACCELERATED THE DIVIDING UP OF LAND
The law which prohibited lending with interest – no matter what the interest rate was – was still in force at the close of the eighteenth century. Turgot informs us that even in 1769 it was observed in many places. These laws persisted, he says, although they were often violated. Consular judges allowed interest without ceding the capital whereas ordinary courts condemned it. We still see dishonest debtors prosecuting their creditors in criminal court for having lent them money without ceding the capital.

Quite apart from the effects this legislation could not fail to have upon trade and upon industrial practice in general, it had a great effect upon the dividing up of land and the conditions of tenure. It had endlessly multiplied perpetual rents – ground rents along with others. Instead of borrowing in times of need, it had led the old landowners to sell off small plots from their estates either for a cash sum or in the shape of perpetual rents. This had contributed on the one hand to the splitting up of the land and on the other to burdening small landowners with a host of perpetual debts.

10. (p. 42) EXAMPLE OF THE STRONG FEELINGS ALREADY
    AROUSED BY TITHES TEN YEARS BEFORE THE REVOLUTION
    In 1779, a minor lawyer from Lucé complained in very bitter
    terms which already smacked of the Revolution that the priests
    and other major tithe-holders sold back to farmers at an exorbi-
    tant price the straw they had received as tithes and which they,
    the farmers, needed vitally for manuring their land.

11. (p. 42) EXAMPLE OF THE WAY THE CLERGY ALIENATED THE
    PEOPLE BY EXERCISING PRIVILEGES
    In 1780, the prior and canons of the priory of Laval complained
    of being made to pay duty on consumables and materials needed
    to repair their buildings. They claimed that, since the duty was
    the equivalent of a tithe and since they were exempt from paying
    it, they owed nothing. The minister told them to take their case
    to the local authority, with an appeal to the tax court.

12. (p. 42) FEUDAL RIGHTS POSSESSED BY PRIESTS. ONE
    EXAMPLE FROM A THOUSAND

The Abbey of Cherbourg (1753)

This abbey at that time owned manorial rights payable in cash
or goods throughout all the parishes in the vicinity of Cherbourg
– one parish alone owed three hundred and six bushels of wheat.
It owned the barony of Sainte-Geneviève, the barony and manorial mill of Bas-du-Roule and the barony of Neuville-au-Plein,
situated at least ten leagues away. It further received the tithes of
twelve parishes on the peninsula, several of which were located
very far away from it.

13. (p. 45) FRUSTRATIONS FELT BY THE PEASANTRY FROM
    FEUDAL RIGHTS AND THOSE IN PARTICULAR EXERCISED BY
    THE PRIESTHOOD
    A letter written just before the Revolution by a farmer to the
    Intendant himself does not carry any authority of proof for the
    accuracy of the facts it states but does indicate perfectly the state
    of mind of the class the writer belonged to:
       'Although we have few nobles in this area,' he says, 'it should
    not be supposed that landed property is any less encumbered
    with fees. On the contrary, almost all the fiefs belong to the
    cathedral, or to the archbishopric, or to the collegiate church of
    St Martin or to the Benedictines of Noirmontiers, of St Julien
    and to other clerics who never cancel any fees and who are
    constantly bringing to light old musty parchments concocted by
    God only knows!

The whole of this area is infected with dues. The greater part of the land owes annually a seventh of the wheat grown per acre; others owe wine. One man owes a quarter of the fruit to the manor; another man, a fifth, etc. In all cases, the tithe is taken first – now a twelfth, now a thirteenth. All these rights are so unusual that I know examples from a quarter of the produce down to a fortieth.

What should we think of all these payments in all types of grain, vegetables, money, poultry, forced labour, wood, fruit and candles? I have heard of strange payments in bread, wax, eggs, headless pigs, wreaths of roses, bunches of violets, gilded spurs, etc. Besides these there is a countless collection of other manorial dues. Why has France not been released from all these extravagant payments? Finally, we are starting to open our eyes and there is everything to hope for from the wisdom of the present government. It will proffer a helping hand to these poor victims of the demands of the old financial regime, called manorial rights, which we were never able to buy or sell.

What should we think of this tyranny called *lods et ventes*? A purchaser spends his last sou to acquire a property and is forced to pay large fees on adjudication and contracts when taking possession, written transcripts, stamp duty, registry, the hundredth penny, the eight sous per pound etc. And above all that he must present his contract to his lord who will make him pay *lods et ventes* on the capital outlay of his purchase – some charging a twelfth, others a tenth. Some claim a fifth; others a fifth and a twenty-fifth. Finally there are some who charge all the rates and I even know others who charge a third of the price paid. No, the most ferocious and the most barbarous nations of the known world have never invented such a set of extortions as our tyrants heaped upon the heads of our forefathers. (This philosophic and literary tirade has almost no grasp of spelling.)

What! Would the late king have allowed the repayment of ground rents on inherited property in the towns and not included those situated in the country? It was the latter he had to begin with. Why would he not allow poor farmers to break their chains, to buy back and free themselves from the manorial dues and ground rents which cause so much harm to vassals and bring such small profits to lords? There should not be any distinction between city and country repayments or between lords and individuals.

The managers of the holders of Church property, at each

change of ownership, rob the farmers and exact a contribution from them. We have a quite recent example of this. The manager of our new archbishop, on his arrival, announced that all the tenant farmers of his predecessor M. de Fleury would be turned out, declaring as null and void all the leases which they had contracted with him and throwing out of the door all those who were unwilling to double their lease payments or to pay large bribes which they had already paid to M. de Fleury's Intendant. Thus they had been deprived of the seven or eight years still remaining to them on their leases, legally executed. This forced them to quit immediately on Christmas Eve – a most critical time of year because of the difficulty of feeding their cattle – without any idea where they would live. The king of Prussia would have done nothing worse.'

In fact, it would appear that, in the case of Church property, the leases of the preceding title-holder created no legal obligation for any successor. The author of this letter highlights a well-established fact when he notes above that feudal rents in the towns could be redeemed even if they could not be in the country-side – a new proof of the abandonment of the peasant farmer and, by contrast, of the way in which all his superiors found methods of avoiding their obligations.

Any institution which has long been dominant, after it has established itself in its natural sphere of influence, moves beyond that sphere and finally exercises a great deal of sway upon the very area of legislation it does not govern. Feudalism, although it primarily belonged to political law, had transformed the whole of civil law and fundamentally altered the condition of men and property in every area of private life. It had acted on inheritances through inequality in dividing up estates, the principles for which had drifted down in certain provinces to the middle classes themselves (as Normandy testifies). It had, one might say, taken over all the real estate for there were scarcely any stretches of land situated entirely beyond its control or whose owners did not feel the consequences of its laws. Not only did it affect the property of individuals but also that of the townships. It impinged upon industry through the payments levied upon it. It impinged upon incomes by the inequality of taxation and in general upon the financial involvement of men in almost every area of business; upon landowners by the fees, payments and forced labour; upon the farmer in a thousand ways but among others by the mon-opolies, the land taxes, the *lods et ventes*, etc.; upon merchants by market dues; upon traders by the toll charges, etc. In knocking feudalism to the ground, the Revolution had, one might say, made itself both seen and felt at every tender point of an individual's concerns.

14. (p. 52) PUBLIC CHARITY GIVEN BY THE STATE – FAVOURITISM
In 1748, the king granted 20,000 livres of rice – that was a year of great distress and famine as were so many in the eighteenth century. The Archbishop of Tours claimed that he had been the one to obtain this help which should be distributed only by him and only in his diocese. The Intendant stated that the help had been granted to the whole area and should be distributed by him to all the parishes. After a prolonged struggle the king, to effect a reconciliation, doubled the amount of rice which he designated for the whole region so that the Archbishop and the Intendant might each distribute half. Both, however, agreed that the distribution would be made by parish priests – it was not a question of either lords or syndics. From the correspondence between the Intendant and the Controller-General, we can see that, according to the former, the Archbishop did not wish to give the rice to anyone but his favourites and notably to distribute the greater share to the parishes owned by the Duchess of Rochechouart. In addition, we find in this bundle, letters from important noblemen asking for special treatment for their parishes and letters from the Controller-General drawing attention to the parishes of certain individuals.

Legal charity gives rise to abuse whatever the system but it is impracticable when directed from a distance and without transparency by central government.

15. (p. 52) ONE EXAMPLE OF THE WAY THIS LEGAL CHARITY WAS GIVEN
In a report given before the provincial assembly of Upper Guyenne in 1780 we find the words: 'of the sum of 385,000 livres granted by his Majesty to this region from 1773 (the time of the establishment of charitable projects) to 1779 inclusive, the electoral district of Montauban, county town and residence of M. the Intendant, has, itself alone, received more than 240,000 livres, the greater part of which sum has been spent in the town of Montauban exclusively'.

16. (p. 53) POWERS OF THE INTENDANT TO REGULATE INDUSTRY
The archives of Intendancies are full of files which relate to the regulation of industry.

Not only was industry subjected to the hindrances imposed by state bodies, the guilds, etc., but was additionally victim of all the whims of government in the guise more often than not of general regulations from the Council and by the special administrative decisions of the Intendants who endlessly busied themselves with the length of cloth, the materials to choose, the methods to follow and the mistakes to avoid in manufacture. Leaving aside sub-delegates, they had under orders local industrial inspectors. Centralization had spread in this direction to an even greater degree than in our own day but was more unpredictable, more arbitrary; it produced swarms of public officials and generally gave rise to every kind of habit of submission and dependence.

Bear in mind that these habits were granted above all to the middle classes (merchants and traders who were going to triumph) much more than to those classes who would be the defeated. Therefore the Revolution was to spread the influence of these habits and to make them all-powerful rather than to destroy them.

All the above remarks have been suggested by the reading of numerous written letters and documents entitled: *Factories and workshops, cloth, drugs*. Such remarks are found in those papers which remain in the archive of the Île-de-France Intendancy. In the same place we find frequent and detailed reports addressed by the inspectors to the Intendant on visits made by them to manufacturers to see that rules laid down for work done had been followed. In addition we find Council decrees issued on the advice of the Intendant to prohibit or allow the manufacture of certain cloths whether at certain locations or made of specified fabrics or finally using certain processes.

The predominant feature of these remarks from these inspectors (who looked down on the manufacturer) is the idea that the duty and the right of the state are to force the latter to do the best possible not only in the public interest but also in his own. As a result they feel bound to make him adopt the best methods and to join forces with him in the smallest details of his trade. They tack on to all this a rich layer of violations and swingeing penalties.

17. (p. 54) THE SPIRIT OF LOUIS XI'S GOVERNMENT
No document can better convey an appreciation of the real spirit of Louis XI's government than the numerous constitutions granted by him to the towns. I have had the chance to study in particular those which most of the towns in Anjou, Maine and Touraine owe to him.

All these constitutions have been constructed on virtually the same model and the same plans emerge perfectly clearly from them. In them appears a portrait of Louis XI which is a little different from the one we know. The general opinion of this prince is that he was the enemy of the nobility while being, at the same time, the sincere though somewhat brutal friend of the people. In these constitutions he displays the same hatred for the political rights of the people as for the nobility. He exploits the middle classes to diminish those above them and to repress those below. He is both anti-aristocratic and anti-democratic; he is the bourgeois king par excellence. He loads the leading town citizens with privileges, thus wishing to increase their importance. He lavishes noble titles upon them, thus lowering their value. At the same time, he destroys the entire popular and democratic character of town administration, restricting the government to a small number of families committed to his reforms and tied to his power by huge favours.

18.   (p. 55) A TOWN GOVERNMENT IN THE EIGHTEENTH CENTURY
I have extracted the file relating to Angers from the inquiry conducted in 1764 upon the administration of towns. There we find the constitution of this town analysed, attacked and defended variously by the presidial, the town council, the sub-delegate and the Intendant. Since the same facts are mirrored in a great number of other places, we must see in this portrait a description far from unique.

Report of the presidial on the present state of the municipal constitution of Angers and the reforms to be enacted. 'The Angers town council,' said the presidial, 'almost never consults the general population, even for the most important projects, unless they are forced to by special orders. This administration is unknown to all those who do not belong to the town council, even the temporary aldermen who have only a very superficial grasp of things. (The tendency of all small bourgeois oligarchies was, in practice, to consult as little as possible what we are calling here the general population.)

The town council is made up of twenty-one officers following a decree of 29 March 1681:

A mayor raised to noble rank and whose duties last for four years.

Four temporary aldermen who remain in office for two years.

Twelve advisory aldermen who, once elected, serve for life.

Two city prosecutors.

One attorney.

One clerk of the court.

They had various privileges such as the following: their capitation tax was fixed at a modest level; they enjoyed exemption from providing lodging for troops or utensils or the supply of provisions or tax contributions; they enjoyed freedom from tax, from dues on double or triple wall divisions, from old and new excise duty, from the incidental costs on articles of consumption, even from the free gift from which they believed they were exempt because of private authority,' says the presidial; they have, besides, payment for candles and a few of them have salaries and free lodging.

We can observe from these details that it was a good thing to be a permanent alderman of Angers at that time. Take note that this system always and everywhere arranged for tax exemptions to fall on the most wealthy. Thus we find further on in this same report: 'These posts are coveted by the richest inhabitants whose ambition is to obtain a considerable reduction in capitation tax resulting in a surcharge which falls upon the other citizens. At the present time there are several municipal officials whose capitation tax is fixed at 30 livres when they ought to pay 250 to 300 livres. One of them could pay at least 1000 livres of tax considering his wealth.' We find in another place in the same report: 'that among the wealthiest citizens we encounter more than forty officials or the widows of officials whose offices grant them the privilege of not paying the considerable capitation tax imposed on the city; the burden of this tax falls upon a countless number of poor tradesmen who, believing themselves overtaxed, constantly complain against their excessive contributions. Such complaints are groundless because there is no unfairness in the way the rest of the city tax burden is divided up.

The *General Assembly* is made up of seventy-six people:

The mayor,

Two deputies of the cathedral chapter,

One syndic from the clergy,

Two deputies from the presidial,

One deputy from the university,

A lieutenant-general of police,

Four aldermen,

Twelve permanent aldermen,

One royal prosecutor at the presidial,

One city prosecutor,

Two deputies from the Streams and Forests Department,
Two from the electoral district,
Two from the salt warehouse,
Two from the tax collectors,
Two from the mint,
Two from the company of lawyers and attorneys,
Two from the town judges,
Two from the solicitors,
Two from the guild of merchants,
Lastly two deputies from each of the sixteen parishes.

These last were considered to represent the people properly speaking and in particular the trade guilds. It can be observed that things were arranged to keep them permanently in a minority.

Whenever positions became vacant in the town council, the General Assembly chose three candidates for each vacancy.

Most of the positions on the town council were not allocated to fixed professions as I have observed in several other municipal constitutions; in other words the electors were not obliged to choose either a magistrate or a lawyer, etc. This was thought to be very bad by the members of the presidial.

According to this same presidial, which seemed exercised by the most violent jealousy of the town council and which I strongly suspect of objecting to having too few privileges in the municipal constitution, 'the General Assembly, being too numerous and partly composed of unintelligent people, should be consulted only in cases of the disposing of town property, loans, the setting up of tax dues and the election of municipal officials. All other business could be discussed in a smaller assembly, composed of notables. The only people who could be members of this assembly were the lieutenant of the Seneschalsy, the royal prosecutor and twelve other notables chosen from the six groups – the clergy, the judiciary, the nobility, the university, businessmen and the middle class – and others not belonging to these groups. The choice of notables would on the first occasion be granted to the General Assembly; thereafter to the assembly of notables itself or to the group from which each notable has to be chosen.'

All these state officials, who thus entered the municipal government as holders of office or notables, often resemble those we have today either by the titles of the office they performed or sometimes even by the nature of that office. But they were quite different from them in their position. This is a fact we must note with care, if we wish to avoid quite erroneous conclusions.

Almost all these officials had been, in effect, city notables before being invested with public office or had striven for public office in order to become a notable. They had had no idea of leaving the city or any hope of further promotion, all of which was enough to make them entirely different from what we know today.

Report of the municipal officials. In this report we see that the town council had been created in 1474 by Louis XI on the ruins of the town's former democratic constitution and always following the system outlined above, namely a restriction of most political rights in the hands of the middle class alone; the removal or weakening of the people; a great number of municipal officials in order to involve more members of society in matters of reform; a profusion of hereditary titles and privileges of all kinds granted to that section of the bourgeoisie that conducted the administration.

We find in this same report letters patent from the successors of Louis XI who acknowledged this new constitution while still restricting the power of the common people. We learn that, in 1485, letters patent granted for this purpose by Charles VIII had been attacked by the townsfolk of Angers in the *parlement*, exactly as in England lawsuits would have been presented to a court of law relating to the charter of a town. In 1601, it was once more a decree of the *parlement* which set the political rights arising from the royal charter. From then on it is only the Royal Council which features.

The consequence of this same report was that, not only for the positions of mayor but for all other posts, the General Assembly put forward three candidates from whom the king made his choice by virtue of an order in council of 22 June 1708. Yet another consequence was that, by virtue of orders in council of 1733 and 1741, tradesmen had the right to one place as an alderman or councillor (that is, a permanent alderman). Finally, we discover that at that time the town council had been given responsibility for the division of the sums to be raised for the capitation tax, the equipment, the billeting of the military, the support for the poor, for the troops, coastguards and waifs and strays.

There follows a very long list of the burdens which municipal officials had to fulfil and which, according to them, amply justified the privileges and their permanent status which we can see they were very frightened of losing. Several reasons they give for their work are strangely interesting, such as these: 'Their most essential occupations,' they state, 'consist in the scrutiny of financial questions constantly on the increase because of the endless extensions to the aid dues, salt tax, stamp and registry dues, the illegal collection of registry dues and freehold dues. The endless disputes raised by the financial companies concerning the various taxes have forced them to pursue lawsuits on behalf of the town, before different courts, from *parlement* to Royal Council, in order to stand up to the oppressive practices under which the town is forced to groan. The experience of thirty years of public service has taught that a man's span of life is hardly sufficient to ward off the ambushes and pitfalls which the agents of the tax farmers are continuously laying before the citizens so as to preserve their brokers fees.'

What is strange is that all these things were written to the Controller-General himself to persuade him to look favourably upon the continuation of the privileges of those who were speaking to him, so deeply embedded was the habit of regarding the companies responsible for collecting taxes as an enemy whom everyone could attack from all sides without objection from anyone. In the end, this habit, as it spread and gradually grew stronger, cemented the view of the Treasury as an untrustworthy and odious tyrant; not everyone's agent but a common enemy.

The same report adds: 'All offices were first joined together into a town council by a Royal Council decree of 4 September 1694 in return for 22,000 livres.' That indicates that the offices had been redeemed that year for that sum. By the decree of 26 April 1723, the municipal offices, created by the decree of 24 May 1722, had been once again joined together into the town council; in other words, the town had been allowed to buy them back. By another decree of 24 May 1723, the town had been allowed to borrow 120,000 livres for the purchase of these said offices. Another order of 26 July 1728 had granted permission for a loan of 50,000 livres to buy back the offices of the clerical secretary in the town hall. 'The town,' it says in the report, 'has paid the money to preserve the freedom of its elections and to allow its elected officials to enjoy, some for two years, others for life, the various prerogatives attached to their jobs.' When some of the municipal offices had been established by the edict of November 1733, a Royal Council decree, requested by mayors and permanent aldermen, intervened on 11 January 1751 to dictate that the sum for redemptions was fixed at 170,000 livres.

This purchase granted the suspension of city tolls for fifteen years.

This is a good example of the administrative practices of the Ancien Régime concerning towns. They were forced to incur debts, then authorized to impose extraordinary and temporary taxes to bale themselves out. And to that must be added that these temporary taxes became permanent, as I have so often observed and, at that point, the government has taken its cut.

The report continues: 'The municipal officials have been deprived of those great legal powers granted to them by Louis XI only by the setting up of royal courts.' Until 1669, they had jurisdiction over disputes between employers and workers. The accounts of the town tolls are presented to the Intendant according to all the decrees which created or renewed these said tolls.

Equally we see in this report that the deputies from the sixteen parishes dealt with above and present in the General Assembly were chosen by guilds, corporate bodies and communities and were strictly representative of the small group which sent them. They had binding instructions on every item of business.

Finally, this whole report reveals that in Angers, as everywhere else, every kind of expenditure had to be authorized by the Intendant and the Council. We must recognize that, whenever the sole ownership of the administration of a town was given to a few men and whenever these men were granted privileges instead of fixed salaries, exempting them personally from the consequences that their administration may have upon the private fortunes of their fellow citizens, central administrative supervision can appear a necessity. The whole report, which is furthermore badly drawn up, discloses on the part of the officials an unusual fear of seeing any changes in the existing state of affairs. Every sort of good and bad reason is gathered in by them in the interests of maintaining the status quo.

The sub-delegate's report. The Intendant had received these two contradictory reports and thus wished to sound out the opinion of his sub-delegate who gave it in his turn.

'The report of the municipal officials does not deserve any attention; its intention is merely to justify these officials' privileges. The one from the presidial may be usefully consulted; but there is no reason for granting all the prerogatives claimed by these magistrates.'

According to this sub-delegate, the town hall administration had long needed some improvements. Beyond the immunities which we already know about and which the municipal officials of Angers already possessed, he tells us that, during his term of office, the mayor enjoyed housing worth 600 francs rent at least, as well as 50 francs in salary, and 100 francs for expenses and fees. The prosecutor-syndic also had housing, as did the town clerk. In order to obtain exemption from the aid dues and tolls, the municipal officials had established for each of them a presumed level of consumption. Each man could annually allow entry into the town, free from dues, so many barrels of wine and similarly all their fresh goods.

The sub-delegate did not suggest removing the tax immunities from the municipal officials but he would like to have had their capitation tax, instead of being fixed and inadequate, settled by the Intendant each year. He wished that these same officials should be subject like the others to the free gift contribution, their exemption from which depended on heaven knows what precedent.

The municipal officials, the report says again, were responsible for the compilation of the capitation tax lists for the citizens. This they performed carelessly and arbitrarily. Thus, annually, there were a host of complaints and requests addressed to the Intendant. It would have been desirable, from then on, for this division to be decided in the interests of each guild or community by its members in a general and set manner. The municipal officials would have remained responsible only for the capitation tax list of the middle classes and others who belonged to no recognized body, such as a few tradesmen and the servants of the privileged.

The sub-delegate's report confirms what the municipal officials had already stated, namely that the municipal offices had been repurchased by the town in 1735 for the sum of 170,000 livres.

Letter from the Intendant to the Controller-General. Armed with all these documents, the Intendant wrote to the minister: 'It is important,' he says, 'to the citizens and the public interest to reduce the size of the town council whose too large numbers have become an infinite burden on the public because of the privileges enjoyed.'

The Intendant continues: 'I am struck by the enormous size of the sums paid out in all periods to redeem the town offices in Angers. The total amount if spent for useful purposes would have profited the town which, on the contrary, simply experienced the burden of the authority and the privileges of these officials.

The internal abuses of this administration deserve the whole attention of the Royal Council,' the Intendant goes on to say, 'leaving aside the fees and the candles which absorb the annual sum of 2,127 livres (which was the sum noted for these kinds of expenses by the normal budget imposed on the towns by the king from time to time), the public coffers are wasted and used at the bidding of these officials for secret purposes. The royal prosecutor having held his post for thirty or forty years has made himself the master of the administration to such an extent that he alone knows how things work, thus making it impossible for citizens ever to obtain the smallest amount of information about the use of these communal revenues.' As a result, the Intendant requested the minister to reduce the town council to one mayor appointed for four years, to six permanent aldermen appointed for six years, to a royal prosecutor appointed for eight years, to one town clerk and to one rate-collector, both permanent posts.

In other respects the constitution proposed by him for this town council is exactly that proposed elsewhere by the same Intendant for Tours. According to him it is necessary:

1. To preserve the General Assembly but solely as an electoral body which would choose the municipal officials;
2. To establish an extraordinary Council of Notables which would have the duty of fulfilling all the functions granted to the General Assembly by the 1764 edict. This council was to be composed of twelve members whose term would last six years and who would be elected not by the General Assembly but by the twelve bodies deemed to be notable (each body electing his own member). He lists as notable bodies the following:

The presidial,
The university,
The electoral district,
The officials from the Streams and Forests Department,
The salt warehouse,
The tax collectors,
The mint,
The lawyers and attorneys,
The town judges,
The solicitors,
The merchants,
The middle class.

As we have noticed, almost all these notables were public servants and all these public servants were notables. From this we might conclude that, as in a thousand other places in these files, the middle classes were then as keen for government positions as today they are lukewarm about any field of activity outside public positions. The only difference was, as I have said in the text, that at that time the trivial importance conferred by public positions was bought whereas today job-seekers ask the favour of being given such positions for nothing.

We can see in this project that the entire reality of municipal power was vested in this extraordinary council which ended by squeezing the administration into one very small collection of middle-class citizens. The only assembly where the common people continued to put in a slight appearance was no longer responsible for anything except the election of town officials and no longer had any advice to give them. Again we must observe that the Intendant was more restrictive and anti-commoner than the king who had appeared in his decree to grant the main functions to the General Assembly and that, in his turn, the Intendant was much more liberal and democratic than the middle classes, at least to judge from the report I have quoted in this text. This report indicated that the notables of another town even had it in mind to exclude common people from the election of the town officials which the king and Intendant had left to them.

It is possible to note that the Intendant uses the terms *bourgeois* and *merchants* to define two distinct categories of notables: it is useful to give an exact definition of these terms to demonstrate the number of small components into which the bourgeoisie was divided and how many small vanities were at work among them.

The term 'bourgeois' had both a general and a restricted meaning: it stood for the members of the middle classes and furthermore designated a certain number of men at the heart of this class. 'The bourgeois are people whose birth and wealth allow them to live comfortably without the need to work for money,' states one of the reports produced for the 1764 inquiry. From the rest of the report we can see that the term 'bourgeois' should not be applied to men who belonged to trade guilds or industrial companies but it is a much more difficult task to say what it should apply to in precise terms. The same report also notes: 'For among those who claim the title of bourgeois, we quite often come across people it cannot appropriately describe except for their life of leisure alone; for the rest they have no wealth and lead an undistinguished and uneducated life. The bourgeois should, on the contrary, always be distinguished by their wealth, talents, manners and way of life. The tradesmen who make up the guilds have never been summoned to the rank of notable.'

The merchants were, along with the bourgeois, the second kind of men who belonged neither to a trade company nor corporation. But what were the limits of this small class? 'Should we,' says the report, 'confuse the shopkeepers from a low background and possessed of little business experience with the wholesalers?' To resolve these difficulties the report suggests an annual list of notable shopkeepers drawn up by the aldermen which will be sent to their leader or syndic to enable him to summon to town hall deliberations only those on the list. Care would be taken to mention on this list no one who had been domestic servants or peddlers or carters nor anyone engaged in other lowly trades.

19. (p. 57) One of the most striking features of the eighteenth century with respect to town administration was less the abolition of all representation and any intervention of the public in government business than the extreme instability of the rules controlling this administration since rights were granted, then withdrawn, returned, increased, diminished and endlessly altered in a thousand ways. Nothing reveals better the degradation into which these local freedoms had fallen than the constant shifts in their laws to which no one seemed to pay attention. This mobility alone would be enough to destroy in advance any individual ideas, any feeling for the past, any local patriotic fervour in the institution which is best suited to it. Thus preparations were being made for the great destruction of the past which the Revolution was about to instigate.

20. (p. 58) A VILLAGE GOVERNMENT IN THE EIGHTEENTH CENTURY, TAKEN FROM THE PAPERS OF THE INTENDANCY OF THE ÎLE-DE-FRANCE

The situation I am about to mention is taken from many others in order to show as an example some of the forms followed by parish government, to demonstrate the slowness which often characterized it and to reveal the nature of a General Assembly in an eighteenth-century parish.

The matter concerns the repair of the priest's house and the church steeple in a country parish, namely Ivry, Île-de-France. To whom should application be addressed to obtain permission for these repairs? How should it be decided who was to pay for them? How should the necessary funds be procured?

1) A request from the priest to the Intendant to highlight the urgent need for repairs to church steeple and priest's house, saying that his predecessor had had useless buildings added to the said priest's house which had completely altered and deformed the character of the site and that, since the villagers had allowed this to happen, it was up to them to bear the expense of putting things back in order, along with recovering the sum needed from the heirs of the previous priest.

2) A ruling from my Lord the Intendant (29 August 1747) which orders that an assembly should be summoned at the request of the syndic to discuss the need for the claimed repairs.

3) Discussion by the villagers by which they declare no opposition to the repair of the priest's house but only to that of the church steeple seeing that this steeple is constructed above the choir and that the priest as receiver of the great tithe is responsible for the repair of the choir. (A council decree from the end of the previous century (April 1695) tied the repair of the choir to whomsoever held the right to collect the tithes from the parish, while the parishioners were responsible for the maintenance of the nave only.)

4) New ruling from the Intendant who, considering the conflict of claims, sends an architect, M. Cordier, to visit and examine the priest's house and church steeple, to draw up an estimate for the work and instigate an inquiry.

5) A report of all these dealings which notably states that at the inquiry a certain number of landowners in Ivry stood in the presence of the Intendant's envoy. These people appeared to be gentlemen, bourgeois and local peasant farmers and gave evidence for or against the priest's claims.

6) Fresh ruling from the Intendant directing that the estimates drawn up by the architect he sent should be laid before the landowners and villagers at a new assembly summoned at the syndic's request.

7) A new parish assembly resulting from this ruling, at which the villagers declare that they still adhere to their views.

8) A ruling from my Lord the Intendant which stipulates i) that in the presence of his sub-delegate in Corbeil, in his house,

the contract for the works shown on the estimate shall be presented and confirmed before the priest, syndic and chief inhabitants of the parish; ii) that, given the perilous state of the building, a tax for the whole sum shall be levied upon the villagers except that those who persist in believing that the steeple is part of the choir and should be repaired by the main tithe-holder can lodge an appeal before the ordinary courts.

9) A notice to all parties to attend at the sub-delegate's house in Corbeil where the bids shall be made and the contract decided.

10) Request from the priest and several villagers to ask that the expenses resulting from the administrative procedures should not be placed, as was normal, upon the contractor since these costs amounted to a high figure and were bound to stop them finding a contractor.

11) Ruling from the Intendant which directs that the expenses incurred by the issue of a contract shall be settled by the sub-delegate so that the total sum shall be part of the contract and the tax levied.

12) Authority given by certain village notables to M. X to be present at the said contract and to agree to it according to the wishes of the architect's estimates.

13) Certificate from the syndic directing that the usual notices and advertisements have been posted.

14) Transcript of the contract:
Total sum for the repairs   487 livres
Expenses incurred pertaining 237 livres 18s 6d
                                               724 livres 18s 6d

15) Finally, a decree in Council (23 July 1748) to authorize the tax intended to cover this sum.

We may note that there were several occasions in this affair when it was a question of summoning the parish assembly. Here are the minutes of the conduct of one of these assemblies. This will show the reader how things generally happened on such occasions.

Act drawn up by the notary: 'Today, at the close of the parish mass, in the usual and customary place, after the ringing of the bell, there appeared in the assembly held by the villagers of the said parish, before M. X, the notary from Corbeil, the undersigned and the witnesses named hereafter, M. Michaud, winegrower, syndic of the said parish who presented the Intendant's directive authorizing the assembly, had it read out and requested action at his behest.

'And there and then appeared a villager from the said parish who stated that the steeple stood above the choir and consequently was the responsibility of the priest; there also appeared . . . (here follow the names of some others who, taking a contrary view, agreed to support the priest's request), then fifteen peasants appeared, labourers, masons and winegrowers who declared their agreement with the preceding persons. Then M. Raimbaud, winegrower, stood before them saying that he was in complete agreement with whatever the Intendant would decide. M. X also appeared, a doctor of the Sorbonne, a priest, who persisted in the content and conclusions of the request. Those attending have requested action – done and passed in the said place of Ivry in front of the cemetery of the said parish, in the presence of the undersigned. This has been dealt with by the report of the notary present from eleven o'clock in the morning to two in the afternoon.'

We can see that this parish assembly is simply an administrative inquiry with the procedures and costs of judicial inquiries. It never concludes in a vote nor, consequently, in the manifestation of the will of the parish. It contains only individual opinions and in no way constricts the decisions of the government. Many other documents inform us in fact that parish assemblies were created to clarify the Intendant's decisions, not to check them, even when the interest of the parish was involved.

We note equally in the same documents that this affair gives rise to three inquiries: one in the presence of the notary, a second before the architect and, finally, a third before two notaries to ascertain whether the villagers persist in their earlier statements.

The tax of 524 livres 10s ordered by the decree of 23 July 1748 bore upon all landowners, privileged or not, but the basis used to divide the share of it among them was different. Those eligible for the *taille* were taxed in proportion to that tax whereas the privileged paid with respect to their presumed wealth which bequeathed a great advantage to the latter over the former.

Finally we can see, in this same episode, that the division of the sum of 524 livres 10s was made up by two tax collectors, inhabitants of the village, neither elected, nor chosen when their turn came round as is most often the case, but chosen and appointed for the post by the sub-delegate and the Intendant.

The pretext used by Louis XIV to destroy the municipal

freedom of towns had been the poor management of their financial affairs. However, the same situation, as Turgot rightly stated, persisted and became worse from the moment of this ruler's reform. He added that most towns at that time were heavily in debt partly because of the funds they had loaned to the government and partly through the expenses and decorations which the town officials – who handle other people's money and do not have to render account to the citizens or to receive any instructions from them – multiplied with a view of gaining personal prestige and sometimes of lining their own pockets.

21. (p. 62) THE STATE WAS GUARDIAN OF THE CONVENTS AS WELL AS THE TOWNS; AN EXAMPLE OF THIS SUPERVISION
When the Controller-General authorized the Intendant to pay over 15,000 livres to the Carmelite convent to which money was owed, he recommended that the Intendant should reassure himself that this money, which represented capital, would be usefully invested. Similar events happened all the time.

22. (p. 68) HOW IT WAS IN CANADA THAT ONE COULD BEST JUDGE THE ADMINISTRATIVE CENTRALIZATION OF THE ANCIEN RÉGIME
It is in the colonies that we can best judge the shape of metropolitan governments because there all the features which characterize them are normally exaggerated and become more obvious. When I wish to judge the spirit of Louis XIV's administration and its defects, I must go to Canada, where the misshapen aspects of the object can be seen as under a microscope.

In Canada a host of obstructions which past factors or the previous social state had placed, either openly or secretly, in the way of the free development of the government's ideas, did not exist. The nobility was almost non-existent, or at least had lost almost all its roots. The Church no longer held its dominant position. Feudal traditions had disappeared or receded into the shadows. The legal system was no longer rooted in ancient institutions and customs. Nothing stopped the central power from indulging all its natural inclinations or from shaping all the laws in harmony with the ethos which gave it inspiration. In Canada, therefore, there was not a shadow of town or provincial institutions; no collective force was authorized, no individual initiative allowed. An Intendant occupied a position which was powerful in quite a different way from his counterparts in France. The administration still meddled in many more things than in metropolitan France and wished to control everything from Paris despite the eighteen hundred leagues which separated them. Canada never adopted the great principles which enable a colony to increase its population and its wealth. Quite to the contrary it employed every kind of petty artificial device and petty regulatory tyranny to expand and spread the population: forced methods of farming; all the lawsuits springing from land concessions were withdrawn from the courts and returned to the arbitration of the government alone; the requirement to cultivate in a particular way; the obligation to live in certain places rather than others, etc. All those things occurred under Louis XIV and those edicts were countersigned by Colbert. One might already imagine one-self in the heart of a modern centralized state or in Algeria. Canada was, in effect, the faithful image of what has always been seen there. In both places we are in the presence of an administration which is almost as numerous as the population – dominant, energetic, regulatory, restrictive, anxious to anticipate everything, taking everything over, always more aware of the concerns of the governed than they are themselves, endlessly on the move and sterile.

In the United States, the English system of decentralization went beyond limits: the townships became almost independent municipalities, kinds of democratic republics. The republican element which constitutes the basis of English government and customs surfaces and develops with no opposition. The so-called administration achieves little in England while individuals achieve a great deal. In America, the administration interferes in nothing while individuals unite together to do everything. The absence of an upper class, while making the Canadian still more obedient to the government than was the Frenchman during the same period, made the citizen of the English provinces increasingly independent of central authority.

In both colonies, they ended up with the establishment of a wholly democratic society whereas in Canada, at least as long as it remained in French hands, equality fused with absolute government. In America, equality was linked with freedom. As for tangible results from both colonial systems, we know that in 1763, at the time of the conquest, the population of Canada stood at 60,000 souls whereas that of the English provinces stood at 3 million.

23. (p. 69) ONE EXAMPLE AMONG MANY OTHERS OF THE ENDLESS GENERAL REGULATIONS CREATED BY THE COUNCIL OF STATE WHICH CARRIED THE FORCE OF LAW

THROUGHOUT FRANCE AND ESTABLISHED SPECIAL
OFFENCES WHICH COULD BE DEALT WITH ONLY BY
ADMINISTRATIVE COURTS

I take the first that come to hand: decree of the Council 29 April
1779 which establishes that in the future throughout the kingdom, ploughmen and wool merchants will have to mark their
sheep in a certain way on pain of a 300 livres fine. 'His Majesty
orders the Intendant to see to the execution of this decree,' it
says. Consequently, it is up to the Intendant to settle the penalty
for any contravention. Another example: decree of the Council
21 December 1778 which prohibits waggoners and carters from
warehousing the goods they are carrying on pain of a 300 livres
fine. 'His Majesty orders the lieutenant-general of police and his
Intendant to see to it.'

24. (p. 78) The provincial assembly of Upper Guyenne demanded
vociferously new brigades of mounted police in absolutely the
same way that, these days, the general council of Aveyron or Lot
probably seeks the establishment of new brigades of gendarmes.
Always the same idea: gendarmes mean order and order cannot
be achieved except with gendarmes via the government. The
report adds: 'There are complaints daily that the countryside has
no police (how could there be? The nobleman is not involved in
anything, the bourgeois is in town and the community furthermore, in the guise of a coarse peasant, has no power) and we
must admit that, with the exception of a few cantons where
fair-minded and benevolent lords use the power over their vassals
created by their position to anticipate these assaults to which
country folk are naturally drawn because of the crudeness of
their ways and the harshness of their character, nowhere else
does there exist any means of constricting these ignorant, coarse
and hot-headed men.'

    That is the way in which the nobles of the provincial assembly
allowed people to refer to themselves and in which the members
of the Third Estate, who alone formed half the assembly, referred
to the people in public documents!

25. (p. 79) Tobacco licences were as sought after under the Ancien
Régime as now. The most important people sought them for
their dependants. Some, I find, were granted on the recommenda-
tion of society ladies, others at the request of archbishops.

26. (p. 80) This disappearance of all local public life had gone beyond
what was credible. One of the roads leading from Maine to
Normandy was impassable. Who asks for it to be repaired? The

district of Touraine which it crosses? The province of Normandy or Maine who are so involved in the business of moving cattle on this route? Some canton which is especially harmed by the poor condition of this road? The district, the province, the cantons have no voice. The traders following this road and sinking into its mud must take it upon themselves to draw the attention of central government in their direction. They wrote to the Controller-General in Paris begging him to come to their help.

27. (p. 87) GREATER OR LESSER IMPORTANCE OF MANORIAL
      DUES AND PAYMENTS ACCORDING TO THE PROVINCE
Turgot says in his works: 'I must remark that the importance of these kinds of payments is very different in most wealthy provinces, such as Normandy, Picardy and the environs of Paris. In these, the main source of wealth comes from the very produce of the land which is divided into large farms from which landowners draw high rents. The manorial dues of the largest estates amount to only a modest share of the revenues and this sum is considered as almost honorary. In the less wealthy provinces, farmed on different principles, the lords and nobles own almost no land themselves. Inheritances, which are much subdivided, are weighed down with heavy grain payments, which burden all the co-tenants equally. These dues often swallow up the best part of the land's produce and the lord's income derives almost wholly from them.'

28. (p. 93) THE INFLUENCE OF DISCUSSION OF SHARED
      INTERESTS WORKS AGAINST CLASS DIFFERENCES
We can see from the unimportant work of agricultural societies in the eighteenth century that shared discussion of common interests militated against class differences. Although these meetings took place thirty years before the Revolution when the Ancien Régime still thrived, and although it was merely a question of theory – by the very fact that people debated questions in which the different classes felt involved and which were discussed together – the closeness and fusion of men are immediately felt and we can see the idea of reasonable reform taking hold on the privileged as on others. Yet it only involved questions of conservation and agriculture.

I am convinced that only a government which never sought strength outside itself and always treated men as separate units, as did that of the Ancien Régime, could have upheld the ridiculous and senseless inequality existing in France at the time of the Revolution. The slightest contact with *self-government* would have profoundly altered and speedily transformed or destroyed it.

29.   (p. 93) Freedoms at a provincial level can survive for some time without there being freedom at a national level, whenever such freedoms are ancient, linked with habits, customs and memories and when despotism on the other hand is new. But it is unreasonable to believe that we can create local freedoms at will or even maintain them for long when we suppress general freedom.

30.   (p. 94) Turgot, in a report to the king, summarized in the following, and for me, very accurate way, the real extent of the nobles' privileges in relation to tax.

    1) 'The privileged are able to manage an exemption from any imposition of tax for any farm which uses four ploughs which, in the environs of Paris, normally carries 2,000 francs of taxes.

    2) These same privileged persons pay absolutely nothing for woodland, pastures, vineyards, ponds, any more than for enclosed lands which belong to their chateaux whatever their size. There are cantons whose main source of production comes from pastures or vines. Then the lord who has his lands managed frees himself from all tax burdens which fall upon those who pay the taille. This second advantage is immense.'

31.   (p. 94) INDIRECT PRIVILEGES IN MATTERS OF TAX. THE DIFFERENCES IN TAX COLLECTION EVEN WHEN THE TAX IS DUE FROM ALL ALIKE

Turgot once again draws a picture of this which I have reason to believe is accurate according to the documents:

'The indirect advantages for the privileged with respect to the capitation tax are very considerable. By its very nature the capitation is an arbitrary tax. It is impossible to divide it up among the total population other than blindly. It was thought more convenient to take the ready-made records of the *taille* as a starting point. A special roll was drawn up for the privileged classes but, since they can defend themselves and those burdened with the *taille* have no one to speak for them, the capitation of the former gradually lessens in the provinces to an excessively small sum while the capitation of the latter is almost the same as the amount demanded by the *taille*.'

ANOTHER EXAMPLE OF THE UNEQUAL COLLECTION OF A COMMON TAX. We know that in local taxes the money was raised on everyone. 'These sums,' stated the orders in Council authorizing these kinds of expenditure, 'shall be raised from all those eligible, exempt or non-exempt, privileged or not, without exception, together with the capitation or in proportion to it.'

Notice that, since the capitation of the *taille* payers, together with the *taille* itself, always rose proportionately higher than that of the privileged, inequality was present in the very scheme which seemed to exclude it.

SAME SUBJECT. I find in the proposed bill of 1764, which was leaning towards establishing equality of taxation, all kinds of provisions aiming to preserve a special category for the privileged classes when it came to the collection of taxes. In it I note, among other matters, that all measures concerned with settling the value of taxable property in the case of the privileged classes could not be taken except in their presence or in that of their authorized representatives.

32. (p. 94) HOW THE GOVERNMENT ITSELF RECOGNIZED THAT THE PRIVILEGED CLASSES WERE ADVANTAGED IN THE COLLECTION OF TAXES EVEN WHEN THE TAX WAS DUE FROM ALL ALIKE

The minister wrote in 1766: 'I can see that the most difficult aspect of the taxes which have to be collected resides in the debts owed by the nobility and the privileged and this is because of the consideration which the tax-collectors feel obliged to display towards them. The result of this is that long-standing and far too large arrears exist with respect to their capitation and *vingtième* (taxes they shared with the common people).'

33. (p. 104) We find in Arthur Young's *Journey* in '89 a brief portrait in which the condition of the two societies is so pleasantly depicted and so well outlined that I cannot resist the urge to include it here.

When Young was travelling through France immersed in the initial feelings brought on by the fall of the Bastille, he was arrested in a certain village by a crowd of people who wished to throw him into prison since he was not wearing the revolutionary cockade on his hat. To extricate himself from this situation he took it into his head to give this small speech:

'Gentlemen,' he said, 'it has just been said that taxes must be paid as before. Of course, taxes must be paid but not like before. They should be paid as they are in England. We have many taxes which you do not have but the Third Estate, the common people, does not pay them; they fall upon the rich only. In our country we pay for every window but the man with only six windows in his house pays nothing. A lord pays the *vingtième* and the *taille* but the small landowner of a garden pays nothing. The wealthy pay for their horses, carriages and servants; they even pay for the freedom to shoot their own partridges. The small landowner is a stranger to all these taxes. Furthermore, in England, we have a tax paid by the rich to help the poor. So, if you must go on paying taxes, they must be paid differently. The English method is much better.

'As my wretched French,' adds Young, 'suited their local speech, they understood me well enough. There was not a single word of this speech which did not meet with their approval and they considered that I might be a good fellow. This I confirmed by shouting: *Long live the Third Estate*. Thereupon they allowed me to go with a cheer.'

34. (p. 105) The church of X in the electoral district of Chollet was falling into ruins. It was a question of repairing it using the method outlined in the decree of 1684 (16 December), namely with the help of a tax levied on all the citizens. When the collectors set out to gather this tax, the Marquis of X, lord of the parish, declared that, since he was responsible alone for repairing the choir, he did not wish to share in the tax. The other citizens replied with considerable justification that, in his capacity as lord and titleholder (doubtless he owned all the feudal tithes), he was obliged alone to repair the choir and, that consequently, that repair could not exempt him from the common dues. At that point, the Intendant intervened with a ruling declaring the Marquis' case invalid and authorized the collectors to continue. There are, in the files, more than ten letters from this Marquis, each one more urgent than the one before, vociferously demanding that the rest of the parish should pay in his stead. He condescended to address the Intendant as *My Lord* and even to beg him, in order to get his way.

35. (p. 107) AN EXAMPLE OF THE WAY IN WHICH THE GOVERNMENT OF THE ANCIEN RÉGIME RESPECTED ACQUIRED RIGHTS, FORMAL CONTRACTS AND TOWN OR ASSOCIATION FREEDOMS

Declaration by the king who 'suspends in time of war repayment of all the loans made to the crown by towns, colleges, communities, hospital managements, charitable institutions, arts and crafts guilds and others which are repaid with the returns from tolls or rights conceded by us,' it is said in this declaration, 'with effect that interest will continue to accrue on all these borrowings'.

Not only was the suspension of the repayment at the time

stipulated in the contract with the creditors but also it was an
attack against pledges given for the payments to creditors. Never
would such measures – found in their swarms in the Ancien
Régime – have been allowed in practice in a government scrutin-
ized by the public or general assemblies. Let us compare this sort
of thing in England or even America. Here the contempt for the
law was as flagrant as the contempt for freedoms at a local level.
36. (p. 108) The instance quoted here in the text is far from being
the only one where the privileged classes realized that the feudal
dues, which weighed heavily upon the peasant, affected them
too. This is what was being said thirty years before the Revolution
by an agricultural society made up entirely of privileged people:
    'Unredeemable payments, whether on land or feudal, which
are connected to real estate become, when they are quite considerable, such a burden to the debtor that they cause his ruin and in
turn that of the land itself. He is forced to neglect the land
because he is unable to find the means to raise loans against an
already overmortgaged property nor to find purchasers if he
wishes to sell. If these dues could be redeemed, this ruined taxpayer would not fail to find opportunities to borrow money to
cancel the due payments or purchasers able to pay for both land
and tax dues. People are always content to maintain and improve
free property, which they believe they peaceably own. It would
be a very encouraging gain to agriculture if practical means could
be found to make these kinds of dues redeemable. Many estate
lords, convinced of the truth of this, would not need asking
to support such an arrangement. It would, therefore, be very
interesting to discover and note practical means to arrive at such
a freeing up of land dues.'
37. (p. 110) All public offices, even that of tax collector, were paid
by immunities from taxes – privileges granted to them by the
1681 ruling. In a letter addressed to the minister in 1782 by an
Intendant, it is stated: 'Among the privileged classes, there is no
class of persons more numerous than the clerical officers of the
salt tax, of those who draft bills, of royal estates, of the postal
service, of financial aid and of every other kind of state agency.
There are few parishes where no such official exists and we even
encounter several with two or three.'
    It was a matter of dissuading the minister, of suggesting the
passing of an order of council to extend tax immunities to
the employees and servants of these privileged agents – immunities which the farmers-general, said the Intendant, never stopped

asking to be extended so as to free themselves from having to pay those who were granted the immunity.

38. (p. 110) Such offices were not completely unknown elsewhere. In Germany a few minor rulers had introduced several of them but in small numbers and in unimportant sections of public administration. The system was pursued on a grand scale only in France.

39. (p. 114) We should not be surprised (even though it appears very odd and indeed is so) to see in the Ancien Régime public officials, several of whom belonged to the administration proper, taking their case to the Parlement in order to know the limit of their various powers. The explanation for this emerges when we realize that all these questions, while being issues of administration, were also issues of private property. What we take here to be an encroachment of judicial power was only a result of the mistake the government had made in turning public employment into offices for sale. Since positions were held as public offices and each official was remunerated on the basis of the decisions he passed, the nature of the job could not be altered without damaging a right which had been purchased from his predecessor. One example among a thousand: a lieutenant-general of police in Le Mans pursued a long lawsuit against the financial department of that town. He sought to prove that, since he policed the streets, he should be in charge of all decisions relating to their paving and should be paid a fee for those decisions. The department replied that the paving of the streets was granted to it by the very title of its duties. On this occasion the Royal Council did not make the decision. Since it was mainly a matter of the interest on the capital involved in the purchase of the office, the Parlement pronounced judgement. Administrative business had been transformed into a case at law.

40. (p. 115) ANALYSIS OF THE GRIEVANCES (*CAHIERS*) OF THE NOBILITY IN 1789
The French Revolution is the only one, I believe, at the beginning of which the various classes were able to issue separately an authentic testimony of the ideas they had in mind and to express the feelings which inspired them before this very Revolution had disfigured or altered those ideas or feelings. This authentic testimony, as everyone knows, was collected in the *cahiers* which the three orders drew up in 1789. These *cahiers*, or reports, were drafted in complete freedom, amid the widest publicity, by each of the orders involved. They were discussed at length between

the interested parties and considered maturely by their authors, for the government of the time, whenever it addressed the nation, never undertook to give any reply to the questions it asked. When the *cahiers* were drawn up, the principal sections of them were collected into the three volumes we see in every library. The originals were lodged in the national archives together with the written transcripts of the assemblies which published them and with, in part, the correspondence which took place at the time between M. Necker and his agents concerning these assemblies. This collection forms a lengthy series of folio volumes. It is the most serious document of ancient France that remains to us and the one which must always be consulted by anyone wishing to know our fathers' state of mind at the moment when the Revolution broke out.

I had been supposing that perhaps the three-volume digest, referred to above, was the work of one party and did not exactly reproduce the character of this extensive inquiry. On comparing the two, however, I found the closest resemblance between the full picture and the reduced copy.

The extract from the *cahiers* of the nobility which I present here is a true version of the way the great majority of this order felt. We can see clearly what the nobility stubbornly wished to retain from the old privileges, what they were not too far from conceding and what they were offering to sacrifice. Above all, we discover for all to see the spirit which animated them at that time in relation to political liberty. A strange and sad picture!

Individual rights. Above all, the nobles asked there to be made an unequivocal declaration of the rights which belong to all men and that this declaration should outline their freedoms and guarantee their safety.

Freedom of the person. They wished serfdom to be abolished wherever it existed and that the means be sought to destroy the trade and enslavement of blacks; each citizen should be free to travel or to settle where he wished, either within or outside the kingdom, without being liable to arbitrary arrest; that the abuses in police regulations be reformed and that the police should from then on be managed by judges, even in the case of a riot; that no one could be arrested and judged by any other than his natural judges; that, consequently, the state prisons and other places of illegal detention should be suppressed. Some asked for the demolition of the Bastille – notably the Paris nobility insisted upon this.

All the secret letters, or *lettres de cachet*, should be banned. If a threat to the state made it necessary to arrest a citizen without his being immediately handed over to the ordinary courts of justice, measures must be taken to avoid any abuses either by informing the Council of State of the detention or by all other means.

The nobility wanted all special commissions, all exceptional courts, all *committimus* privileges, decrees of reprieve, etc., to be abolished and that the most severe punishments should be imposed upon those who ordered or carried out an arbitrary order; that in the usual courts of justice – the only ones which should be preserved – necessary measures should be taken to safeguard individual liberty especially in what concerned criminals; that justice should be offered free of charge and useless jurisdictions be suppressed. As one *cahier* states: 'Magistrates are established for the people not people for magistrates.' They even request that in every district counsel and defence lawyers should be arranged free of charge for the poor; that all investigations should be in public and that the freedom of self-defence should be granted to litigants; that, in criminal matters, the accused should be provided with a lawyer and that, at every stage of the proceedings, the judge should be assisted by a certain number of citizens from the order to which the accused belonged, which men shall have the responsibility for passing the verdict on the crime or misdemeanour of the defendant (in this respect they are returning to the English constitution); that punishments should be in line with the crimes and be equal for all; that the death penalty be used more rarely and all corporal punishments and torture abolished; finally, that the condition of prisoners should be improved and above all that of litigants held in custody before trial.

Following the *cahiers*, means had to be found to have individual liberty respected in the recruitment of the army and navy. It should be allowed to convert obligatory military service into a payment of money; no lots would be drawn except in the presence of a deputation from all three orders. Finally, the duties of discipline and military obedience would be accompanied by the rights of the citizen and freeman. Blows with the flat blade of the sword would be abolished.

Freedom and inviolability of property. They asked for property to be inviolable and to suffer a damaging attack only for reasons of indispensable public usefulness. In such cases the government should not delay in paying compensation at a high price. Confiscations should be abolished.

Freedom of trade, work and industry. Freedom of trade and industry should be protected. As a result professional confederations and other privileges granted to certain companies should be removed. Customs barriers should be withdrawn to national borders.

Freedom of religion. The Catholic religion would be the only dominant one in France but every individual would be allowed freedom of conscience and non-Catholics would have their civil rights and properties restored to them.

Freedom of the press; inviolability of the postal service. The freedom of the press should be protected and a law should settle in advance the restrictions which could be brought to bear in the general interest. No one would be subjected to Church censorship except for books about doctrine. As for the rest, all that was needed was the necessary care to know the names of authors and publishers. Several asked that press misdemeanours should be subject to the judgement of juries only.

The *cahiers* insisted above all and with a unanimous voice that private contents in the post should be respected without interference in such a manner that letters could not be used as the subject or the means of any accusation. The opening of letters, they said bluntly, was the most odious of spying practices since it involved the violation of public trust.

Teaching, education. The *cahiers* of the nobility merely asked for an active policy to support education and for it to be extended to town and country, directing it according to principles suited to the assumed careers of the children. Above all, these children should be given a national timetable which would teach them their duties and rights as citizens. They even wished to have drawn up for them a catechism in which the principle elements of the constitution would be included for them to understand. However, they did not specify the methods to use for promoting and spreading learning; they simply claimed educational establishments for the children of poor noblemen.

The care which should be taken of the people. A great number of *cahiers* insisted that more consideration should be shown to the common people. Several complain against the abuse from police regulations which, they said, habitually dragged off into prisons or detention centres crowds of workmen and useful citizens without reason or regular trials, often for mistakes or even for mere suspicion, which is an attack against natural freedom. All the *cahiers* asked for forced labour to be abolished. The majority of districts wanted permission to buy back the lord's right to hire out equipment or charge tolls. A great number asked for the collection of several feudal dues to be less burdensome and for the abolition of the freehold duty. One *cahier* stated that the government was involved in helping the purchase and sale of land. This was precisely the reason given for the abolition at a stroke of all manorial rights and for the sale of all entailed lands. Many *cahiers* wished to see the right of owning dovecotes made less damaging to farming. As for the establishments aimed at the conservation of the king's game reserves, known by the name of *capitaineries*, they asked for the immediate removal of these as hostile to the right to own property. They wanted a tax collection less burdensome for the people to replace the current imposition of taxes.

The nobles asked for an effort to spread prosperity and comfort throughout the countryside; to establish the spinning and weaving of coarse cloth in the villages to give work to country people in the off season; to create in each district public grain stores under the surveillance of the provincial government in order to anticipate food shortages and to maintain the price of produce at a fixed rate; to strive to improve farming and to better the lot of the countryside; to increase public works and in particular to put effort into the draining of marshes and to prepare against flooding, etc.; finally, to foster throughout all provinces every encouragement to trade and agriculture. The *cahiers* would have liked hospitals to be divided into small establishments built in each district; to get rid of poorhouses to be replaced by charity workshops; to set up charitable funds under the control of provincial estates and to see that surgeons, doctors and midwives be placed in the town districts – paid for by the provinces – in order to give free treatment to the poor; to give free access to the law for the common people; finally, to consider the creation of institutions for the blind, deaf and dumb and foundlings.

However, in all these matters, the order of the nobility restricted itself generally to the mere expression of its desire for reforms without entering into great detail on how to achieve them. We can see that the nobles had lived among the lower classes less than the minor clergy and that they had thought less about the ways of achieving a remedy for the wretchedness they had had less contact with.

Accessibility to public office; the hierarchy of ranks and the honorary privileges of the nobility. It was above all, or, rather simply, in what concerned the hierarchy of ranks and the difference in status, that the nobility departed from the general spirit of the reforms requested and that, while making a few important concessions, it clung on to the principles of the Ancien Régime. It felt that it was fighting for its very existence. Its *cahiers*, therefore, pursued insistently the continuation of the clergy and the nobility as separate orders. They even sought the means to preserve the order of the nobility in all its purity: thus it should be forbidden to purchase the title of nobleman; it should no longer be associated with certain jobs; no one should obtain it except through merit after long and useful service rendered to the state. They hoped that false noblemen would be discovered and prosecuted. Finally, all the *cahiers* insisted that the nobility should be preserved with all its honours. Some wished noblemen to be granted some distinctive mark which would single them out in public.

One could not imagine anything more typical than such a request or more apt to display the similarity which existed between the nobleman and the commoner despite the difference in their social status. In the *cahiers* in general the nobility, which showed itself to be quite flexible about its practical rights, hung on grimly and anxiously to its honorary privileges. It wished to preserve all those it possessed and would like to have been able to invent some it had never enjoyed, such was its feeling of being dragged away already in the waves of democracy and its fear of being dissolved. What a strange thing! It felt this danger intuitively, yet had no perception of it.

As for the distribution of public burdens, the nobles asked that the sale of posts in the legal profession be suppressed; that, in the case of these sorts of post, all citizens could be put forward by the nation to the king and appointed by him regardless of rank, except for conditions of age and ability. For military positions, the majority thought that the Third Estate should not be excluded and that any soldier who had deserved well of his country had the right to reach the highest ranks. Several *cahiers* say: 'The order of the nobility does not approve of any law which closes entry into military positions to the order of the Third Estate.' Nobles simply wanted that the right to enter the regiment as an officer without having first of all risen through the lower ranks should be reserved for them alone. However, almost all the *cahiers* asked for the establishment of fixed rules, applicable to everyone, for military promotion and that these posts should not be left entirely to favour. Men should attain positions, other than the highest, through length of service.

As for clerical offices, they asked for the re-establishment of elections for the distribution of livings or at least for the king to create a committee to be able to advise him in the sharing out of those livings.

Finally, they said that from then on pensions should be distributed with more discrimination, that it was agreed they should no longer be concentrated on certain families and that no citizen could have more than one pension or receive the salary from more than one office at a time. Inherited pensions should be abolished.

Church and clergy. When it was no longer a question of its own rights and its individual constitution but of Church privileges and organization, the nobility did not look so closely. In this case, it focused its gaze firmly on abuses committed.

They requested that the clergy should not enjoy any tax privileges and should pay its debts without having the nation bear them. Monastic orders should be fundamentally reformed. Most *cahiers* declared that these establishments were far removed from the spirit of their founders.

Most districts wanted tithes to cause less harm to agriculture. There was even a large number who sought their abolition. 'The largest share of the tithes,' said one *cahier*, 'is collected by those priests who work least hard to supply spiritual help to the people.' We have seen that the second order was none too tactful about the first in its remarks. They scarcely showed more respect towards the Church itself. Several districts issued a formal acknowledgement of the Estates-General's right to suppress certain religious orders and to sue their assets for other purposes. Seventeen districts stated that the Estates-General had the competence to control discipline. Several said that feast days were too frequent, damaged agriculture and encouraged drunkenness. Consequently, a great number should be removed. They should revert to Sundays.

Political rights. As for political rights, the *cahiers* acknowledged that every Frenchman had the right to take part in government, directly or indirectly – that is, the right to elect and to be elected while preserving the separation of the classes. Thus no one could appoint or be appointed outside his order. Once this principle had been settled, the system of representation should

be established so as to guarantee to each of the national orders
the means of taking part seriously in the management of public
affairs.

As for the manner of voting in the assembly of the Estates-
General, opinions were divided: the majority advocated a separate vote for each order; some thought that an exception should
be made to this ruling in the case of taxation; others, finally,
asked for the following arrangement: 'Votes shall be counted
individually and not by order, since this method is the only
reasonable one and the only one to sideline and destroy the
selfishness of the group which has been the unique source of all
our misfortunes, which might bring men together and lead them
to the outcome which the nation has the right to expect from an
assembly where patriotism and lofty virtues will be strengthened
by enlightened attitudes.' However, as this innovation might, if
adopted too hastily, be dangerous in the present state of minds,
several thought that it should be accepted only cautiously and
that the assembly should assess whether or not it would be wiser
to postpone individual voting to future Estates-General. In all
these contingencies, the nobility wanted each order to be able to
preserve the dignity owed to any Frenchman. As a result, they
wanted the abolition of all humiliating procedures inflicted on
the Third Estate, for example the need to kneel. One *cahier*
stated: 'The sight of a man kneeling before another wounds
human dignity and proclaims, among beings equal by nature, an
inferiority which is incompatible with their fundamental rights.'

*Of the system which needed to be established in the form of
government and of the principles of the constitution.* As for the
form of government, the nobility required the continuance of
royalty, the preservation of legislative, judicial and executive
powers in the person of the king but, at the same time, the
establishment of fundamental laws aimed at safeguarding the
rights of the nation in the exercise of the king's powers.

As a result the *cahiers* all announced that the nation had the
right to convene in the Estates-General, made up of a sufficiently
large number of delegates to guarantee the independence of these
assemblies. They wanted these Estates to meet henceforward
periodically, at fixed times, as well as at every new accession to
the throne without any need for letters of convocation. Many
districts even declared that it would be desirable for this assembly
to be permanent. If the summoning of the Estates-General did
not take place within the legal time limit, they would have the

right to refuse to pay taxes. A small number of districts requested that, during the time between one meeting of the Estates and another, an intermediate commission should be established responsible for the overseeing of the government of the kingdom. But, generally speaking, the *cahiers* formally opposed the setting up of this commission, declaring that such a body would be entirely incompatible with the constitution. The reason given for this is strange: they were afraid that such a small assembly in the face of the government would allow itself to be led astray by government pressure.

The nobility did not want ministers to have the right to dissolve the assembly and wanted them to be punishable by law when they disturbed its orderliness with their intrigues; no public official, no person in any way connected with government, could be a deputy; the persons of deputies should be inviolable and could not, said the *cahiers*, be liable for prosecution for any opinions they had expressed; finally, that the meetings of the assembly should be in public and that, furthermore, in order to invite the nation to be part of its deliberations, the latter should be circulated in print.

The nobility made a unanimous request that the principles which should regulate central government be applied to the administration of the various parts of its territory and that, as a consequence, in every province, district and parish, assemblies should be established composed of members elected freely and for a limited period.

Several *cahiers* thought that the offices of Intendant and Receiver-General had to be removed; all of them reckoned that, from then on, provincial assemblies should alone be responsible for the division of taxes and for the supervision of the particular interests of the province. They intended the same arrangements for district assemblies and those of parishes, both of which would henceforth be subordinate to the provincial administration only.

Division of powers.

Legislative powers. As for the division of powers between the assembled nation and the king, the nobility requested that no law should take effect until it had received consent from the Estates-General and the king, as well as being written into the registers of those courts responsible for its execution; that the right to establish and settle the amounts of taxes should belong solely to the Estates-General; that the subsidies which might be sanctioned could not last longer than the time between one session of the Estates and the next; that all taxes which had been collected or established without the consent of the Estates-General should be declared illegal and that the ministers and collectors who had ordered or collected said taxes should be prosecuted as embezzlers.

The nobility added that, in the same way, no loans should be raised without the consent of the Estates-General; only a line of credit should be fixed by the Estates-General for use by the government in the event of war or major disaster with the proviso that a meeting of the Estates-General should be called as soon as possible thereafter.

All the national treasury should be placed under the supervision of the Estates-General who would fix the expenditure of every department and the most careful measures should be taken to ensure that the resources voted could not be exceeded.

Most of the *cahiers* asked that the suppression of vexatious taxes be pursued, those known by the name of rights of insinuation, hundredth penny, ratification dues – all collectively known as the Régie (or Administration) of the king's domains. One *cahier* said: 'The word Régie would alone be enough to wound the nation since it denotes objects belonging to the king but which are really a part of the citizens' property.' All the royal domains which were not sold should be placed under the administration of the provincial estates and no ruling, no fiscal edict, could be issued without the consent of the three Orders of the nation.

It is quite clear that the idea of the nobility was to confer on to the nation the whole financial administration whether in the regulation of loans and taxes or in the collection of these taxes through the representation of the national and provincial assemblies.

Judicial power. Similarly in the organization of the law the nobility tended to make the power of judges dependent, at least to a great extent, upon the assembled nation. Thus several *cahiers* declared: 'that magistrates will be responsible for their actions to the assembled nation'; that they could not be dismissed except by the agreement of the Estates-General; that no court of law would, under any pretext whatsoever, be disturbed in the exercise of its functions without the agreement of these Estates; that the corrupt practices of the supreme court, as well as those of the Parlements, would be judged by the Estates-General. According to most *cahiers*, judges should not be appointed by the king except upon the nomination of the people.

Executive power. As for the executive power, it belonged exclusively to the king but necessary limitations were placed upon it to guard against abuses.

Thus, as far as government was concerned, the *cahiers* required state accounts from the various departments to be printed and made public and that ministers should be answerable to the assembled nation; similarly that, before using troops for external defence, the king should explain his intentions precisely to the Estates-General. At home these same troops could not be deployed against citizens except at the command of the Estates-General. The number of troops should be limited and only two-thirds would normally be kept in active service. As for foreign troops which the government might have in its pay, the king would have to remove them from the heart of the kingdom and dispatch them to the borders.

On reading the *cahiers* of the nobility the most striking feature, and one which no extract can reflect, is the degree to which these nobles belonged to their age. They displayed its prevailing ethos and fluently used its language. *They speak of the inalienable rights of man and the principles central to the social contract.* When it came to the individual they usually concerned themselves with his rights and when it came to society, with the latter's duties. Political principles seemed to them *as absolute as those of morality and both held reason as their common base.* When they wished to abolish the remnants of serfdom, *it became a matter of removing the final traces of the degradation of the human race.* They sometimes called Louis XVI *a citizen king* and on several occasions spoke of the charge of high treason which would so often be levelled at them. In their eyes, as in those of everyone else, everything should be expected from state education and it was the state which should control it. One *cahier* said: *The Estates-General would see it as their business to inspire a national character through the changes in children's education.* Like the rest of their contemporaries, they displayed a lively and sustained enthusiasm for the uniformity of legislation except, however, in all that concerned the existence of the three Orders. They, as much as the Third Estate, wanted government and its measures to be uniform. They outlined every kind of reform which they intended to be radical. According to them, all taxes without exception should be abolished or transformed; the whole system of justice should be changed except the law administered by lords of the manor and that simply needed to be improved. For them and all other Frenchmen, France was a trial ground, a sort of model farm for politics in which everything should be turned over, everything tried out except for a small corner where their private privileges grew. Yet we have to admit in their honour that even that spot was scarcely spared by them. Briefly, we may conclude that the only thing missing in these nobles to effect the Revolution was to become commoners.

41.   (p. 116) EXAMPLE OF THE RELIGIOUS GOVERNMENT OF AN ECCLESIASTICAL PROVINCE IN THE MIDDLE OF THE EIGHTEENTH CENTURY

1)   The archbishop.

2)   Seven vicars-general.

3)   Two ecclesiastical courts, called officialities. The one, called the metropolitan officiality, had charge over the verdicts of suffragan bishops. The other, called the diocesan officiality, had charge over:

   a)   Personal affairs among the clergy.

   b)   The validity of marriages according to the sacrament. This last court was made up of three judges along with solicitors and prosecutors.

   c)   Two financial courts. The one called the diocesan office, had, in the first instance, charge over all those affairs connected with the tax imposition on the clergy in the diocese (we know that the clergy taxed itself). This court, presided over by the archbishop, was composed of six other priests. The other court judged on appeal those cases brought before the other diocesan offices in the ecclesiastical province. All these courts admitted lawyers and held hearings.

42.   (p. 117) THE SPIRIT OF THE CLERGY IN PROVINCIAL ESTATES OR ASSEMBLIES

What I am saying here in the text about the Estates of Languedoc is applicable just as well to the provincial assemblies meeting in 1779 and 1787, notably in Upper Guyenne. The members of the clergy in that provincial assembly were among the most enlightened, active and liberal. The Bishop of Rodez it was who supported making public the minutes of the assembly.

43.   (p. 117) The priests' liberal attitude in political matters, evident in 1789, was not prompted simply by the excitement of the moment; it was already apparent at a much earlier time. It was notably displayed in Berry as early as 1779 when the clergy

offered 68,000 livres as a free gift solely on condition that the provincial administration was preserved.

44. (p. 119) Pay careful attention to the fact that political society was without ties whereas civil society still had them. People were bound to each other at the heart of the class system. There even existed something of the narrow bond between the noble class and the common people. Although this had happened within civil society its consequences made themselves felt indirectly in political society. Men linked in this way formed irregular and ill-organized groups who were refractory under the hand of power. The Revolution, having broken these social bonds without replacing them with political ties, paved the way for both equality and enslavement.

45. (p. 120) EXAMPLE OF THE WAY IN WHICH THE COURTS EXPRESSED THEMSELVES ON THE OCCASION OF CERTAIN ARBITRARY ACTS

From a report offered to one Controller-General in 1781 by the Intendant of the Paris region, it appeared that this region was used to allowing parishes to have two syndics, one elected by the inhabitants in an assembly presided over by the sub-delegate, the other appointed by the Intendant, the latter being the supervisor of the former. In the parish of Rueil, a quarrel arose between the two syndics when the elected officer did not wish to obey the appointed one. The Intendant managed to persuade M. de Breteuil to have the elected syndic thrown into La Force prison for two weeks. He was, in fact, arrested, then relieved of his duties and replaced by someone else. Thereupon the Parlement, meeting at the request of the imprisoned syndic, began proceedings whose outcome I have been unable to discover. It declared that the imprisonment of the plaintiff and his quashed election could not be considered as anything other than arbitrary and tyrannical acts. The justice of that time was sometimes very badly muzzled!

46. (p. 123) The educated and wealthy classes, including the bourgeoisie, were far from being oppressed and enslaved under the Ancien Régime and one may say that all of them were often much too free to do what suited them since the royal power did not dare stop their members from establishing an elevated position to the detriment of the common people, and almost always felt the need to abandon the latter in order to purchase their goodwill or to bring their resentment to an end. We can state that, in the eighteenth century, a Frenchman belonging to these classes often possessed a much greater capacity to resist the

government and to force it to humour him than an Englishman of the same period and in the same situation. The royal power would sometimes have felt obliged to treat him more temperately and in a more reserved manner than the English government would have felt itself so constrained, faced with a man of the same standing. It would be so wrong to muddle independence with freedom. No one is less independent than a free citizen.

47. (p. 123) THE REASON WHICH OFTEN FORCED THE ABSOLUTE GOVERNMENT TO USE MODERATION UNDER THE OLD ORDER
There is scarcely anything except the increase of old taxes and, above all, the introduction of new ones, which can, in ordinary times, create great embarrassment for the government or arouse the common people. In the ancient financial constitution of Europe, when a ruler had expensive tastes, when he rushed into wild political schemes, when he allowed disorder to creep into his finances or when again he needed money to support himself by winning over many people – paying them large profits or huge salaries when they had not earned them, maintaining huge armies or embarking on public works, etc. – he immediately had recourse to taxes which straightway disturbed and worried all classes, especially that class which foments violent revolutions, namely the common people. Nowadays, in the same situation, money is borrowed, the immediate effect of which is almost imperceptible and whose final result will be felt only by the next generation.

48. (p. 124) One of the many examples of this is to be found in the district of Mayenne. The main estates situated there had been leased out to farmers-general who took as sub-tenants wretched smallholders who had nothing and to whom they supplied the most necessary tools. One can understand that such farmers-general were not obliged to accommodate these tenants or debtors of the old feudal lord who had put them in his place and that feudalism, as exercised by their hands, could often appear harsher than in the Middle Ages.

49. (p. 124) Another example. The citizens of Montbazon had listed on the *taille* roll the stewards of the duchy owned by the prince of Rohan, even though these stewards were acting in his name. This prince (who was doubtless very rich) not only put an end to what he called *this abuse* but managed to reclaim the sum of 5,344 livres 15 sous which he had wrongly been made to pay and which would now be charged to the citizens.

50. (p. 127) EXAMPLE OF THE WAY IN WHICH THE PECUNIARY RIGHTS OF THE CLERGY ALIENATED THE HEARTS OF THOSE

WHO OUGHT TO HAVE DRAWN CLOSE TO THEM BECAUSE OF
THEIR ISOLATION

The priest of Noisai claimed that the citizens were obliged to
repair his barn and wine press. He asked for a local tax to be
raised for that purpose. The Intendant replied that the citizens
were only responsible for repairs to his house. The barn and
the wine press would remain the expense of this pastor, more
preoccupied with his farm than with his flock (1767).

51. (p. 129) We found the following in one of the reports sent in 1788
by peasant farmers in reply to an inquiry from the provincial
assembly. It is written in clear terms and in a moderate tone: 'To
the abuses of the collection of the *taille* is added that of the
bailiffs. They normally make five visits during the collection of
the *taille*. They are usually invalid soldiers or Swiss. At each visit
they stay for four or five days in the parish and are charged for
by the office of the *taille* collection at 36 sous per day. As for the
distribution of the *taille*, we will not expose the all too well-
known arbitrary abuses, nor the damaging effects caused by the
legal functions of officials who are often incapable and almost
always biased and vindictive. They have, however, been the
source of disturbance and quarrels. They have given rise to lawsuits, expensive for litigants and very beneficial for the districts
where the courts sit.'

52. (p. 130) THE SUPERIORITY OF THE METHODS FOLLOWED
IN THE INDEPENDENT PROVINCES (*PAYS D'ÉTATS*)
ACKNOWLEDGED BY THE OFFICIALS OF THE CENTRAL
GOVERNMENT ITSELF

In a confidential letter written 3 June 1772 by the director of
taxation to the Intendant it is stated: 'In the independent provinces, since the tax was a fixed percentage, every taxpayer is
subject to it and indeed pays it. Any increase in the levy of this
percentage is in proportion to the increase demanded by the
king upon the total sum which must be raised (one million, for
example, instead of 900,000 livres). That is a simple operation,
whereas in most places the tax levy is personal and virtually
arbitrary. Some pay what they owe, others pay only half, others
a third, a quarter or nothing at all. How then does one subject
the tax to an increase of one-ninth?'

53. (p. 132) THE MANNER IN WHICH, AT THE BEGINNING, THE
PRIVILEGED CLASSES UNDERSTOOD THE PROGRESS OF
CIVILIZATION BY ROADS

The Count of X complained in a letter to the Intendant about the lack of urgency in building a local road. It was, he said, the fault of the sub-delegate who did not expend enough energy in his job and did not force the peasants to fulfil their forced labour.

54.   (p. 133) ARBITRARY PRISON FOR FORCED LABOUR
Example: we see in a letter from a chief provost in 1768: 'Yesterday I had given the order for the imprisonment of three men at the request of M.C., the assistant engineer, for not having fulfilled their forced labour commitments. Whereupon there has been uproar among the village women who cried out: "Just look at that! You think about the poor when you consider the forced labour duty but do not bother about giving them food to eat."'

55.   (p. 133) There were two kinds of resource for road building:
  1)   The most important was the forced labour gang for all the heavy work which required only manual effort.
  2)   The least important was the general imposition of a tax, the proceeds of which were placed at the disposal of the Highways Department to help with structural work. The privileged classes, namely the main landowners more interested than anyone else in roads, did not contribute to the *taille* and, furthermore, since the highways tax was linked to the *taille* and raised in the same way, they were exempt from paying that too.

56.   (p. 133) EXAMPLE OF FORCED LABOUR TO TRANSPORT CONVICTS
We see in a letter addressed to the Intendant in 1761 from a commissioner appointed to police the chain gangs, that peasants were forced to carry convicts in their carts. This they did very unwillingly and were often maltreated by the warders, 'seeing,' says the commissioner, 'that they are brutal and coarse individuals and that the peasants reluctantly performing this service are often insolent'.

57.   (p. 133) Turgot depicts the discomforts and harshness of forced labour used to transport military equipment in descriptions which, having read the files, do not seem exaggerated to me. Among other remarks, he says the primary inconvenience was the extreme inequality of a burden which was, in itself, very considerable. It fell entirely upon a small number of parishes exposed to it by the misfortune of their location. The distance they had to travel was often five, six and sometimes ten or twelve leagues; then it was necessary to expend three days for the round trip. The payment allotted to the landowners was only a fifth of their costs. This forced labour took place almost always in the

summer at harvest time. The oxen were almost always overloaded
and often sick after being used, to the point where a great number
of landowners preferred to pay out 15 to 20 livres rather than
supply a cart and four oxen. Finally, inevitably, disorder reigned
and the peasant was constantly exposed to the violence of the
soldiers. The officers almost always demanded more than was
due to them. Sometimes they forced the drivers to harness saddle
horses to carriages at the risk of laming them. The soldiers had
themselves carried on vehicles already heavily laden. At other
times, frustrated by the slowness of the oxen, they poked at them
with swords and, if the peasant wished to raise some objections,
he was roughly treated.

58. (p. 133) EXAMPLE OF THE MANNER IN WHICH FORCED
LABOUR WAS APPLIED TO EVERYTHING
The Intendant of the navy at Rochefort complained about the ill
will of the peasants who were obliged during their forced labour
to haul building timber bought by naval suppliers from the various provinces. We can see from this correspondence that peasants
were still, in 1775, bound to this forced labour for which the
Intendant fixed their remuneration. The naval minister, who sent
this letter on to the Intendant at Tours, told him to arrange for the
vehicles requested to be supplied. The Intendant, M. Ducluzel,
refused to authorize such kinds of forced labour. The naval
minister wrote him a threatening letter announcing that he would
report his resistance to the king. Immediately the Intendant
replied, on 11 December 1775, saying firmly that, for the ten
years he had been Intendant in Tours, he had never given authorization for these kinds of forced labour, because of the inevitable
abuses that they entailed, abuses which the price fixed for the
carts never compensated. 'For often,' he said, 'the animals are
lamed by the weight of the huge equipment they have to haul
along roads which are as bad as the weather in which they are
required to work.' The thing which prompted the Intendant's
firm tone appears to be a letter from M. Turgot together with
documents, dated 30 July 1774, when he entered the ministry.
In these, he said that he had never authorized the forced labour
at Limoges and supported M. Ducluzel in not doing so in Tours.

It appears from other parts of this correspondence that suppliers of timber quite often demanded this forced labour without
authorization by means of deals between themselves and the state
because they could save at least a third on transport costs. A
sub-delegate gave an example of this profit: 'The distance to

transport the wood from the place where it is felled to the river along almost impassable roads,' he says, 'is six leagues; the time for the return journey is two days. By paying the haulage gangs, as their wage, at the rate of six liards a league per cubic foot, this will amount to 13 francs 10 sous per trip. This is hardly enough to cover the expenses of the small landowner, his helper, the oxen and horses harnessed to his cart. His effort, his time, the work of his animals, all that is wasted.' On 17 May 1776 the king's express command to have this forced labour performed was notified to the Intendant by the minister. M. Ducluzel, having died, his successor, M. Escalopier hastened to obey and to post orders which stated that 'the sub-delegate will divide the duty between the parishes by virtue of which the different gangs from these said parishes will be required to meet at the prescribed place and time set down by the syndics where the timber was sited and to transport it at the price set by the sub-delegate.'

59. (p. 142) It has been said that the character of eighteenth-century philosophy was a kind of worship of human reason, a boundless trust in its omnipotence to transform laws, institutions and habits at will. We must be clear about this. If truth be told, it was less human reason that the philosophers worshipped than their own reason. Never has less trust been placed in common sense than by them. I could quote several of them who despised the crowd almost as much as they did God. They manifested the pride of competitors towards God and the pride of the upstart towards the crowd. Real and respectful deference to the will of the majority was as alien to them as deference to divine will. Almost every revolutionary since then has displayed this double character. It is a long way from that attitude to the respect shown by the English and Americans to the opinions of the majority of their citizens. With them reason is proud and self-confident but never insolent. Therefore this leads to freedom, whereas our kind of reason has scarcely achieved anything but invent new forms of slavery.

60. (p. 153) INSTANCE OF THE WAY IN WHICH THE PEASANTRY WAS OFTEN TREATED

1768. The king granted 2,000 francs reduction in the *taille* to the parish of Chapelle-Blanche near Saumur. The priest intended to set aside a part of this sum to have a belfry constructed and to rid himself of the noise of the bells which, he said, he found irksome in his vicarage. The villagers objected and complained. The sub-delegate took the side of the priest and, at night, had three of the leading inhabitants arrested and imprisoned.

Another example: order from the king to have a woman, who had insulted two riders from the mounted police, imprisoned for two weeks. Another order to have a stocking-maker, who had spoken ill of the mounted police, imprisoned for two weeks. The Intendant replied to the minister that he had already had this man put in jail; the minister fully approved this. The insults aimed at the mounted police had occurred in relation to the violent arrest of beggars – an action which had apparently offended the people. The sub-delegate, on the arrest of the stocking-maker, had let it be known to the public that those people who might continue to insult the mounted police would be more severely punished.

We can see from the sub-delegate's and the Intendant's correspondence that the Intendant had given them the order to have these nuisances arrested, not in order to have them brought to trial but to have them restrained.

The sub-delegate asked the Intendant to keep two dangerous beggars he had had arrested in permanent confinement. A father complained against the arrest of his son as a vagabond because he had been travelling without papers. A landowner of X asked for a neighbour of his to be arrested. This man, he said, had settled in his parish and had been helped by him but was now acting badly towards him and annoying him. The Paris Intendant begged his colleague in Rouen to do this landowner this favour as he was his friend.

To anyone wishing to free beggars the Intendant replied that 'the poorhouses should not be considered as prisons but simply as an establishment intended for the *administrative correction* of beggars and vagabonds'. This idea has found its way into the Penal Code which shows to what degree these Ancien Régime traditions in this matter have been so well preserved.

61.   (p. 154) Frederick the Great has written in his Memoirs: 'The Fontanelles, the Voltaires, the Hobbeses, the Shaftesburys and the Bolingbrokes, these great men dealt a mortal blow to religion. Men now began to look closely at what they had stupidly worshipped. Reason flattened superstition. Disgust was felt for fables which had been believed. Deism made numerous converts. If Epicureanism was fatal to the idolatrous religion of pagans, Deism was no less so for the Jewish visions adopted by our ancestors. Freedom of thought which prevailed in England had contributed much to the progress of philosophy.'

From the above passage, we can see that Frederick the Great,

NOTES

at the time he was writing these lines – namely the middle of the eighteenth century – still looked upon the England of that period as the home of anti-religious doctrines. In this we can see something more striking: a sovereign, who was one of the most steeped in human science and human affairs, appeared to have no idea about the political usefulness of religions, so much had the intellectual shortcomings of his teachers debased his own mental qualities.

62. (p. 172) This spirit of progress which manifested itself at the end of the eighteenth century appeared throughout Germany at the same time. Similarly, it was accompanied everywhere by the desire to change institutions. Look at the picture drawn by a German historian of the events of that period in his country:

'In the second half of the eighteenth century,' he says, 'the new spirit of the times is gradually being introduced into ecclesiastical dominions themselves where reforms are being instigated. Industry and tolerance are spreading everywhere. Enlightened absolute government which had already taken hold in the important states is appearing even here. One must state that at no period in the eighteenth century had we seen quite so clearly in these ecclesiastic dominions rulers as remarkable and as impressive as during the final decades preceding the French Revolution.'

We must note how the picture seen there resembles that in France where the movement towards improvement and progress was beginning at the same time and where the men most worthy of governing appeared just when the Revolution was about to devour everything.

Also we must acknowledge just how far this entire area of Germany was obviously drawn into the French movement of civilization and politics.

63. (p. 173) HOW THE JUDICIAL LAWS OF THE ENGLISH PROVE THAT INSTITUTIONS MAY SUFFER FROM MANY SECONDARY DEFECTS WITHOUT THAT PREVENTING THEM FROM ATTAINING THE MAIN AIM PROPOSED WHEN THEY WERE ESTABLISHED

Nations have this ability to prosper despite the imperfections encountered in secondary areas of their institutions as long as the general principles and the very spirit giving them life are fertile. This phenomenon could not be better in evidence than when we examine the constitution of justice in the England of the last century such as is illustrated in Blackstone.

Two great areas of surprising diversity meet the eye:

1)   Diversity of laws.

2)   Diversity of the courts which implement them.

1)   *Diversity of Laws.*

    i.   The laws are different for England itself, for Scotland, for Ireland, for various European possessions of Great Britain such as the Isle of Man, the Channel Islands, etc., and finally for the colonies.

   ii.   In England itself we can see four kinds of law: common law, statutes, Roman law and equity. Common law is itself divided into general customs applicable to the whole kingdom; into customs which are peculiar to certain manors or towns or sometimes to certain isolated classes such as, for instance, merchants. Sometimes these customs reveal large differences one from another, such as, for example, those at variance with the general trend of English law, which demand the equal division of inheritances among all offspring (*gavelkind*) or, even more strangely, give the right of primogeniture to the youngest child.

2)   *Diversity of the Courts.* The law, says Blackstone, has instituted an amazing variety of different law courts. This can be illustrated from the following very brief summary.

    i.   First of all we encounter those courts established outside England itself such as those in Scotland and Ireland, which did not always fall within the province of the upper English courts even though they must, I think, have been subject to the final arbitration of the House of Lords.

   ii.   As for England itself, if I remember rightly, among Blackstone's classifications, I find that he counts:

       a)   Eleven types of court according to the common law, four of which seem already to have fallen into disuse.

       b)   Three types of court whose jurisdiction extended to the whole country applying to certain matters only.

       c)   Ten types of court with a special character. One of these types is composed of local courts, created by different acts of Parliament or existing by virtue of tradition either in London or in provincial towns and cities. The latter are so numerous and offer such a great variety in their constitution and in their regulations that the author abandons a detailed description of them.

Thus in England itself alone, if we can rely upon Blackstone's text, there existed for the period he was writing – namely the second half of the eighteenth century – twenty-four types of court, several of which were subdivided into a great number of single courts each bearing a particular character. If we set aside the types which, from then on, have almost disappeared, there still remain eighteen or twenty.

Now, if we analyse this judicial system, we can see easily that it contains all sorts of imperfections.

Despite the multiplicity of courts, there was a shortage of small lower courts within range of those on trial which are suitable for judgement over small cases on the spot and at small cost. This made justice awkward and expensive. The same cases fell within the competence of several courts; this cast a vexing uncertainty over how to start proceedings. Almost all courts of appeal judged certain cases in the first instance, on some occasions in courts of *common law*, others in *courts of equity*. Appeal courts were of very different kinds. The only central point was the House of Lords. Litigations against the government were not separated from ordinary disputes; such would appear a considerable flaw in the eyes of most of our lawyers. Finally, all these courts would draw justification for their decisions from four different legislative areas, one of which was established by precedent and another, equity, which was established on nothing exact since its object was more often than not to challenge custom or statutes and to correct any outdated or overharsh decisions meted out by these customs or statutes by relying upon the discretion of the judge.

Those are a lot of flaws and, if we compare this huge and ageing machine of English justice with the modern creation of our own legal system, and if we compare the simplicity, the consistency and the interdependence we can perceive in the latter with the complication and confusion we note in the former, the flaws of the first will appear even greater. And yet there is no country in the world where, from Blackstone's time, the mighty ends of justice were as completely achieved as in England, where, that is to say, each citizen of whatever rank, whether he pleaded against an individual or against the ruler, was more sure of being heard and could find in all the courts of his land better guarantees for the defence of his wealth, his liberty and his life.

That does not mean that the flaws in the English judicial system served what I am calling here the mighty ends of justice; this simply proves that there are in every legal organization secondary defects which may harm only slightly these ends and other fundamental defects which not only harm them but destroy them, even though they are linked to many good secondary qualities. The secondary defects are more easily spotted and are normally the first to strike the minds of common people. They leap to the eye, as the saying goes. The fundamental defects are often more concealed and not always discovered or highlighted by the jurists and other professional practitioners.

Furthermore, take note that the same qualities may be secondary or fundamental according to the times and the political organization of society. In periods when aristocracy and inequalities prevail, anything which tends to diminish a privilege for certain individuals before the courts, to guarantee safeguards for the weak plaintiff against the strong, to underline the action of the state – impartial, of course, when it is only a matter of a dispute between two citizens – all that becomes a fundamental quality. Yet it lessens in importance as the state of society and the political constitution turn towards democracy.

If we study the English judicial system according to these principles, we find that, in allowing the existence of all those defects which might make our neighbours' legal system obscure, awkward, slow moving, expensive and inconvenient, they had taken endless precautions to make sure that the strong could never be favoured at the expense of the weak, the state at the expense of the individual. We can see, as we delve further into the detail of this law-making, that each citizen has been provided with all kinds of defensive arms and that things have been so arranged as to grant each citizen the maximum number of safeguards possible against biased judgements, against the venality as understood from judges and against that more common and above all more dangerous venality which arises in times of democracy from the subservience of the courts towards public power.

From every point of view, the English judicial system, despite the numerous secondary faults which we encounter there, seems to me superior to our own, which is not prey to any of these flaws, it is true, but neither does it offer, to the same extent, the fundamental qualities which are found there. Our system, though excellent as far as the safeguards it offers to every citizen in disputes between individuals, is weak on the side which should always be reinforced in a democratic society such as ours, namely the safeguards for the individual against the state.

64. (p. 174) ADVANTAGES ENJOYED BY THE PARIS DISTRICT
This region was just as favoured in relation to government chari-

ties as it was by tax collections. For example: a letter from the Controller-General to the Intendant for the Île-de-France district, 22 May 1787, to inform the latter that the king had fixed, for the Paris district, the sum which should be used for charity works during that year at 172,800 livres. Beyond that, 100,000 livres were earmarked for the purchase of cows to be given to farmers. We can see from this letter that the sum of 172,800 livres was to be distributed by the Intendant alone as long as he conformed to the general rules indicated by the government and as long as he sought approval for this division from the Controller-General.

65.   (p. 175) The administration of the Ancien Régime was composed of a mass of different powers, created at different times, most frequently for financial purposes and not for the government proper; these sometimes featured in the same area of operation. Confusion and conflict could be avoided only if each power operated only rarely or not at all. The instant they decided to escape from this lethargy, they hindered each other and became embroiled. As a result the complaints against the complexity of administrative machinery and against the confusion over the scope of these powers were a lot more lively in the years immediately before the Revolution than thirty or forty years earlier. The political institutions had not become worse; quite the reverse, they had greatly improved but political life had become more active.

66.   (p. 180) THE ARBITRARY INCREASE IN TAXES
What the king says here of the *taille* he could have said with as much justification of the *vingtième*. We can work this out from the following correspondence. In 1772, the Controller-General, Terray, had decided upon a considerable increase, 100,000 livres, in the *vingtièmes* in the district of Tours. We can see the pain and embarrassment this measure caused M. Ducluzel, the Intendant, an able administrator and a good man, in a confidential letter in which he wrote: 'It is the ease with which the previous increase of 250,000 livres was obtained which has probably encouraged this cruel interpretation and the June letter.'

In a highly confidential letter written by the director of taxes to the Intendant on the same occasion, he says: 'If the tax increases asked for always seem to you as serious and revolting with regard to the general distress as you have kindly witnessed to me, it would be desirable for the province which can find no defender or protector but your generous feelings, that you could at least spare it the supplementary tax roll which is always a retrospective and hateful imposition.'

We can also see from this correspondence the absence of any standard procedure and how much arbitrariness was practised even when attitudes were well intentioned. Intendant as well as minister aimed the burden of supplementary taxes now on agriculture rather than industry, now on one sector of agriculture rather than another (for example, vineyards) according to whether they considered industry or some branch of agriculture in need of kindly consideration.

67. (p. 182) THE WAY IN WHICH TURGOT SPEAKS OF COUNTRY PEOPLE IN THE PREAMBLE TO A ROYAL DECLARATION
'The royal communities are composed,' he says, 'in the greater part of the kingdom, of poor, ignorant and brutish peasants, incapable of administering themselves.'

68. (p. 186) HOW REVOLUTIONARY IDEAS TOOK ROOT QUITE NATURALLY IN PEOPLE'S MINDS AT THE HEIGHT OF THE ANCIEN RÉGIME
In 1779, a lawyer addressed the Council and asked for a decree to re-establish a maximum price for straw throughout the kingdom.

69. (p. 187) The chief engineer wrote in 1781 to the Intendant about a request for an extra indemnity: 'The claimant seems not to realize that the indemnities granted are a special favour for the Tours district and that he is very lucky to recover a part of his loss. If we reimbursed in the way the claimant indicates, four millions would not be enough.'

70. (p. 192) The Revolution did not come about because of this prosperity. However, the spirit which was to produce the Revolution – this active, agitated, intelligent, innovative, ambitious, democratic spirit of new societies – was beginning to invigorate everything and, before overturning society in a brief moment, was already strong enough to shake and develop it.

71. (p. 193) THE CONFLICT BETWEEN THE DIFFERENT ADMINISTRATIVE POWERS IN 1787
An example of this: The intermediary commission of the Île-de-France provincial assembly claimed the management of the poor-house. The Intendant wished to retain control of it, 'because,' he says, 'this house is not maintained by funds from the province'. During the debate, the intermediary commission had contacted intermediary commissions from other provinces to obtain advice. We find among other replies the one received from the intermediary commission of Champagne which announced to the

Île-de-France's commission that it had met the same problem and
that it was exercising the same resistance.

72. (p. 196) I have come across in the minutes of the first provincial
assembly in the Île-de-France this statement in the mouth of the
committee's spokesman: 'Up to now the tasks of syndic, being
much more burdensome than honourable, were bound to deter
all those who combined wealth and intelligence commensurate
with their status.'

73. (p. 207) (*Relating to several passages in this book.*) FEUDAL
RIGHTS STILL IN EXISTENCE AT THE TIME OF THE
REVOLUTION ACCORDING TO THE FEUDAL LAWYERS OF THE
TIME

I have no intention at this point of producing a treatise on feudal
rights, nor, above all, of finding out what might have been their
origin. I wish simply to show which of them were still in force
throughout the eighteenth century. Then, these rights played such
a great role and since have preserved such a great place in the
imagination of those who no longer suffer from them that it
seemed very interesting to me to know what they were exactly
when the Revolution destroyed them all. With this aim in mind,
I have first of all studied a certain number of 'terriers' or manorial
registers, choosing those which were of a more recent date. This
method led me nowhere. For the feudal rights, although regulated
by one system of laws, which was the same throughout Europe,
were infinitely varied in kind, according to the province and even
the cantons. The only system which appeared to me suitable for
showing approximately what I was seeking was the following
one.

Feudal rights gave rise to all kinds of cases of dispute. It was
a matter of knowing how dues had been acquired, how they
were lost, of what exactly they were composed, which could be
collected only on the strength of a royal patent, which could be
founded only on a private title, which, by contrast, had no need
of formal titles and could be collected according to the terms
of local customs or even by virtue of long-standing practice.
Finally, when one wished to sell them, one needed to know
how to value them and what sum represented each kind of tax
according to its importance. All these points which concerned a
thousand financial interests were subject for debates and a whole
order of jurists had been formed whose sole occupation was to
cast light upon them. Several of these men wrote in the second
half of the eighteenth century, some even as the Revolution was

approaching. They were not learned jurists as such; they were legal practitioners whose sole aim was to clarify for men in the profession the rules to follow in this specialized field which was so attractive for lawyers. After a careful study of these experts in feudal law, we can reach a quite detailed and quite clear idea of a subject whose bulk and confusion are at first astonishing. Below I give the most abbreviated summary of my efforts that I have been able to make. These notes are principally drawn from the work of Edme de Fréminville who was writing around 1750 and that of Renauldon, written in 1765 and entitled: *Historical and Practical Treatise on Manorial Dues*.

The *cens* (that is perpetual payments in kind and in money attached by feudal law to the ownership of designated lands), in the eighteenth century, still altered to a profound degree the condition of a great number of landowners. The *cens* continued to be indivisible, that is, one could approach any one of the owners of the property subject to this *cens* and ask him for the whole sum of the *cens*. It was always free from any regulations. The owner of a property liable to *cens* is unable to sell it without being subject to withdrawal of *cens*, which meant that he had to allow the property to be repurchased at the sale price. But this practice took place only under certain conditions; the Paris practice, which was the most widespread, did not recognize this right.

Lods et ventes: in areas administered according to custom, it was generally the rule that a sale of any inherited property liable to *cens* carried with it *lods et ventes* which were sales taxes which had to be paid to the lord. These dues were more or less considerable according to custom but quite sizeable everywhere. They did exist equally in areas governed by written law. They normally amounted to one sixth of the price and were called *lods*. But in these areas it was up to the lord to establish his right. In areas of written law, as in those governed by custom, the *cens* created for the lord the privilege of taking precedence over all other debts.

Terrage or *champart*, *agrier*, *tasque*: this was a certain portion of produce which the lord received from any properties subject to the *cens*. The amount varied according to contracts and customs. Quite often one still encountered this right in the eighteenth century. I believe that the *terrage*, even in regions governed by custom, always had to be founded on a legal title. The *terrage* could be manorial or attached to the land. It is useless to explain here the indicators which governed these two different kinds. Suffice it to say that the land-based *terrage*, like ground rents, lapsed after thirty years whereas manorial *terrage* could never lapse. Land subject to the *terrage* could never be mortgaged without the consent of the lord.

Bordelage: a tax which existed only in Nivernais and Bourbonnais; it consisted of an annual payment in cash, grain and poultry, due on property held under the *cens*. This obligation had very severe consequences: a failure to pay for three years running gave rise to *commise*, or confiscation to the lord. A man owing *bordelage* was furthermore subject to a host of inconveniences on his property: sometimes the lord could inherit it even though there were legal successors. This contract was the most stringent in feudal law and the legal code had ended up by restricting it to rural properties 'for the peasant is always the mule ready to bear any load,' said the author.

Marciage: this was a special tax collected in very few places from the owners of properties or land tied to *cens* which consisted in a certain payment due only on the natural death of the lord of the property.

Pledged tithes: in the eighteenth century there were still a great number of pledged tithes. In general they had to grow out of a contract and were not demanded simply by the fact that the land belonged to the lord.

Parcière: *parcières* were taxes collected from the harvest of the produce of properties. Quite similar to *champart* or pledged tithes, they were in use mainly in Bourbonnais and the Auvergne.

Carpot: used in the Bourbonnais, this tax is to vineyards what *champart* is to arable land, namely, the right to receive a share of the produce. This was a quarter of the grape harvest.

Serfdom: the term 'serf customs' was given to those still containing some traces of serfdom – these were few in number. In the provinces governed by them, there were no lands or very few in which some traces of the former enslavement were not in evidence. (This was written in 1765.) Serfdom or, as the author calls it, servitude, was either *personal* or *real*.

Personal servitude was an inherent part of a person and followed them everywhere. Wherever the serf went, into whatever place he transferred his savings, the lord could claim these by levy rights. The authors reported several decrees which established this right, one of which was that of 17 June 1760 by which the court cancelled the claim of a lord of Nivernais for the inheritance of Pierre Truchet, deceased in Paris. Under the custom of Nivernais, he had been the son of a serf who had married a free woman of Paris and who had died there just like his son. But the decree appears to have been based on the fact that Paris was a place of sanctuary where the claim could not be followed up. If the right of sanctuary forbade the lord from taking possession of goods owned by the serfs in such a place of sanctuary, it did not oppose his inheriting any goods left within his seigneury.

Real servitude resulted from the holding of a piece of land and could come to an end when the land had been vacated or the owner had moved to some other place.

Corvées: a right which the lord exercised over his subjects, by virtue of which he might use for his own profit a certain number of their oxen and horses. The *corvée* at will, that is according to the lord's pleasure, was completely abolished. It had been reduced for a long time to a certain number of days a year.

The *corvée* could be *personal* or *real*. Personal *corvées* were due from all workmen with homes on the lord's land, each man according to his own trade. Real *corvées* were tied to the ownership of certain property. Noblemen, churchmen, clergymen, law officers, lawyers, doctors, notaries, bankers and notables had to be free from the *corvée*. The author quotes a decree of 13 August 1735 which exempted a notary whose lord had wanted to force him to come to the seigneury where the notary lived and spend three days drawing up deeds for nothing. Another decree of 1750 declared that, whenever the *corvée* was due, either in person or in money, the choice should be left to the debtor. All *corvées* needed to be ratified by written title. The manorial *corvée* had become very rare in the eighteenth century.

Banalités: the provinces of Flanders, Artois and Hainaut alone were free from *banalities*. The Paris custom was very strict about the exercise of this right without proper entitlement. Everyone dwelling within the boundaries of the *banalité* were subject to it even, most often, nobles and priests.

Independently of the banality of mills and ovens, there were many others:

1) *Banalités* of industrial mills, such as cloth mills, cork mills, hemp mills. Several custom areas (among others Anjou, Maine and Brittany) established this banality.

2) *Banalités* of the wine press. Very few customs spoke of it. Lorraine established the custom, as did Maine.

3) The *banal* bull. No customs alluded to this but there were certain deeds which established it. The same was true for *banal* slaughterhouses.

In general, the secondary *banalités* which we have just mentioned were less common and viewed still less favourably than the others. They could not be established except on a very clear text from the customs or, if that were missing, on a very exact deed.

Ban of the grape harvest: this was still in use throughout the whole kingdom in the eighteenth century. It was purely a policy linked to the lord's function as high justice. To exercise it, the lord did not need any deed. The *ban* of the grape harvest was binding on everyone. The customs of Burgundy gave the lord the right to harvest his grapes one day before any other vineyard owner.

Right of *banvin*: A right enjoyed by a good number of lords, say the authors, either by virtue of custom or by special deeds, to sell the wine from their manorial estates for a specified period of time (generally one month or forty days) before anyone else. Among the big custom areas only Tours, Anjou, Maine and Marche established and regulated it. A decree from the tax court, 28 August 1751, authorized, as an exemption, bars to sell wine during the *banvin*, but only to strangers. It was still necessary for the wine to be the lord's, from his estate. These customs which established and regulated this right of *banvin* normally required that it be founded on a deed.

Right of *blairie*: a right belonging to the lord as high justice because of the permission he granted to the inhabitants to pasture their animals on land situated within the boundaries of his jurisdiction or on common grazing land. This right did not exist in areas of written law but was very well known in areas of customary law. It was particularly found, under different names, in Bourbonnais, Nivernais, Auvergne and Burgundy. This right assumed that originally all the land belonged to the lord in such a manner that, having distributed the best parts of it in fiefs, *censives* and other land concessions for payments, some still remained to serve only as common pasture which he allowed to be used on a temporary basis. *Blairie* was established in several customs but there was only the lord high justice who could claim it. It had to be based on a special deed or at least upon ancient acceptance supported by long-standing ownership.

Tolls: in the beginning, say the authors, an enormous number of manorial tolls existed on bridges, rivers and roads. Louis XIV destroyed a great number of them. In 1724, a commission appointed to inquire into all the toll title deeds eliminated twelve hundred and more were eliminated every day (1765). The primary principle, says Renauldon, in this context was that the toll, being a tax, should not only be based on a title but upon one issued by the sovereign. The toll carried the heading: *By order of the king.* One of the conditions of this is that a list of all the dues payable on each kind of merchandise should be attached to them. This list of fees always needed the approval of the Royal Council. As the author says: the title of concession had to be followed by uninterrupted possession. In spite of all these precautions which the legislator took, the value of some tolls had increased considerably in modern times. 'I know of a toll,' he adds, 'which was leased for only 100 livres a century ago and which brings in 1400 today; another, leased for 39,000 livres brings in 90,000 livres.' The chief judicial rulings and edicts which regulated the right of tolls were Title 29 of the ruling of 1669 and the edicts of 1683, 1724 and 1775.

The authors I quote, although quite favourable in general terms to feudal rights, acknowledged that great abuses were committed in the collection of tolls.

Bacs: the right of ferries differed markedly from that of tolls. The latter was levied on goods only, the former upon persons, animals and vehicles. In order for this right to be exercised, it also had to be authorized by the king and the dues levied had to be fixed by decree of the council which created or sanctioned them.

The right of *leyde* (according to the place, it was given several different names) is a tax levied on goods brought to fairs or markets. A good many lords considered this right as linked to high justice and entirely manorial, say the feudal lawyers I am quoting, but this was not so for it was a tax which had to be authorized by the king. In any case, this right belonged to the lord high justice who collected the police fines arising from that right. However, although according to theory the right of *leyde* could stem from the king alone, it appears that, in fact, it was often based simply upon feudal deeds and long usage.

Certainly, fairs could be established only upon royal authorization.

Lords, in order to enjoy the right to regulate the weights and measures which their vassals should employ in fairs and markets of the manor, did not need precisely established deeds nor permission from the king. It was enough for this deed to be based upon custom and continuous ownership. Every king in turn, who had wanted to bring back uniformity into weights and measures, failed, say the authors. Things have remained where they were at the time of the drawing up of customs.

Roads: rights exercised by lords over the roads. The main roads, those called the king's roads, belonged in fact to the crown. Their creation, upkeep and the crimes committed upon them were beyond the jurisdiction of the lords or their judges. As for private roads within the bounds of the manor, they belonged without doubt to lords high justice who exercised over them all the rights of maintenance and supervision while their judges had jurisdiction over all the crimes committed upon them, outside royal lawsuits. In former times, lords had been responsible for the maintenance of the main roads which crossed their boundaries. To cover the expenses laid out upon these repairs they had been granted for these roads rights of toll, boundary and access. However, since then the king had recovered general control over the main roads.

Waters: all rivers navigable by boat or raft belonged to the king even if they crossed lords' lands, despite any deed to the contrary. (Ruling of 1669.) If lords collected a few dues on these rivers, they were those of fishing, mills, ferries or landing stages, etc., by virtue of concessions perforce granted them by the king. There were lords who claimed rights of policing and law enforcement over these rivers but only as a result of an obviously unlawful occupation or of concessions seized illegally.

Small rivers belonged unquestionably to the lords through whose land they flowed. They exercised over them the same rights of ownership, law-enforcement and policing as the king over navigable rivers. All lords high justice were universal lords of non-navigable rivers flowing through their domains. In order to enjoy ownership over them they needed no other title than that granted by high justice. A few custom areas, such as Berry, granted individuals to raise, without the lord's permission, a mill on a lord's river which flowed through their property. The custom of Brittany granted this right only to particular nobles. In general, the lord high justice was certainly the only one who had the right to allow the construction of a mill within the boundaries of his jurisdiction. No one could cross over a lord's river in order to defend his property without the permission of his judges.

Fountains, wells, flax-wetting pits, ponds: the rainwater flow-ing along the main roads belonged to the lords high justice who had exclusive rights to dispose of it. The lord high justice could have a pond constructed within the boundaries of his jurisdiction even on the property of his subjects by paying them the value of the land submerged. This was the clear arrangement of several custom areas, for example Troyes and Nivernais. As for indi-viduals, they could make ponds only on their land. Nevertheless, in such a case, several custom areas forced the owner to ask the lord's permission. Those custom areas, which forced an indi-vidual to obtain the lord's consent, did demand that such consent should be free.

Fishing: fishing in rivers navigable by boat or raft belonged solely to the king who alone could grant concessions. His judges alone had the right to arbitrate over fishing infringements. Many lords had the right to fish in rivers of this kind but they held the concession from the king and had seized it unlawfully. As for non-navigable rivers, permission was not granted to fish in them even with a rod and line except by the lord high justice within whose boundaries they flowed. A decree of 30 April 1749 con-demned a fisherman in just such a case. Lords themselves, more-over, if they fished, had to submit to the general angling regulations. The lord high justice could grant the right to fish in his river either as a fief or for a *cens*.

Hunting: hunting could not be leased like fishing. It was a right granted to the individual. It was held to be a royal right which noblemen themselves enjoyed within the bounds of their jurisdic-tion or on their own fief only with the king's permission. This principle was outlined in the ruling of 1669, title 30. The lord's judges were competent to sit in all cases of hunting infringements, with the exception of the hunting of red beasts (these are, I believe larger animals – stags and hinds), which are royal cases.

The right to hunt was the one most forbidden to commoners; even free-holding commoners did not possess it. The king did not grant it in his favours. So strict was this principle that a lord could not even allow it. The law was that rigorous. Yet, every day lords were observed granting permission to hunt not only to noblemen but to commoners. The lord high justice could hunt within the boundaries of their jurisdiction, but by himself. He had, within these limits, the right to make all regulations, prohib-itions and restrictions concerning hunting. All the lords of fiefs, although they did not have legal rights, could hunt throughout their fief. Noblemen possessing neither fiefs nor legal status could also hunt over land belonging to them in the neighbourhood of their homes. It was judged that a commoner who owned a park within an area of high justice had to keep it open for the pleasure of the lord but this decree was very ancient, dating from 1668.

Rabbit warrens: none can now be established without legal title. Commoners, like noblemen, were allowed to open warrens but noblemen alone could own ferrets.

Dovecotes: certain custom areas granted the right to dovecotes to lords high justice alone; others granted it to all with fief ownership. In Dauphiné, Brittany and Normandy no commoner was allowed to possess dovecotes, small pigeon coops or aviaries. Only nobles could have pigeons. Penalties pronounced against those killing pigeons were very harsh, often culminating in corporal punishment.

According to the authors quoted, such were the chief feudal rights still collected in the second half of the eighteenth century. They add: 'the rights in question so far are the ones generally established. There are still many others, less well known and less extensive, which featured only in a few custom areas or even in some manorial estates by virtue of special title-deeds.'

These uncommon or restricted rights referred to here by name by the authors totalled ninety-nine, several of which were a burden upon agriculture because they gave lords certain rights over harvests, or because they established tolls over the sale of produce and transport as well. The authors state that several of these rights had fallen into disuse in their time. However, I think that a great number must still have been collected in certain places in 1789.

Having identified, among the feudal experts in the eighteenth century, the chief feudal rights still in force, I wished to know what their importance was in the eyes of contemporaries, at least from the point of view of the income of those collecting these dues and of those who paid them.

One of the authors I have just mentioned, Renauldon, informs us of the above by exposing the rules which lawyers had to follow to estimate in inventories the various feudal rights existing in 1765, that is twenty-four years before the Revolution. According to this legal expert, the following were the rules that had to be observed in this regard.

Rights of jurisdiction. He states: 'Some number of our custom areas put the value of high, low and average justice at a tenth of land revenue. Manorial justice at that time had great importance. Edme de Fréminville thinks that, nowadays, justice should be valued at a twentieth of land revenues. I believe this estimate is still too high.'

Honorary rights. However difficult it might be to value these rights, our author, a very positive man, little impressed by appearances, is confident that it was, nonetheless, wise for experts to set the value at a very modest level.

Manorial forced labour. The author states the rules for the valuation of forced labour which establishes that this right was still sometimes met. It sets the value of a day's work with oxen at twenty sous and that of a man at five plus food. This is quite a good indication of the level of wages in 1765.

Tolls. When these tolls were valued, the author says, 'No manorial right should be valued at a lower level than tolls. They fluctuate greatly; since the maintenance of the roads and bridges most useful for trade are now the responsibility of king and provinces, many tolls today are useless and are regularly being abolished.'

Fishing and hunting rights. Fishing rights could be leased and could be expertly valued. Hunting rights belonged purely to individuals and could not be leased. Thus they were in the honorary category but were not useful. Experts could not include them in their estimates.

Then the author speaks particularly about the rights of *banalité*, *banvin*, *leyde* and *blairie*, which reveal that these rights were the most frequently exercised and still retained the highest importance. He adds: 'A good many other manorial rights are still encountered from time to time. It would take too long and even be impossible to report here but, among examples we have just cited, intelligent experts will find rules to value separately the rights we do not mention.'

The value of the *cens*. Most custom areas decided that the *cens* should be valued at three per cent. The reason why the valuation of the *cens* is set so high is because this right represented, beyond the tax itself, variable sources of income such as *lods et ventes*.

Feudal tithes, *terrage*. Feudal tithes could not be estimated at less than four per cent since this type of property was liable neither to care, nor labour, nor financial outlay. When *terrage* or *champart* entailed *lods et ventes*, that is when a field subject to these dues could not be sold without paying a transfer fee to the lord controlling it, this occasional fee had to raise the valuation to three per cent. Otherwise it should be equal to the tithe.

Ground rents which carried no *lods et ventes* nor right of redemption (namely without manorial fees) should be valued at five per cent.

ESTIMATE OF THE DIFFERENT METHODS OF OWNING PROPERTY IN FRANCE BEFORE THE REVOLUTION

We know, says the author, of only three types of property.

1) *Freehold.* This is free tenure, exempt of every charge and not subject to any manorial duties or rights, either useful or honorary.

   Both nobles and commoners could be freeholders. The nobleman owning the freehold had the right of jurisdiction or fiefs depending on him or lands paying *cens* to him. He followed the laws of the feudal system when dividing the land. The commoner with freehold had neither jurisdiction, nor fief, nor the right to claim *cens* and divided the land according to commoner practice. The author does not acknowledge anyone but freeholders as having full ownership of land.

   The valuation of freehold property. It had to be the highest form of tenure. The customs of the Auvergne and Burgundy set their valuation at two and a half per cent. The author considers that an estimate of three per cent would be accurate.

   We must note that commoner freeholders living within the jurisdiction of the manor were subject to this jurisdiction. In this case this was not subservience to the lord but submission to a jurisdiction standing in the place of the state courts.

2) The second type of property was that held in *feudal tenure*.

3) The third was composed of property held *subject to the cens* or, in legal language, common tenure.

The valuation of property held in feudal tenure. The valuation was bound to be less since the feudal dues which burdened it were great.

1) In the districts of written law and in several custom areas fiefs owed only the dutiful homage of *hand and mouth*.

2) In other custom areas, fiefs outside the scope of hand and mouth were what was called *at risk* as in Burgundy and were subject to feudal confiscation (*commise*) whenever the owner took possession without having sworn an oath and paid homage.

3) Other custom areas such as Paris and many others subjected

the fief, beyond the pledge of faith and homage at purchase, to a tax of a fifth or twenty-fifth.

4) In yet others such as Poitou and some others they are subject to the right of a payment against an oath and to service on horseback, etc.

Property owed in the first category had to be valued more highly than the others.

The custom of Paris set the estimate at five per cent, which the author seems to see as quite reasonable.

The valuation of property owned by common tenure or governed by cens. To reach this valuation, it is best to divide them into three classes.

1) Those properties held in simple *cens*;
2) Beyond the *cens* they could be subject to other kinds of servitude;
3) They could be entailed, subject to the real *taille* or *bordelage*.

Of these three forms of commoner-held property outlined here, the first and second were quite normal in the eighteenth century; the third was uncommon. The assessments made of them, says the author, would be lower as you reached the second and especially the third. The owners of property in the third class were not even, if truth be told, real owners since they could not dispose of their belongings without the lord's permission.

The *terrier*. These were the regulations outlined by the feudal lawyers quoted above about the way in which the manorial registers, called *terriers*, were drawn up and kept up to date; I have mentioned these in several places in the text. This *terrier*, as we know, was a single register in which were listed all the title deeds stating the dues belonging to the manor, either in property or in honorary rights, real, individual or mixed. Inserted there were all the declarations of those subject to *cens*, the customs of manor, the leases, etc. In the custom of Paris, say our authors, the lords could rewrite their *terriers* every thirty years at the expense of those subject to *cens*. They add: 'We are nonetheless very happy when we come across a new one every century.' One's *terrier* could not be rewritten (this was an inconvenient process for all those dependent on the manor) without obtaining an authorization called *lettres à terrier* either from the great chancellory when it concerned manors situated within the jurisdiction of different *parlements* or from the Parlement in other cases. The notary was appointed by the court. It was before him that all the vassals, nobles, commoners, those subject to *cens*, those

under a perpetual lease and those bound by the lord's jurisdiction
had to appear. A map of the manor had to be attached to the
terrier.

Independently of the *terrier* could be found other registers,
called *lièves*, in the manor in which the lords or their tax farmers
listed the sums of money received from those subject to *cens*,
with their names and the date of their payment.

Glossary

Argenson René-Louis de Voyer, marquis d', 1694–1757. Friend of Voltaire (q.v.), Foreign Minister, wrote several interesting Memoirs.

Ban and **Banalités** The monopoly exercised by the lord to hire out mills, bread ovens, wine presses, bulls for stud, etc.

Baudeau Nicolas, 1730–92. A physiocrat who wrote an introduction (1781) to economic philosophy which Tocqueville had read.

Beaumarchais Pierre-Augustin Caron de, 1732–99. Playwright author of comedies *The Barber of Seville* (1775) and *The Marriage of Figaro* (1784).

Blackstone Sir William, 1723–80. The greatest legal commentator on English constitutional matters. His *Commentaries on the Laws of England* was published 1765–9.

Bolingbroke Henry St John, 1678–1751. English Foreign Minister who negotiated the Treaty of Utrecht, 1713, to close the War of Spanish Succession. A deist philosopher, he wrote political and literary letters. Entertained Voltaire (q.v.) in England, 1726.

Boulainvilliers Henri, comte de Saint-Saire, 1658–1722. French historian and political writer who deplored the rise of absolute monarchy and government by the people. From Normandy (like Tocqueville), he was a supporter of feudalism. He was among the first to believe that a study of history can help the understanding of contemporary society.

Burgundy Duke of Burgundy, Louis de France, 1682–1712; grandson of Louis XIV, father of Louis XV. Pupil of Fénélon (q.v.).

Burke Edmund, 1729–97. A leading Whig MP. The first and greatest ideological opponent of the French Revolution (*Reflections on the Revolution in France*, 1790). He profoundly influenced Tocqueville, who both admired him and disagreed with him. *The Ancien Régime* is, among other things, a sustained critique of Burke's views. The quotation on p. 18 comes from *Substance of the Speech on the*

Army Estimates (1790); on p. 20 from *Letters on a Regicide Peace*, Letter 1. The reference on p. 34 is a paraphrase in *Reflections on the Revolution in France*, pp. 179–81. The reference, on p. 83 is a paraphrase taken mid-sentence from *Reflections*, volume 4, p. 301.

Cahiers Each Electoral district of the three Orders drew up petitions of grievances (*cahiers de doléances*) to present to their Estates-General (q.v.) at their meeting in 1789. Tocqueville was not the first or the last historian to recognize their immense value as evidence.

Carlyle Thomas, 1795–1881, Scottish essayist and historian. He wrote *The French Revolution*, his most famous work, from 1834 to 1837.

Charles VII 1403–61, King of France (1422–61). Under him, and inspired by Joan of Arc, the royal army drove the English from France. Tocqueville's reference highlights Charles's attempts to stabilize the revenue.

Chateaubriand François-René de, vicomte, 1768–1848. The greatest French writer of his generation and the father of French Romanticism. A leading politician under the Restoration (1814–30), his rupture with the Bourbons helped to precipitate the 1830 Revolution. He was related by marriage to Tocqueville and greatly influenced him.

Châtelet Émilie, marquise du, 1706–49. Mathematician, physicist and philosopher. Voltaire (q.v.) was her lover.

Choiseul Étienne François, duc de, 1719–85. Louis XV's chief minister, 1758–70, he did much to make good France's losses in the Seven Years War but nothing to reform the government of the Ancien Régime.

Colbert Jean-Baptiste, 1619–83. Louis XIV's Controller-General of Finances; his capable management made possible the triumphs of the Sun King's first twenty years as active ruler of France.

Committimus Royal permission given to individuals to take legal cases to certain courts outside the usual judicial system.

Commynes Philippe de, c. 1447–1511. Wrote Memoirs on the reigns of Louis X (q.v.) and Charles VIII. He served Charles the Bold, Duke of Burgundy, Louis XI, Charles VIII and Louis XII.

Democracy in America Tocqueville's first masterpiece, published in two parts, 1835 and 1840. Making the United States his field of observation, Tocqueville explored the question of whether a free government of equality under the law was possible in modern times (he argued it was); discussed the changes that, he believed, the advance of democracy would make in civil society and warned his readers against various dangers which he saw. (Available in Penguin Classics since 2003.)

Diderot Denis, 1713–84. A man of letters and philosopher, chief editor of the *Encyclopédie*, a fine letter writer, admired by Catherine the Great, translated by Goethe, he was one of the most brilliant thinkers of the eighteenth century.

Dragonnades 1681–85, the persecution of French Protestants under Louis XIV after the revocation of the Edict of Nantes.

Encyclopédie A literary and philosophic publication inaugurated by d'Alembert in 1745 and edited from 1747 by Denis Diderot (q.v.). Publication started in 1751. At first suppressed, it became a national treasure. It extended knowledge beyond previous encyclopaedias to include 'trades'. Many of the names mentioned by Tocqueville were contributors: Voltaire, Forbonnais, Turgot, Morelly, Necker and Quesnay (qq.v.). Rousseau (q.v.) wrote on music. The first edition ran to twenty-eight volumes and continued throughout the Revolution.

Estates-General France's medieval quasi-parliament (not to be confused with the Parlement de Paris) did not meet between 1614 and 1789; when at last it again convened the Revolution followed immediately. By August the Estates, which had met separately, had merged into one body, calling itself the National Assembly (soon after that it was usually referred to as the Constituent Assembly, having taken up the task of giving France a constitution).

Evocation A procedure by which the king's officers could remove a law case from the jurisdiction of the *parlements* and settle it themselves.

Farmers-General Under the Ancien Régime the government 'farmed out' the collection and administration of taxes to bodies of private citizens – the farmers-general – who took enormous percentages of the monies collected as commission for their trouble. They were exceedingly unpopular and the system grew into one of the worst inefficiencies of the Ancien Régime.

Fénelon François de Salignac de la Mothe, Bishop, 1651–1715. Churchman in Louis XIV's court; writer on theology and education. A liberal humanist, an advanced thinker in the fields of spirituality and political theory. His most famous book, *The Adventures of Telemachus* (1699) features Salentum (q.v.) as a Utopia.

Feudalism The word used loosely and universally in the eighteenth and nineteenth centuries to describe the social system of the eighteenth century, characterized by the privileges accorded to those of noble rank, especially those relating to taxation and land-ownership. The term was derogatory and meant to imply that the system was as obsolete as it was unjust. In fact 'feudalism', although

it had evolved from the structures of the Middle Ages, was quite
distinct from the 'feudal society' described by, for example, Marc
Bloch.

Fief The ancient Frankish word *fehu-od* (meaning cattle) for land held
by the vassal of a king or a lord in return for specified services,
military or judicial. By the end of the Middle Ages such fiefs had
lost this character almost completely and were held as simply private
property, which could be bequeathed or sold.

Fleury André Hercule de, 1653–1743. Cardinal, tutor of Louis XV
(q.v.) in 1715. Became *de facto* first minister from 1726. He vigorously disciplined the *parlements* (q.v.).

Forbonnais François Véron de, 1722–1800, writer in 1758 of a two-
volume work on French finances from 1595 to 1721.

Frederick the Great 1712–86, King of Prussia (1740–86). A great
admirer of the French Philosophes (q.v.) and of Voltaire (q.v.) until
they met. The epitome of what the eighteenth century called an
enlightened despot. His great achievement was to use the rationalism
of the Enlightenment to transform Prussia into a Great Power and,
in many ways, the first modern state in European history. His mili-
tarism and Machiavellianism made it difficult for the Philosophes
to accept him as one of their own.

Frederick William XI 1744–97, King of Prussia (1786–97). An insig-
nificant ruler with no political or military gifts. His main interests
were cultural, especially musical. He squandered financial resources
and failed to carry out any reforms.

Fréminville Edmé de. Writer of a practical treatise on Manorial dues,
five volumes, Paris (1746–57).

Fronde There were two Frondes: that of 1648, a rising against royal
authority led by the Parlement of Paris and the Fronde of the Princes
(1649–53), in which factions and frivolous nobles showed themselves ready to plunge France into anarchy. The experience convinced the young Louis XIV (q.v.) that he must be absolute master
of his kingdom. He never forgot or forgave the 'frondeurs', individually or collectively.

Gavelkind A name for land tenure which developed into the custom
of dividing a tenant's land equally among his sons at death.

Guilds The medieval system of associations to protect artisans. There
were three grades of membership: master, journeyman and appren-
tice. By the end of the seventeenth century their power and influence
had gone into decline.

Helvétius Claude Adrien, 1715–71. Philosopher and educationalist
whose works were banned. He pursued a hedonistic philosophy

based on self-interest, the physical sensations and the equality of intellect.

Henri III 1551–89, last of the Valois kings of France (1574–89). His reign was disrupted by the Wars of Religion. Financial crisis induced the king to raise revenue by selling administrative and judicial posts; his example was followed by his successors. In the long run this greatly weakened royal authority and was thus one of the causes of the French Revolution.

Henri IV 1553–1610, first Bourbon king (1589–1610). His aim was to stabilize government and end religious strife (1598 Edict of Nantes). He ruled absolutely through Councils and developed the Intendant system. During a period of religious peace and along with his excellent finance minister Sully (q.v.) he oversaw a period of prosperity.

d'Holbach Paul Henri Thiry, baron, 1723–89. Atheist and materialist. He wrote scientific articles for the *Encyclopédie*. He saw man as a machine; free will and the soul did not exist. He had a great influence on Goethe and Shelley.

Hume David, 1711–76. Historian, essayist and philosopher. His interest was in causality and the nature of the mind.

Île-de-France The region around Paris.

Insinuation To register an agreement, which was originally enacted verbally, into a written form of words so as to give it official authority.

Intendant Lost in obscurity, created formally in 1625 and given full authority by Louis XIV (q.v.), Intendants were, under the Ancien Régime, the king's supervisors in governmental control of public order, military and financial affairs of the country, having authority over a province or '*généralité*'. They were a solution to the loss of royal power brought about by the selling of offices over the centuries. Each Intendant worked with sub-delegates and was generally unpopular. They were suppressed on 22 December 1789.

Jacquerie The 1358 great peasant rebellion in the reign of Jean II (q.v.).

Jean II 1319–64, King of France (1350–64), taken prisoner by the English at the Battle of Poitiers (1356).

Lavoisier Antoine-Laurent, 1743–94. Brilliant scientist and the father of modern chemistry. As a farmer-general, he had a wall erected round Paris in 1787, was accused by Marat of cutting off the air from the capital and was executed.

Law John, 1671–1729. Scottish financier and money reformer. In 1716 he was invited to repair the financial damage caused by

Louis XIV's campaigns. Political intrigue and speculation destroyed his scheme to issue bank notes instead of gold.

Le Trosne/Letronne Guillaume François, 1728–80. Physiocrat, author of a financial study of tax reform in 1779.

Louis IX 1215–70, Saint Louis, King of France (1226–70). A just ruler; a brilliant man concerned with the rule of law and sound moral principles, especially from his officials. He died of plague on his second crusade.

Louis XI 1423–83, King of France (1461–83). A supporter of the common people, he attempted to discipline the nobility and to centralize government in royal hands. He strengthened the army and quadrupled the *taille* (q.v.). The central purpose of his reign was to weaken the great semi-independent nobles (the Duke of Brittany and, especially, the Duke of Burgundy) and strengthen the power of the crown. Unscrupulous and devious, he was largely successful in this undertaking.

Louis XII 1462–1515, King of France (1498–1515). He simplified and improved the administration of justice, seeking to protect his lowliest subjects against oppression. He managed to leave taxes alone, kept his kingdom free from civil war and invasion. He promoted the theory of royal absolutism.

Louis XIII 1601–43, King of France (1610–43). Inherited the throne as a boy and, until he reached maturity, the government of France was threatened by noble factionalism (as it was during the minority of his son). But in Cardinal Richelieu he found a chief minister of iron will and immense ability and, in spite of occasionally cool personal relations, stuck to him until the cardinal's death in 1642. His support enabled Richelieu to found the absolutist state that became the Ancien Régime.

Louis XIV 1638–1715, King of France (1643–1715). Building on the foundations laid by Richelieu and Mazarin (q.q.v.), he turned the traditional French monarchy into a personal autocracy which neither of his immediate successors was able or willing to exercise adequately, one of the greatest weaknesses of the Ancien Régime. In spite of this, and of the unsuccessful wars of his last twenty years and of his intolerance of religious dissent, the Sun King is remembered as the incarnation of royal greatness. He built Versailles.

Louis XV 1710–74, King of France (1715–74). Known in his youth as 'Louis the Well-beloved', he wasted the years of his prime by involving France in a succession of unprofitable wars, which left the country and its monarchy badly weakened. Towards the end of his life he at last made a serious effort to reform French government but his sudden death from smallpox came before his new institutions had taken root. His successor immediately abolished them.

Louis XVI 1754–93, King of France (1774–92). Of good character and mediocre abilities, Louis was always anxious to do the right thing but never very clear as to what that was. He reversed the policy of Louis XV by recalling the *parlements* (q.v.) but suspended them in his turn some twelve years later. Turgot (q.v.), his first Controller-General, might have made good his master's weaknesses and introduced successful reforms but Louis let him be driven from office after only two years. It was the first in the series of mistakes that eventually brought Louis to deposition and the guillotine.

Louis-Philippe 1773–1850, King of the French (1830–48). After the overthrow of his cousin Charles X in the July Revolution, the Duke of Orléans accepted the crown and for a few years seemed to have established a new dynasty as 'the Bourgeois king'. He was very intelligent, very vain and unable to adjust to the demands of the age. His failings were among the chief causes of the 1848 Revolution. Tocqueville despised him.

Luther Martin, c. 1483–1546. Theologian who launched the Protestant Reformation; most famous for his attack on papal indulgences sold to replenish Vatican coffers.

Machault d'Arnouville Jean-Baptiste, 1710–94. A lawyer who as Controller-General of Finances from 1745 to 1754 attempted to reform Louis XV's tax laws. He introduced the *vingtième* (q.v.) as a universal tax. This was opposed by the clergy and right-wing nobility. He was disgraced in 1757 and died in prison under the Terror.

Maillotins The name given to the Parisian rebels of 1382 who protested against the imposition of new taxes.

Maistre Joseph de, 1753–1821. Diplomat and thinker, conservative in politics, devoted to the papacy and opposed to the French Revolution.

Malesherbes Chrétien Guillaume de Lamoignon de, 1721–94. Administrator and statesman known for his tolerance in the last decade of the Ancien Régime. Great-grandfather to Tocqueville. He had supported the Philosophes (q.v.) during his time as head of press censorship. In the 1770s he had defended the people against Louis XVI's despotism; he emerged from retirement to defend that king from the people. His reward was death by the guillotine along with his daughter (Tocqueville's mother's mother) and granddaughter, 22 April 1794.

Maria Teresa of Austria, 1717–80. Energetic and courageous ruler.

Mother of Marie-Antoinette, wife of Louis XVI (q.v.). Promoted the alleviation of the hardships of her serfs.

Mazarin Cardinal Jules, 1602–61. Protégé of Richelieu and chief minister to the Regent, Queen Anne of Austria, during the minority of Louis XIV (q.v.). The Fronde (q.v.) was largely inspired by the desire to get rid of him as a foreign favourite – he was Italian. He was a statesman of first-rate ability who completed the work of Richelieu, contrived the Peace of Westphalia and the Peace of the Pyrenees, which confirmed France as the first Power in Europe, trained Louis XIV for the work of kingship and brought forward the men who were to be his earliest and most successful ministers.

Mercier de la Rivière 1720–93. An important Physiocrat. Author of *The Natural and Essential Order of Political Societies* (1767), a book studied by Tocqueville.

Michelet Jules, 1798–1874. Historian known for his monumental *History of France* and *History of the French Revolution* (1847–53, seven volumes).

Mill John Stuart, 1806–1873. Philosopher and economist, outstanding scholar and Tocqueville's greatest student and interpreter. He profoundly admired *Democracy in America* and *The Ancien Régime*. His *On Liberty* (1859) was deeply influenced by Tocqueville's thought.

Mill of Sans-Souci A probably fictional story tells how Frederick the Great (q.v.) tried to force a mill owner to sell him his windmill, near the king's Potsdam palace called Sans-Souci (Carefree). The owner suggested that the king should obey his own laws.

Mirabeau Honoré Gabriel Riqueti, comte de, 1749–91. A colourful figure, enemy of despotism, whose moment came in 1789 with his support for the Third Estate and his hope to reconcile the monarchy and the Revolution, in which he failed. 'The Shakespeare of eloquence', he was among the greatest of orators.

Mirabeau Victor Riqueti, marquis de, 1715–89 (the elder). Criticized Louis XIV's (q.v.) centralized government. Supported the Physiocrats' (q.v.) aim to reform taxation, with a scheme to tax land and income alone. He supported the *pays d'états* (q.v.). The father of the more famous Honoré (q.v.). Tocqueville took copious notes on his 1756–8 two-volume work, *L'Ami des Hommes*.

Molé Louis-Mathieu, comte, 1781–1855. His career in administration began under Napoleon; he held important posts under the Restoration and the July Monarchy, including that of Prime Minister (1837–9). Overshadowed by Guizot until 1848, he made a political comeback under the Second Republic but unwisely first supported

302 GLOSSARY

and then opposed the ambitious Louis-Napoleon. The *coup d'état*
of 1851 ended his career. He was Tocqueville's friend and cousin.

Molière Jean-Baptiste Poquelin, 1622–73. French comic playwright
who satirized contemporary manners with an acute insight into
human nature. The quotation refers to the *Malade Imaginaire* of
1673, where learning with no common sense is one theme of the
play.

Mollien François Nicolas, comte de, 1758–1850. He left four volumes
of Memoirs (1845, Paris) after a life in public service in finance
under Louis XVI and later under Napoleon.

Montesquieu Charles Louis de Secondat, baron de, 1689–1755. One
of the most famous critics of Louis XIV's reign in the 1721 book *The
Persian Letters*, mocking the Church. He hated despotism and, like
Tocqueville, was devoted to liberty. His *L'Esprit des Lois*, published
in 1748, was one of the most influential works on political theory.

Morelly André, 1727–1819. Contributor to the *Encyclopédie* (q.v.)
and follower of Turgot's (q.v.) views. In *Le Code de la Nature* he
expounded a primitive communism.

Napoleon I The greatest general of his era and a superb, if despotic,
ruler of France. Emperor of the French, 1804–14, and for a hundred
days in 1815. Tocqueville was fascinated by him.

Napoleon III Emperor of the French, 1852–70. The Bonaparte
pretender from 1832 to 1848; president of the Second Republic,
1848–52; seized dictatorial power in the *coup d'état* of December
1851. Tocqueville detested his despotism and *The Ancien Régime*
is, in part, an anti-Bonapartist tract.

Necker Jacques, 1732–1804. A Swiss Protestant banker, twice served
as Louis XVI's Controller-General. He sedulously cultivated his
own popularity, which was much greater than his actual achievements and ability warranted. News of his dismissal precipitated the
assault on the Bastille, 1789. He was the father of Madame de Staël.

Notables The class of former nobles, upper bourgeoisie, administrators, lawyers, businessmen and so on who, for most of the nineteenth
century, were the clearest beneficiaries of the French Revolution.
The word became current in 1787 when Louis XVI's minister
Calonne summoned an Assembly of Notables which he erroneously
hoped would facilitate his programme of reform.

Orry Philibert, 1689–1747, Controller-General of France in 1730.
His father had worked in Spain, introducing a system of Intendants.

Parlements The law courts established by the medieval kings of France,
first in Paris, then in various provinces. Over the centuries, especially
after their members acquired property rights in their offices, they

became strongly resistant to royal authority. In the eighteenth century they clamoured for reform but were one of the chief obstacles in its way.

Pays d'Élection The Royal Provinces. The majority of French provinces which were under the direct control of the king.

Pays d'États Described in this translation as the Independent Provinces, they were independent of the king and they had considerable privileges and rights. (v. The Appendix)

Péréfixe Hardouin de Beaumont de, 1606–71. Archbishop of Paris (1662), tutor to Louis XIV (q.v.) and opponent of the Jansenists. He published his *History of King Henry the Great* in 1661.

Philosophes The term used collectively for most of the leading French writers of the eighteenth century such as Voltaire (q.v.) and the group round the *Encyclopédie* (q.v.). They embodied the Enlightenment. Rousseau (q.v.) was at first their protégé but then attacked them for their rationalism.

Physiocrats (Greek *phusis* – nature; *kratein* – to rule). An eighteenth-century economic movement that sought the harmony of natural law with legal and ethical practice. Founded by François Quesnay (q.v.), it was in opposition to any regulation of trade as a source of wealth, preferring the products of the soil. His followers included Mirabeau (the elder, q.v.), Mercier de la Rivière (q.v.), Le Trosne (q.v.), Baudeau (q.v.) and Rouband. Their best hope of influence came and fell with Turgot's (q.v.) ministry. They preferred the title Economists and the term Physiocrats took over only in the nineteenth century.

Pitt William, the Younger, 1759–1806. Prime Minister of Britain 1783–1801, 1804–6. Initially a reforming Whig, believing in free trade, he led his country in the wars against the French Revolution and became, in effect, the founder of the modern Conservative (or Tory) Party.

Prefectural Council The law of 17 February 1800 (28 Pluviôse Year VIII) had created such councils of government-appointed members to arbitrate contentious legal issues. These were condemned by Tocqueville who was always against special privileges accorded to public officials to avoid equality before the law.

Préfét/préfecture Post-Revolution official created by Napoleon (q.v.) in 1800 to replace the Intendant of the Ancien Régime to look after the French departments, which replaced the provinces.

Présidial Court of Appeal. Established in 1551 in certain towns to deal with less important cases. Otherwise appeals were made to the *parlement* (q.v.)

Provost An officer placed in charge of Church, military and administrative groups carrying a right of jurisdiction, e.g. taxes, military discipline, royal palaces.

Quesnay François, 1694–1774. A doctor who turned to economics at the age of sixty, became the leader of the Physiocrats (q.v.). Supported free competition and the harmonization of the class system under a strong central government.

Rajah of Hindustan From 1842 to 1843 Tocqueville had taken notes on the history of India which he thought of writing about.

Reformation The sixteenth-century religious revolution which split medieval Christendom for good. The so-called Protestant revolt against the authority of the papacy, led by Luther (q.v.) and Calvin, divided Europe along confessional lines; but its most important consequence was probably the liberation of the individual mind and conscience to reason for itself, not only in matters of religion.

Régie The system of raising taxes.

Revolution of 1830 Charles X, 1757–1836, last king of the senior line of Bourbons (1825–30), was driven from his throne after the 'three glorious days' of insurrection in Paris, 27–29 July 1830, provoked by his four decrees dissolving the newly elected Chamber of Deputies before it had ever met, reducing the electorate to 25,000 landholders and abolishing freedom of the press. He was replaced by Louis-Philippe and by a somewhat liberal political system: the so-called July Monarchy.

Revolution of 1848 In its last years, the July Monarchy proved as inflexible and myopic as the Bourbons before it. Economic crisis and political repression eventually provoked another Parisian insurrection (22 February 1848) which overthrew the July Monarchy and replaced it with the Second Republic; but revolutionary turbulence did not die out for nearly four years, when it was at last crushed by the dictatorship of Napoleon III (q.v.).

Richelieu Armand du Plessis, Cardinal de, 1584–1642. Chief minister of Louis XIII. Richelieu's central purpose was to make the king's power unchallengeable in France and to raise France to pre-eminence internationally. He let nothing and nobody stand in his way: not French Protestants, French nobles, the king himself, the Pope or the House of Habsburg.

Rousseau Jean-Jacques, 1712–78. An immensely influential writer. His *Confessions* inspired Robespierre; his *Social Contract* was thought to justify revolutionary dictatorship. His insistence on the importance of a virtuous citizenship left its mark on Tocqueville.

Salentum v. Fénelon. A Utopia found in Fénelon's *The Adventures of Telemachus*. A book very critical of despotism.

Salvian c. 400–c. 490, a Church writer who tried to shame the Romans into better ways by saying that, in some respects, the victorious barbarians, though smelly, were morally superior. His writings highlight the widespread poverty and unequal distribution of wealth.

Schama Simon, published his acclaimed book on the French Revolution, *Citizens*, in 1989.

Schiller Johann Christoph Friedrich von, 1759–1805, German poet, dramatist and philosopher.

Sénéschal Chief law officer in a designated area. The *Sénéschaussée* was the area covered by his jurisdiction.

Sixteen The name of the Paris city council during the Wars of Religion.

Suard Jean-Baptiste, 1734–1817, French journalist and critic, writer of interesting Memoirs.

Suffolk A large agricultural county in the east of England, long famous for sheep-rearing.

Sully Maximilien de Béthune, duc de, 1560–1641. The chief minister of Henri IV (q.v.), who rescued French public finances after the ruin of the Wars of Religion.

Syndic An official elected to take charge of any social body, e.g. a group of creditors, family, worker's meeting.

Tartuffe Play by Molière (1764), France's best-known comic playwright (q.v.), on the theme of hypocrisy and human gullibility.

Taxes

    capitation: personal tax on everyone except the clergy.

    cens: rent on land leased out by a lord to a tenant.

    corvée: days of unpaid labour owed by commoners to the lord for the maintenance of roads, transportation of military equipment and military service.

    lods et ventes: a tax paid to the lord on any property sold.

    hundredth penny: a tax on the transfer of property (*mutation immobilière*).

    octroi: a tax levied from the thirteenth century by a commune or town on certain categories of goods. Abolished by the Revolution for five years, 1791–6, it lasted until the mid-twentieth century.

    quitrent: *la censive*. The area covering all those properties where *cens* (q.v.) was due.

    taille: the chief tax of the Ancien Régime. Levied on persons in the *pays d'éléction* (q.v.) and the *pays d'état* (q.v.). It had many oppressive features, of which the worst was that the nobles and clergy were exempt from it.

306 GLOSSARY

tithe: payment as a proportion of produce or income paid to the Church and sometimes to the lord

vingtième: a 5 per cent tax on the revenue from property imposed on nobles and commoners.

du Terray (abbé) Joseph-Marie, Controller-General of France in 1769, disgraced by Louis XVI.

Thirty Years War 1618–48. A general European war that broke out because of the hatred between Protestants and Catholics but was kept going by the rivalry between the dynasties of Habsburg and Bourbon.

Turgot Anne-Robert-Jacques, baron de'l'Aulne, 1727–81. Statesman and economist, he admired the Physiocrats (q.v.) and wrote for the *Encyclopédie* (q.v.). He was appointed Intendant for Limoges 1761. He fought for the abolition of the *corvée* (q.v.) and for the *taille* (q.v.) to be paid by all classes. Champion of liberty, equality and poor relief. Became Controller-General (q.v.), 1774, tackling the country's financial crisis. Hated by many at court for his views, he was forced to resign in 1776. An idealist of great charm, but awkward with strangers. His ideas and reforms were taken up by the Revolution. Admired by Tocqueville.

Vauban Sébastien Le Prestre de, Marshal of France, 1633–1707. One of Louis XIV's greatest commanders, an expert in fortification. Made rational suggestions for the government of France which the king ignored. One of Tocqueville's ancestors.

Voltaire François-Marie Arouet, 1694–1778. A man of mischief, anti-Church, ritual and dogma; forced into continuous retreat from the authorities. A poet, playwright and polemicist. He paid a stormy visit to Frederick the Great, 1750–53. Champion of the oppressed. His best known book is *Candide* (1759) in which he develops his style of understated irony. He liked the religious tolerance and liberal thought of the English – the theme of *Lettres philosophiques sur les Anglais* (1728).

War of Spanish Succession The war between France, Austria and England, 1701–14.

Westphalia Treaty of (1648), which brought the Thirty Years War (q.v.) to an end.

Young Arthur, 1741–1820. English writer on agriculture, famous for his extensive travels of investigation, especially in France at the outbreak of the Revolution, recorded in his *Travels in France* (1792). Tocqueville studied and cited him and his influence is very clear in *The Ancien Régime*. This edition has retained Tocqueville's versions for obvious reasons.

The quoted references on the following pages are from *Travels in France*, ed. M. Bentham Edwards (London, 1915). p. 18 v.98:

p. 38 this looks like a précis of the above, v. p. 330

p. 82 a free treatment of v. p. 153

p. 83 15 July 1789, Young is at Nancy. v. p. 201

p. 103 the quotation is from p. 146

p. 172 from pp. 44–5. Tocqueville might even be saying the opposite to Young!

p. 212 maybe a quotation from memory. From p. 67?

PENGUIN CLASSICS

A VINDICATION OF THE RIGHTS OF WOMAN
MARY WOLLESTONECRAFT

Writing in an age when the call for the rights of man had brought revolution to America and France, Mary Wollstonecraft produced her own declaration of female independence in 1792. Passionate and forthright, *A Vindication of the Rights of Woman* attacked the prevailing view of docile, decorative femininity, and instead laid out the principles of emancipation: an equal education for girls and boys, an end to prejudice and a plea for women to become defined by their profession, not their partner. Wollstonecraft's work was received with a mixture of admiration and outrage – Walpole called her 'a hyena in petticoats' – and it established her as the mother of modern feminism.

This revised edition contains a new chronology, updated further reading, greatly expanded notes and an updated introduction. The text of the second edition of 1792, including original punctuation, is printed with emendations listed.

'Her pioneering demand for equality' Sheila Rowbotham

'She is alive and active … we hear her voice and trace her influence even now'
Virginia Woolf

Edited with an introduction and notes by Miriam Brody

PENGUIN CLASSICS

DIALOGUES CONCERNING NATURAL RELIGION
DAVID HUME

'Were this world ever so perfect a production, it must still remain uncertain, whether all the excellences of the work can justly be ascribed to the workman'

In the posthumously published *Dialogues Concerning Natural Religion*, the Enlightenment philosopher David Hume attacked many of the traditional arguments for the existence of God, expressing the belief that religion is founded on ignorance and irrational fears. Though calm and courteous in tone – at times even tactfully ambiguous – the conversations between Hume's vividly realized fictional figures form perhaps the most searching case ever mounted against orthodox Christian theological thinking and the 'deism' of the time, which pointed to the wonders of creation as conclusive evidence of God's Design. Hume's characters debate these issues with extraordinary passion, lucidity and humour, in one of the most compelling philosophical works ever written.

Based on Hume's own manuscript, Martin Bell provides an accessible modern edition, while his fascinating introduction sets Hume's religious scepticism in the philosophical and scientific context of its time.

Edited with an introduction by Martin Bell

PENGUIN CLASSICS

THE DESCENT OF MAN
CHARLES DARWIN

'With all these exalted powers – Man still bears in his bodily frame the indelible stamp of his lowly origin'

In *The Origin of Species*, 1859, Charles Darwin refused to discuss human evolution, believing the subject too 'surrounded with prejudices'. He had been reworking his notes since the 1830s, but only with much trepidation did he finally publish *The Descent of Man* in 1871. The book notoriously put apes in our family tree and made the races one family, diversified by 'sexual selection': Darwin's provocative theory that female choice among competing males leads to diverging racial characteristics. Named by Sigmund Freud as 'one of the ten most significant books' ever written, Darwin's *Descent of Man* continues to shape the way we think about what it is that makes us uniquely human.

In their introduction, James Moore and Adrian Desmond, acclaimed biographers of Charles Darwin, call for a radical re-assessment of the book, arguing that its core ideas on race were fired by Darwin's hatred of slavery. This reprint of the second and definitive edition also contains suggestions for further reading, a chronology and biographical sketches of prominent individuals.

Edited with an introduction by James Moore and Adrian Desmond

PENGUIN CLASSICS

DEMOCRACY IN AMERICA *AND*
TWO WEEKS IN THE WILDERNESS
ALEXIS DE TOCQUEVILLE

'A new political science is needed for a totally new world'

In 1831 Alexis de Tocqueville, a young French aristocrat and ambitious civil servant, made a nine-month journey throughout America. The result was *Democracy in America*, a monumental study of the strengths and weaknesses of the nation's evolving politics and institutions. Tocqueville looked to the flourishing democratic system in America as a possible model for post-revolutionary France, believing that the egalitarian ideals it enshrined reflected the spirit of the age and even that they were the will of God. His insightful work has become one of the most influential political texts ever written on America and an indispensable authority for anyone interested in the future of democracy. This volume includes the rarely translated *Two Weeks in the Wilderness*, an evocative account of Tocqueville's travels in Michigan among the Iroquois and Chippeway, and *The Excursion to Lake Onéida*.

This is the only edition that contains all Tocqueville's writings on America. Gerald Bevan's translation is accompanied by an introduction by Isaac Kramnick, which discusses Tocqueville's life and times, and the enduring significance of *Democracy in America*.

Translated by Gerald Bevan with an introduction by Isaac Kramnick

THE STORY OF PENGUIN CLASSICS

Before 1946 ... 'Classics' are mainly the domain of academics and students; readable editions for everyone else are almost unheard of. This all changes when a little-known classicist, E. V. Rieu, presents Penguin founder Allen Lane with the translation of Homer's *Odyssey* that he has been working on in his spare time.

1946 Penguin Classics debuts with *The Odyssey*, which promptly sells three million copies. Suddenly, classics are no longer for the privileged few.

1950s Rieu, now series editor, turns to professional writers for the best modern, readable translations, including Dorothy L. Sayers's *Inferno* and Robert Graves's unexpurgated *Twelve Caesars*.

1960s The Classics are given the distinctive black covers that have remained a constant throughout the life of the series. Rieu retires in 1964, hailing the Penguin Classics list as 'the greatest educative force of the twentieth century.'

1970s A new generation of translators swells the Penguin Classics ranks, introducing readers of English to classics of world literature from more than twenty languages. The list grows to encompass more history, philosophy, science, religion and politics.

1980s The Penguin American Library launches with titles such as *Uncle Tom's Cabin*, and joins forces with Penguin Classics to provide the most comprehensive library of world literature available from any paperback publisher.

1990s The launch of Penguin Audiobooks brings the classics to a listening audience for the first time, and in 1999 the worldwide launch of the Penguin Classics website extends their reach to the global online community.

The 21st Century Penguin Classics are completely redesigned for the first time in nearly twenty years. This world-famous series now consists of more than 1300 titles, making the widest range of the best books ever written available to millions – and constantly redefining what makes a 'classic'.

The Odyssey continues ...

The best books ever written

PENGUIN CLASSICS

SINCE 1946

Find out more at www.penguinclassics.com